Angular 5 Projects

Learn to Build Single Page Web Applications Using 70+ Projects

Mark Clow

Apress®

Angular 5 Projects

Mark Clow
Sandy Springs, Georgia, USA

ISBN-13 (pbk): 978-1-4842-3278-1   ISBN-13 (electronic): 978-1-4842-3279-8
https://doi.org/10.1007/978-1-4842-3279-8

Library of Congress Control Number: 2018934214

Managing Director, Apress Media LLC: Welmoed Spahr
Acquisitions Editor: Louise Corrigan
Development Editor: James Markham
Coordinating Editor: Nancy Chen

Cover designed by eStudioCalamar

Cover image designed by Freepik (www.freepik.com)

Distributed to the book trade worldwide by Springer Science+Business Media New York, 233 Spring Street, 6th Floor, New York, NY 10013. Phone 1-800-SPRINGER, fax (201) 348-4505, e-mail orders-ny@springer-sbm.com, or visit www.springeronline.com. Apress Media, LLC is a California LLC and the sole member (owner) is Springer Science + Business Media Finance Inc (SSBM Finance Inc). SSBM Finance Inc is a **Delaware** corporation.

For information on translations, please e-mail rights@apress.com, or visit www.apress.com/rights-permissions.

Apress titles may be purchased in bulk for academic, corporate, or promotional use. eBook versions and licenses are also available for most titles. For more information, reference our Print and eBook Bulk Sales web page at www.apress.com/bulk-sales.

Any source code or other supplementary material referenced by the author in this book is available to readers on GitHub via the book's product page, located at www.apress.com/9781484232781. For more detailed information, please visit www.apress.com/source-code.

Printed on acid-free paper

Table of Contents

About the Author

Mark Clow has worked in IT for the last 28 years and enjoys developing software. An Englishman now living in Atlanta, Georgia, he's worked with Angular since version 1. He is currently working as a full-stack developer with Angular on the front-end and Spring Boot Microservices on the back-end.

About the Technical Reviewer

Massimo Nardone has more than 23 years of experiences in security, web/mobile development, the cloud, and IT architecture. His true IT passions are security and Android. He's been programming and teaching how to program with Android, Perl, PHP, Java, VB, Python, C/C++, and MySQL for more than 20 years. He holds a master of science degree in computing science from the University of Salerno, Italy, and has worked as a project manager, software engineer, research engineer, chief security architect, information security manager, PCI/SCADA auditor, and senior lead IT security/cloud/SCADA architect for many years.

His technical skills include security, Android, cloud, Java, MySQL, Drupal, Cobol, Perl, web, mobile development, MongoDB, D3, Joomla, Couchbase, C/C++, WebGL, Python, Pro Rails, Django CMS, Jekyll, Scratch, and more. Massimo has worked as visiting lecturer and supervisor for exercises at the Networking Laboratory of the Helsinki University of Technology (Aalto University). He holds four international patents (in PKI, SIP, SAML, and Proxy areas).

He currently works as chief information security officer for Cargotec Oyj and is member of ISACA Finland Chapter Board. Massimo has reviewed more than 40 IT books for different publishers and is the coauthor of *Pro Android Games* (Apress, 2015).

Acknowledgments

First and foremost, thanks to my wife Jill and her patience. I hope she is enjoying herself doing her favorite things, like paddle boarding, kayaking, and being at one with nature. I hope she never reads this book because it would bore her.

Thanks go out to the people publishing blogs and articles to the web; without you, I would never have been able to perform as much research as I did.

Even more thanks go out to the people working on Angular, especially those updating the Angular.io website with useful information. It was invaluable to me.

The original version of this book was revised. Some minor edits were made to the Introduction.

Introduction

Disclaimer

Let's get this over with as quickly as possible. I need to mention two things. First, some of the information in this book may be incorrect (I'm a human being that makes mistakes). Also, this book is somewhat opinionated. I have tried my best to be as technically accurate as possible, but I'm still learning a lot and have much yet to learn about Angular. I do have some strong opinions, but please don't take them as gospel. I don't intend to harm anything or anyone—I'm not smart enough for that.

Scope

This scope of this book is to help developers get started in Angular. You're not going to read and learn *all* there is to know about Angular 5. That's not the purpose of this book; getting up to speed as a developer is. In my opinion, *getting up to speed* means having a good overall knowledge—sufficient to start working.

Approach

This book contains chapters with small code examples built with the Angular CLI. You'll be able to try out code without being burdened by setting up a large project. I did it this way because I found this format easier to understand than creating a large project would be.

Example Code

The example code is available at `https://github.com/markclow/learn-angular-fast`.

Remember, you'll need to do an `npm install` on each project to install the dependencies and get it working. Sometimes you may also need to re-install the CLI using the following two commands:

```
npm uninstall --save-dev angular-cli

npm install --save-dev @angular/cli@latest
```

And sometimes you may get the "Environment configuration does not contain environment Source entry" error. This is fixed by editing the file angular-cli.json and changing the setting from this

```
"environments": {
  "source": "environments/environment.ts",
  "dev": "environments/environment.ts",
  "prod": "environments/environment.prod.ts"
}
```

to this:

```
"environmentSource": "environments/environment.ts",
"environments": {
  "dev": "environments/environment.ts",
  "prod": "environments/environment.prod.ts"
}
```

Angular and Naming

The purpose of AngularJS and Angular is to create single page applications (SPAs). I'll soon talk about how web applications have evolved from server-side applications to single page applications. Angular gives us a way of writing SPAs, but there's now more than one version of Angular. As of the time of writing, there are four versions:

- The original Angular, which runs on JavaScript
- Angular 2, 4, and 5, which run on TypeScript

Now that we have four Angulars, developers have rallied around a newer naming convention, which I use in this book:

- The original Angular is called AngularJS because it runs on JavaScript and is very different from the other Angulars.

- Angular 2, Angular 4 and Angular 5 will just be called Angular.

My Opinion as a Developer

I'm a developer who's used to using a typed, comprehensive language (such as Java, .NET C#, VB) on the server, and who enjoys the benefits of a compiler. But I'm also someone who has to do client-side coding, being a "full stack developer." I admit don't like JavaScript much. I have a long complaint list, and you can see it in Chapter 3. But I have to use JavaScript because that's what runs on the browsers. I have little choice. I just need code that runs on current browsers, and I wish there was a structured way of doing it with a proper language.

I also liked the original Angular (AngularJS) because you could get stuff running *fast*. However, AngularJS had some issues (see Figure 1).

```java
package com.mkyong.test.core;

import java.lang.annotation.ElementType;
import java.lang.annotation.Retention;
import java.lang.annotation.RetentionPolicy;
import java.lang.annotation.Target;

@Retention(RetentionPolicy.RUNTIME)
@Target(ElementType.METHOD) //can use in method only.
public @interface Test {

    //should ignore this test?
    public boolean enabled() default true;

}
```

Figure 1. *AngularJS issues*

It had some strange syntax—mostly because it used JavaScript, for example IFFEs—and patterns. This caused the learning curve for AngularJS to be somewhat inconsistent, as I've indicated in Figure 2. Some parts are easy to learn; others are more difficult.

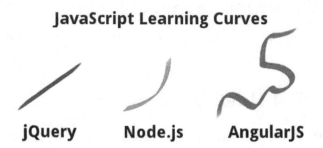

Figure 2. *JavaScript learning curves*

Most AngularJS developers wanted the Google people to take a step back and re-architect Angular to make it simpler, more logical, and more (acceptable) to developers in general, not just UI guys.

And they did so. I think they did a tremendous job when they converted AngularJS to Angular.

Why Is Angular the Answer?

Angular can be used with languages like TypeScript and CoffeeScript. Transpilation (more on that later) is nothing new and has been around since before Angular came out.

You *can* write Angular code in JavaScript (I wouldn't, though), but I believe it's easier to write Angular code in TypeScript because Angular was *written in* TypeScript. TypeScript (like other transpiled languages) gives you the ability to write Angular code in a language similar to Java, .NET C#, or VB on the server. You have classes, interfaces, casting, and a lot more. This will catch on because hordes of developers who are used to writing code in those languages can transition over to Angular 5.

If You Use TypeScript, You Can Use Annotations

Annotations, a form of metadata, provide data about a program that's not part of the program itself. Annotations have no direct effect on the operation of the code they annotate.

Having done a lot of Java Spring development with JPA, I'm used to using annotations and am totally at ease with them. All you're doing is basically adding more information about your code. This information is also conveniently located inline, inside your code, so you can see it.

Annotations have a number of uses, including the following:

- *Information for the compiler*: Annotations can be used by the compiler to detect errors or suppress warnings.

- *Compile-time and deployment-time processing*: Software tools can process annotation information to generate code, XML files, and so forth.

- *Runtime processing*: Some annotations are available to be examined at runtime.

If you decide to stay with JavaScript for your Angular coding, you can say goodbye to annotations.

You Use Dependency Injection with Dependencies Injected Through Constructors

Being a Java Spring guy, I love dependency injection. It makes life simpler. I found Angular dependency injection similar and a breeze to use. We'll go into dependency injection more in Chapter 13.

You Can Develop a Well-Structured, Logical User Interface

Angular user interfaces consisting of components. A *component* can contain other components, which can contain other components. This is known as *composition* and it can form a complex hierarchy of components. Components can also talk among themselves.

Figure 3 shows search user interface. Enter search at top, and list items go underneath.

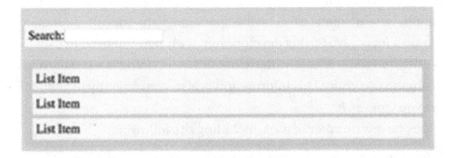

In Angular you could implement this with the following hierarchy of components.

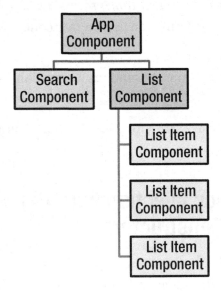

Figure 3. *Search UI*

You Use Instance Variables Bound to the UI (no $scope)

The strength of Angular is its binding, and that remains. In AngularJS, the developer used to bind visual components to variables contained within the scope. Now the developer binds to variables contained within the class. This is similar to how you code a UI in Java or .NET on the server.

Sounds Good, Doesn't It?

There has to be a catch, right? Well, there's good news and there's not-so-good news.

Good News

Here's the good news:

- The good news is that Angular seems to be the answer for mainstream developers like you and me (that is, non-UI gurus). It may make our life easier in the long term. You will still have to deal with CSS though!

- Some Angular stuff won't take much learning because you already know them from the server side.

- The Angular CLI makes code generation a snap.

- There's plenty of Angular sample code available online.

Not-So-Good News

There are a lot of new technologies and concepts to learn:

- TypeScript

- Transpilation of TypeScript to JavaScript

- Editing TypeScript

- Creating and consuming JavaScript modules

- Deploying code, including JavaScript modules

- Angular components.

- Angular dependency injection

- Angular and UI widget libraries

- Angular router

- Reactive extensions

- And, yes, more…

Luckily, those things are covered in upcoming chapters. So, let's get going!

CHAPTER 1

Web Applications and AJAX Communications

This book was written for developers who have a very basic knowledge of web development. It doesn't require software to be installed in advance, but in later chapters you will need to install software to run the example code. The book provides information on how to download and install the software when required.

Before we dive into Angular, I want to introduce some basic concepts of web development. This chapter covers the basic architecture of a web application and how it passes data from the server to the web browser. It also introduces some of the tools that might make your life easier when debugging the communication between the server and the web browser.

More experienced developers can just skip over this chapter.

1

© Mark Clow 2018
M. Clow, *Angular 5 Projects*, https://doi.org/10.1007/978-1-4842-3279-8_1

Introducing the Client and Server

Web applications basically involve two computers communicating with each other, called a *server* and a *client*. This concept is illustrated in Figure 1-1.

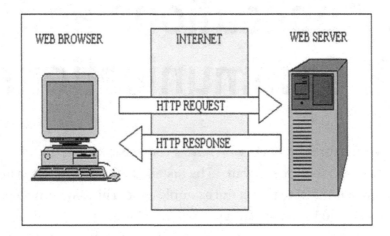

Figure 1-1. *Client/server architecture*

The server sits in the company office or data center, listens to HTTP requests, and responds back with answers. The server also accesses the data (stored in a database) that's used by the web application.

The user uses their web browser to interact with the web application. The user's computer communicates with the server, sending HTTP requests and receiving answers. Client computers may be a variety of machines, from smart watches to cell phones to tablets to computers.

On the web, clients and servers communicate using HTTP (HyperText Transfer Protocol). HTTP works as a request-response protocol between a client and server. Chapter 20 covers HTTP in detail.

Server-Side Web Applications

A *server-side web application* is one where most of the application executes on the server, and the client is only used to display HTML pages one at a time. When the user performs an action in the web application, the client sends a request to the server, which does something and returns a brand-new HTML page to be displayed on the client as a response. The web page is regenerated every time and sent back to be displayed on the client's web browser, as illustrated in Figure 1-2.

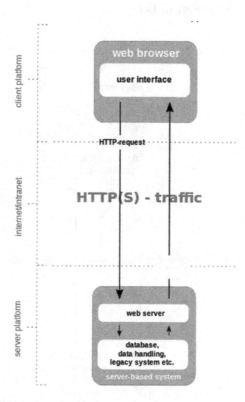

Figure 1-2. *Server-side web application*

Client-Side Web Applications

Client-side web applications (also known as *single page apps*, or SPAs for short) are a more recent phenomenon, and the computing industry is moving more towards this model. Here, a lot of the application still executes on the server, but some code also executes on the client (the web browser) to avoid the frequent regeneration of pages. When the user performs an action in the client, it sends a request to the server, which does something and returns *information about the result—not* an entirely new HTML page. The client-side code listens for an answer from the server and itself decides what to do as a response without generating a new page. Client-side web applications tend to be more interactive and flexible because they can respond more quickly to user interactions—they don't have to wait on the server to send back as much data. They only need to wait for the server to respond back with a result, rather than a whole HTML page. This architecture is illustrated in Figure 1-3.

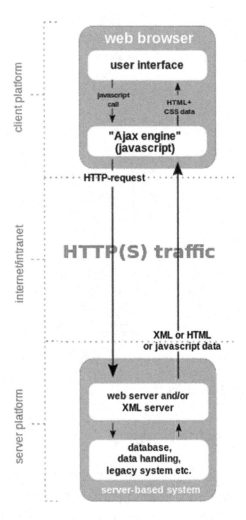

Figure 1-3. *Client-side web application*

Striking a Balance

So there are basically two types of web applications: server-side and client side (SPA). If these are thought of as black and white, your web application should be somewhere in the middle, in the "grey" area.

The server-side should remain the repository for the clever stuff—the business rules, data storage, and settings should remain on the server and be invoked or retrieved from the client-side when required.

The client-side (browser) should use the more modern client-side technology to avoid full-page refreshes. However, it shouldn't be too smart or too bloated. It should know enough to do its job of interacting with the user and nothing more. It should invoke code on the server-side to do smart things or perform business processes. It shouldn't have too much business logic, internal system data (data other than that data the user can view or modify) or hardcoded information because that's better managed on the server.

Caution   You must avoid throwing "everything but the kitchen sink" into the client.

Creating Web Applications with AJAX

AJAX stands for Asynchronous JavaScript and XML. AJAX is a technique for creating better, faster, and more interactive web applications with the help of XML, HTML, CSS, and JavaScript.

When a client-side web application needs to communicate with the server, it uses AJAX to send something out and waits for the result to come back. Remember, it gets back a result that only contains data, *not* an entirely new web page. Also, the client-side code doesn't stop running while it's waiting, because it still has to display the user interface and respond to the user. This is the *asynchronous* part of AJAX.

Client-side web applications use JavaScript to invoke the AJAX request and respond to it. This is the JavaScript part of AJAX.

AJAX requests used to use XML (Extensible Markup Language) as the data format for the request and result data going back and forth between the client and the server. Nowadays, AJAX tends to use JSON (JavaScript Object Notation) as the data format instead of XML. That's because JSON is much more compact and maps more directly onto the data structures used in modern programming languages. But both XML and JSON are commonly used formats for transferring data in text form.

Earlier, I used the term *asynchronous*. You may think of asynchronous this way: you call your spouse to ask a favor. Their phone is busy, so you leave a message asking them to stop at the supermarket and buy you a case of beer. In the meantime, you keep watching TV—because tlhese things are happening *asynchronously*. The outcomes of this process would include the following:

- *Success*: Spouse calls you back and tells you the beer is on the way.

- *Failure*: Spouse calls you back and tells you the store was closed.

In AJAX, the client-side code doesn't stop running while waiting for a response from the server, just as you didn't stop watching TV while waiting for your spouse to get back to you.

Callbacks

Typically, when you make an AJAX call, you have to tell it what to do when the server response is received. This code that the AJAX system code should fire when the response is received is known as the *callback*.

When you perform AJAX operations, you invoke the AJAX code with parameters and one or two functions—the callbacks. There are two types of callbacks:

- *Success*: The success (or done) callback is invoked if the server responds successfully and the client receives the answer without error.

- *Failure*: The fail or error callback is optional and is invoked if the server responds back with an error (or if the AJAX call can't communicate with the server).

Promises

Sometimes you invoke AJAX code, and it returns what's known as a *promise* or a *deferred*. A *promise* is an object that is a "promise of response" from an AJAX operation. When you receive a promise, you can register your success or failure callbacks with the promise, enabling the promise to invoke the callback once a success or failure occurs.

Encoding

When you work with AJAX (or other communication between client and server), you need to ensure that the information is sent in a form that's suitable for transmission. You do that using *encoding*. If you don't use encoding, it's quite possible that some information won't be received exactly as it was sent. This is especially true for some special character information—for example, spaces, quotation marks, and so on.

Table 1-1 lists the three main methods to encode information.

Table 1-1. *Three Main Methods of Encoding Information*

Method	Notes
encodeURI	This is useful for encoding entire URLs into UTF-8 with escape sequences for special characters. It encodes the string in the same manner as encodeURIComponent (see next entry), except it doesn't touch characters that make up the URL path (such as slashes). Example: `http://www.cnn.com` gets converted to `http://www.cnn.com%0A`.
encodeURIComponent	This is useful for encoding parameters. It's not suitable for encoding entire URLs because it can replace important URL path information with escape sequences. Example: `http://www.cnn.com` gets converted to `http%3A%2F%2F www.cnn.com%0A`.
escape	This returns a string value (in Unicode format) that contains the contents of [the argument]. Take care using this because servers don't expect to receive data in Unicode format by default. Example: `http://www.cnn.com` gets converted to `http%3A//www.cnn.com%0A`.

To test these methods, head over to `http://pressbin.com/tools/urlencode_urldecode/`. Figure 1-4 shows what this web interface looks like.

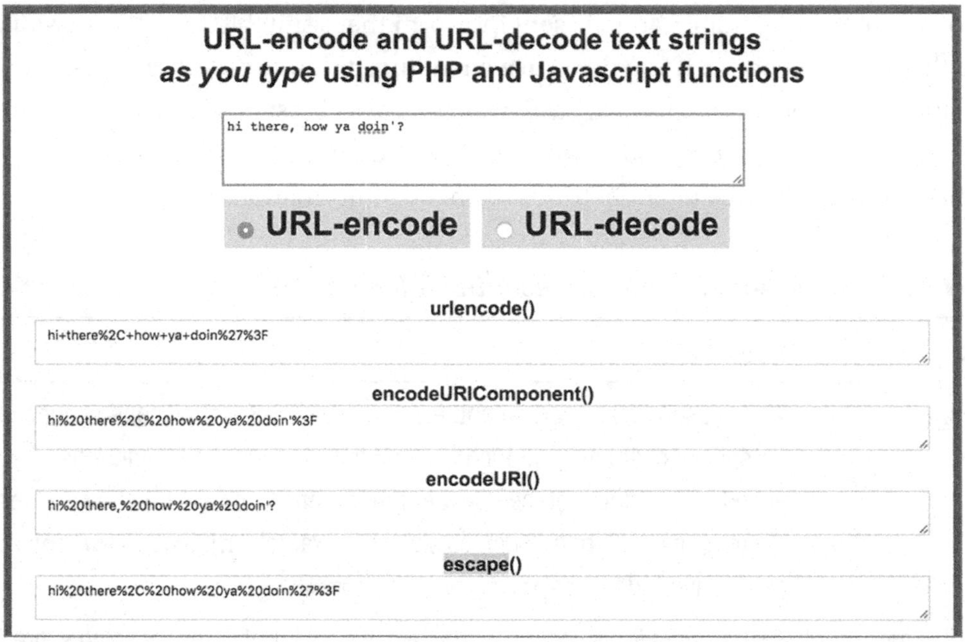

URL-encode and URL-decode text strings
***as you type* using PHP and Javascript functions**

hi there, how ya doin'?

⊙ URL-encode   ○ URL-decode

urlencode()

hi+there%2C+how+ya+doin%27%3F

encodeURIComponent()

hi%20there%2C%20how%20ya%20doin'%3F

encodeURI()

hi%20there,%20how%20ya%20doin'?

escape()

hi%20there%2C%20how%20ya%20doin%27%3F

Figure 1-4. *Web page that displays different encodings for what you type*

HAL and HATEOAS

To talk with the server, the client needs to know to which URLs the server is available on. This information should not be hardcoded on the client. Instead, the server should tell the client what URLs to use to get information. There are various standards for the format of sending this information back to the client, including HAL and HATEOAS.

For example, if the client sends an AJAX request to the server to retrieve a list of customers, the information returned should include the URLS for the AJAX requests for each customer. This avoids hardcoding the customer AJAX request URL on the client. You can read more about HAL and HATEOAS at `https://martinfowler.com/articles/richardsonMaturityModel.html` and `https://en.wikipedia.org/wiki/HATEOAS`, respectively.

Monitoring Data Traffic

Your web browser has developer tools built in. One of these tools is a network tool that allows you to monitor data traffic between the client and the server. This data traffic is presented as a list with a timeline, as shown in Figure 1-5. You can select an item on the list to view it in more detail and see exactly what data was sent to the server and what data came back. You can filter the type of network traffic that you want to follow. For example you can select 'XHR' to view AJAX requests.

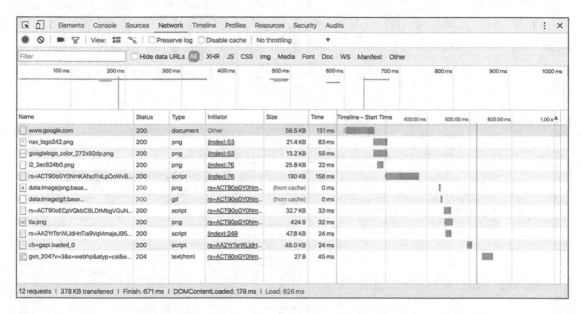

Figure 1-5. *Viewing data traffic with the network developer tool in the Google Chrome browser*

Fiddler is a free web debugging proxy that works in a similar way to the network tab in your browser's developer tools (see Figure 1-6). Fiddler has some extra capabilities, such as creating your own AJAX requests and running scripts. Read more about Fiddler at `www.telerik.com/fiddler`.

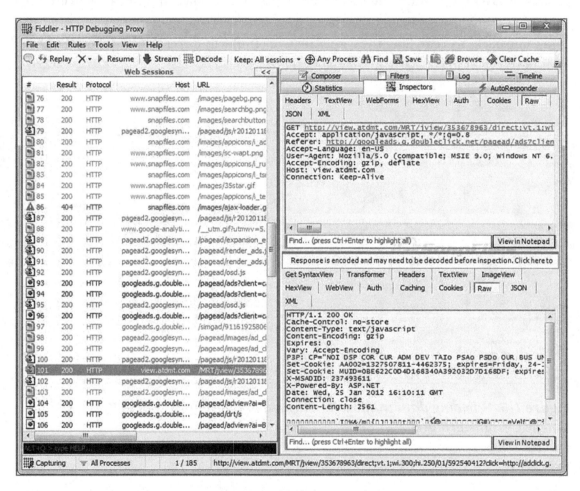

Figure 1-6. *Viewing data traffic with Fiddler*

Postman is very similar to Fiddler (`www.getpostman.com`). Both are very useful.

Analyzing JSON

You'll often receive long JSON responses from the server and need to traverse the response data to extract just the data you need. Your response data will normally be passed to your AJAX success callback as an argument. Here are some tips on examining this data:

- *Convert it to a string*: You can call the JSON.stringify function to convert the response data into a string. This will enable you to output it to the console in your success callback, as shown here:

```
function success(data){
  console.log('success - data:' + JSON.stringify(data));
  //
  // do something with data
  //
}
```

- *Copy the JSON data out of the console*: To copy the JSON data into your clipboard, do the following:

  a. Open your browser.

  b. Go to the developer tools menu.

  c. Click the console opeion.

  d. Select JSON text.

  e. Right-click and select Copy.

- *Format the JSON data to make it more readable*: Now that you have the JSON data in your clipboard, you can copy and paste it into a website to make it more readable:

  a.   Open your browser.

  b.   Go to `https://jsonformatter.curiousconcept.com` (or a similar service—there are lots of these). Figure 1-7 shows what this website looks like.

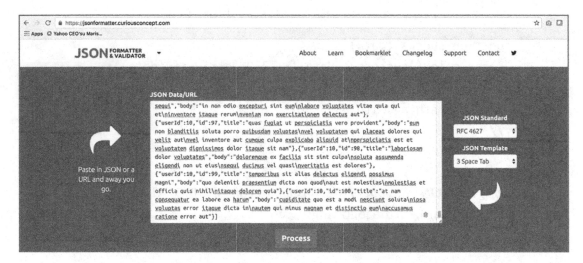

Figure 1-7.   *Formatting JSON data*

  c.   Paste the JSON into the big text box.

  d.   Click the Process button. The website will show you the JSON data in a validated, formatted, easy-to-read web page, as shown in Figure 1-8. You can even view the JSON full-screen.

Figure 1-8. *Formatted JSON data*

- *Copy the JSON data and paste it into your editor*: Then you can apply your editor's format commands. You may need to first save the file as a .js file to ensure it formats it as JavaScript.

Summary

The world of web applications has changed a great deal in recent years. Client-side applications (also known as SPAs) are becoming more common. In this chapter, we saw that one of the most important aspects of an SPA is the AJAX communication between the client (the browser) and the server.

As a developer, it will be important for you to know how to use the network portion of your web browser's development tools so that you can debug this AJAX communication. You may also need to know how to use other tools such as Postman or Fiddler.

In the next chapter, I'll introduce Angular and show how it's changed from version to version.

CHAPTER 2

AngularJS vs. Angular (Old vs. New)

Before learning Angular, it helps to know a bit about the original version, called AngularJS, and talk about the most important differences between the first version and the later ones.

Here are some basic facts about AngularJS and Angular:

- AngularJS, released in 2009, was the original Angular.

- It's a JavaScript framework for dynamic web applications—no page reloads required. Dynamic web applications are also known as SPAs (single page applications).

- It's popular for creating web pages with widgets that work fast on any browser.

- It allows users to extend HTML to add domain-specific tags, such as <CAR>.

- It allows users to bind data from the model to the HTML/domain-specific tags.

- Angular 2 was developed 2009 and 2014.

- Google announced development of Angular 4 in September 2014 and it went into beta in January 2015.

- Angular 4 was released in March 2017.

- Angular 5 was released in November 2017.

© Mark Clow 2018
M. Clow, *Angular 5 Projects*, https://doi.org/10.1007/978-1-4842-3279-8_2

AngularJS took off like wildfire because it was a great tool for prototyping applications quickly. It was also flexible in that you could use the HTML for a page and build quickly on it, turning it from static HTML into a moving, responsive, sexy app. Here's how:

1. Take an HTML template and modify some of the HTML code elements to add data binding.

   Data binding allows a visual control (such as a text box, select box, and so on) to have its value synchronized with a variable. For example, you could have a `city` variable that's bound to a "City" text box. If the user types into the text box, the value of the `city` variable is updated. If the code changes the value of the `city` variable, the "City" text box is updated to match

2. Add a JavaScript Angular controller:

   a. Add the variables for the HTML markup to be bound to.

   b. Add behavioral JavaScript code (code to respond to events like button clicks and so on).

Done!

You could (obviously) do a lot more, but the point is that developers could get *quick* results turning raw HTML into a working, responsive application.

Semantic Versioning

Angular 2, 4 and 5 are very similar and they are all very different from the original AngularJS. It seems very strange that we had AngularJS for several years then Angular 2, 4 and 5 in a short space of time. This is because the people at Google decided to implement Semantic Versioning since version 2. Semantic versioning is the new standard for software versioning and the reason why it is now so popular is that the version number (or the change of version number) provides information about the changes made since the last version.

With semantic versioning, the version number is split into three parts, each part separated by a period.

[major version number] . [minor version number] . [patch version number]

So when Angular changed from 4 to 5, this was a change of major version number.

A major version number change indicates that the software changed in a major way, meaning that your code that used to work may no longer work as the api has been changed.

A minor version number change indicates that the software was changed but it was changed in such a way as to allow your code to still work.

A patch version number is for bug fixes and everything should work.

Angular 5 is Angular 4 with many small improvements, some of which result in a modified api. As indicated by the semantic major version number change, your code may need to be modified when converting from 4 to 5. The most important changes from 4 to 5 include:

- Modification of the http module (this was already included in Angular version 4.3).

- The build optimizer has been modified to generate smaller, more efficient deployment modules. When you deploy the files from your Angular project these files will be smaller.

- There are new tools for transferring state data from the browser and the server (and vise-versa).

- The compiler has been rewritten be faster and more thorough. In the past, Angular was written to use jit (just in time compilation) when running your app. When you loaded components and object, these would be compiled when required. Angular is now moving more towards the aot model, in which your code is compiled in advance rather than when required. These compiler updates in 5 advance the move to aot, which will make your app run faster as it will be performing less compilation when running the app.

- Improved internationalization support for multi-language apps.

Platform

AngularJS runs on web browsers, and web browsers run JavaScript, so, JavaScript is the platform for AngularJS and Angular.

The term *evergreen browsers* refers to browsers that are automatically upgraded to future versions, rather than being updated by distribution of new versions from the manufacturer, as was the case with older browsers. The term is a reflection on how the design and delivery of browsers have changed quickly over the last few years. Now all the widely used browsers are evergreen and update themselves.

Browsers Run JavaScript Using JavaScript Engines

We used to think of a web browser and its ability to run JavaScript as the same thing. Since Node (which uses the JavaScript engine from Google Chrome to run programs away from the browser), this has changed, and you can run these engines standalone, away from the browser.

A *JavaScript engine* is a program or interpreter that executes JavaScript and that may utilize JIT (just-in-time) compilation to bytecode. Since AngularJS, JavaScript engines have steadily improved with new versions of ECMA JavaScript (*ECMA* refers to version). AngularJS ran on web browsers running version of JavaScript called ECMA5. Now most browsers run a later version. With ECMA6 (also known as ECMA 2016), JavaScript took a giant leap toward becoming a structured, typed language like Java or .NET. The two more important changes there are the new syntaxes for creating classes and modules, which are important and relevant for this book.

As you may know, the world of client-side JavaScript changes quickly. The ECMA Wikipedia page is regularly updated with the latest information: `https://en.wikipedia.org/wiki/ECMAScript`.

Shims and Polyfills

Shims and polyfills are software components designed to allow older browsers to run more modern code. A *shim* is a piece of code that intercepts existing API calls on a browser and implements different behavior, which enables standardizing APIs across different environments. So, if two browsers implement the same API differently, you could use a shim to intercept the API calls in one of those browsers and make its behavior align with the other browser. A *polyfill* is a piece of JavaScript that can "implant" missing APIs into an older browser. For example, shims and polyfills enable older ECMA5 browsers to run ECMA6 code.

TypeScript

In between the emergence of AngularJS and Angular, JavaScript was improved and became more of a structured language. But you can take things even further and use the TypeScript language, which is structured and even more like languages like Java, .NET, and C#. In fact, TypeScript was developed by Microsoft to be an improved successor to JavaScript. Figure 2-1 expresses TypeScript in a nutshell.

$$\text{TypeScript} = \text{ECMA6} + \text{Types} + \text{Annotations}$$

Figure 2-1. *How to think of TypeScript*

Why is TypeScript important? Google developed Angular using TypeScript. Angular and the TypeScript language are therefore a great combination, and we're going to talk a lot about that in this book.

Transpilation

How does TypeScript run on a web browser? Well, it doesn't, at least not at the moment. TypeScript gets converted back to compatible JavaScript using a process called transpilation. A *transpiler* is a piece of software that converts the source code of one language into the source code of another. For example, TypeScript, CoffeeScript, Caffeine, Kaffeine, and more than two dozen other languages are transpiled into JavaScript.

If you want to see transpilation firsthand, check out `www.typescriptlang.org/play/` and look at some examples. If you select Using Classes from the pop-up box on that web page, you can see how a modern TypeScript class is transpiled into compatible JavaScript.

Listing 2-1 shows the code you would write for a TypeScript class, and Listing 2-2 shows the transpilation to JavaScript.

Listing 2-1. TypeScript Class

```
class Greeter {
    greeting: string;
    constructor(message: string) {
        this.greeting = message;
```

```
    }
    greet() {
        return "Hello, " + this.greeting;
    }
}
```

Listing 2-2. Transpiled to Browser-Compatible JavaScript

```
var Greeter = (function () {
    function Greeter(message) {
        this.greeting = message;
    }
    Greeter.prototype.greet = function () {
        return "Hello, " + this.greeting;
    };
    return Greeter;
}());
```

Debugging and Map Files

So, you're writing code one way and deploying it in another way—that must be a nightmare to debug, right? Yes, it *would* be a nightmare to debug if you didn't have map files. *Map files* are automatically generated by your transpiler and give the browser the information it needs to *map* the original (TypeScript) code to the deployed (JavaScript) code. That means the JavaScript debugger can let you debug your source code as if the browser were running it. How cool is that? And if you enable .map files in your browser, it will automatically look for them, pick them up, and use them. I use .map files all the time when I'm debugging in Chrome.

Map files do the following:

- Map a combined/minified/transpiled file back to an unbuilt state.

- Map JavaScript lines of code in the browser back to the TypeScript lines of code

- Enable browsers and debuggers to show the original code that you wrote in TypeScript and debug it

Transpilation and the Angular CLI Tool

There are many ways of setting up your project to transpile your TypeScript code into browser-friendly JavaScript. It all depends on your project setup. You have many options in this regard, and it can get complicated and confusing.

I recommend that you get started using the Angular CLI tool. This tool can very simply generate ready-made projects that have a simple build process setup, including transpilation. It can also be of use in larger projects.

Modules

The word *module* refers to small units of independent, reusable software code—for example, code to perform animations. I think of modules like LEGO blocks (Figure 2-2). Each block has its own purpose but is plugged into a larger structure (the application).

AngularJS had its own module system that was simple to use. At that time, JavaScript didn't have its own system of modularizing code. Angular has its own module system to package Angular code into modules, as well as modern JavaScript modules.

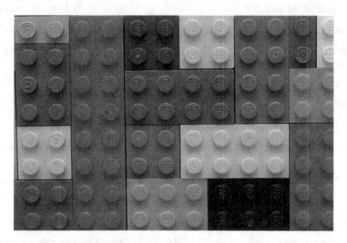

Figure 2-2. *Modules are like software LEGO blocks*

Don't worry, this will all be covered later in more detail.

Controllers and Components

AngularJS used controllers to represent a widget in the user interface on the HTML page.

Angular (from version 2 on) replaces controllers with the `Component` object. Components can have their own tag, such as `<Component1>`. Components have a class that contains data and code.

Chapter 8 covers components in greater detail. Components are the building blocks of Angular 5 applications.

Dependency Injection and Constructor Injection

As I've mentioned, being a Java Spring guy, I love dependency injection because it makes life simpler. We could spend pages and pages on this subject and the benefits that dependency injection provides.

AngularJS provided dependency injection. Modern Angular also provides dependency injection. Because your components have classes, dependencies are now usually injected via the constructor, using the Constructor Injection pattern. This software pattern is another server-side technology that is now being used on client-side. Let's look at an example of Java Spring using Constructor Injection. The following configuration specifies a constructor argument—a string message, `"Spring is fun"`:

```xml
<?xml version="1.0" encoding="UTF-8"?>
<beans xmlns="http://www.springframework.org/schema/beans"
       xmlns:xsi="http://www.w3.org/2001/XMLSchema-instance"
       xsi:schemaLocation="http://www.springframework.org/schema/beans

http://www.springframework.org/schema/beans/spring-beans.xsd">

    <bean id="message"
        class="org.springbyexample.di.xml.ConstructorMessage">
      <constructor-arg value="Spring is fun." />
    </bean>

</beans>
```

The following bean class expects to receive the message in the constructor:

```
public class ConstructorMessage {

    private String message = null;

    /**
     * Constructor
     */
    public ConstructorMessage(String message) {
        this.message = message;
    }
    /**
     * Gets message.
     */
    public String getMessage() {
        return message;
    }
    /**
     * Sets message.
     */
    public void setMessage(String message) {
        this.message = message;
    }

}
```

What's so great about this? In this case, it's a simple example of a String. But it shows how a software object (in this case, a String object) is "plugged into" another software object using the constructor.

For example, in Angular you could create a single reusable oftware object that handles communication with your server. You can pass it into every object (class) that needs it by passing it in through the constructor. Then, in the class, you have a ready-made way of talking to the server.

Write a service once, use it many times in many places.

Scope, Controllers, and Components

In AngularJS, Scope ($scope) used to be the "data container" for the controller. Your variables would be contained in the $scope object. For example, if you had a controller for an input form for an address, each line of the address would probably be a variable inside the $scope for the controller.

In Angular, you no longer have controllers—you have components, and you use these components to construct user interfaces. You can nest components inside other components using composition. Components have a class, similar to Java or .NET. The class is the "data container" and contains your variables. This is far more like conventional server-side coding. For example, if you have a component for an input form with an address, each line of the address would probably be a variable inside the component's class, similar to a Java swing (or Windows Form) class.

- Components use classes to contain their variables and application code.

- Classes have instance variables, constructors, and methods.

- You can inject dependencies into your classes using the constructor.

- Instance variables can be bound to the template to create a responsive user interface.

Chapter 8 covers components in detail.

Forms

Writing code that handles data input on forms is important. It was easy to write AngularJS code that worked with forms, data input, and validation, but Angular has new form modules that make it easier to do the following:

- Create forms dynamically

- Validate input with common validators (required)

- Validate input with custom validators

- Test forms

Templates

AngularJS and Angular both use HTML templates (see Figures 2-3 and 2-4). The HTML in the template is bound to the data variables and the code in order to make a working application. Unfortunately, the template syntax has diverged. Chapter 12 covers the new syntax in detail.

```
1    <input ng-model="thing.item" type="text">
2    <button ng-click="thing.submit(item)" type="submit">
```

Figure 2-3. *AngularJS template*

```
1    <input #item type="text">
2    <button (click)="submit(item)" type="submit">
```

Figure 2-4. *Angular template*

Summary

After this chapter you should have a better understanding of the different versions of Angular. The original AngularJS took off like wildfire because it was a quick way to write cross-browser applications, but it had some inconsistencies and needed updating to use capabilities offered by the updated browsers.

The more modern Angular is like AngularJS, only with a more straightforward development environment, backed up with the ability to work with newer JavaScript and TypeScript.

Angular depends on JavaScript and TypeScript. Chapter 3 introduces JavaScript and how it has changed from version to version.

CHAPTER 3

JavaScript

When Netscape hired Brendan Eich in April 1995, he was told that he had ten days to create and produce a working prototype of a programming language that would run in Netscape's browser.

Ten days to create what we now know as JavaScript! I would say he did a pretty good job considering the time he was given.

JavaScript is continually evolving. Currently, most web browsers support JavaScript ES5, but ES6 will become the norm within the next year or two.

JavaScript ES5: Limitations and Shortcomings

This section discusses currently perceived limitations and shortcomings in JavaScript up to and including the current version ES5. Many of these shortcomings have been addressed in ES6, covered later in the chapter.

Types

When performing operations on variables, a computer may or may not know the type of each variable involved.

If the types **are** known then the operations are simple as the operation is very specific. Example:

```
const a: number = 123;
const b: number = 456;
const c: number = a + b;
```

If the types **aren't** known then things get more complicated. The computer has to attempt to figure out the types of the variables being used or coerce them into the expected type. The logic can get complicated.

M. Clow, *Angular 5 Projects*, https://doi.org/10.1007/978-1-4842-3279-8_3

Example:

```
var foo = 123 + "Mark";
```

What's the answer?

- 123Mark?

- Error—because 123 is a number and "Mark" is a string?

JavaScript supports only six types:

- Undefined

- Null

- Boolean

- String

- Number

- Object

That's right, only one number type. Yet there are so many different types of numbers, including integers and decimals. I don't think I am stretching things when I write that in terms of types, JavaScript doesn't cut it.

Fail Fast Behavior

Code should either work accurately or it should fail fast (immediately). Because JavaScript has so few types and rules, it quite often continues rather than fails, with strange side effects. Things you don't think will work *do* work.

For example, the following code *doesn't* fail:

```
alert((![]+[])[+[]]+(![]+[])[+!+[]]+([![]]+[][[]])[+!+[]+[+[]]]+(![]+[])
[!+[]+!+[]]);
```

Value/Object Comparison

When you compare two variables in Java or a .NET language, you don't need to be a rocket-science to figure out how it is going to compare them. You implement a .equals() method. However, because JavaScript has few types, it uses complicated logic to compare values or objects. To see how JavaScript compares variables, take a look at the equality algorithm shown in Figure 3-1. You may want to take a Tylenol first.

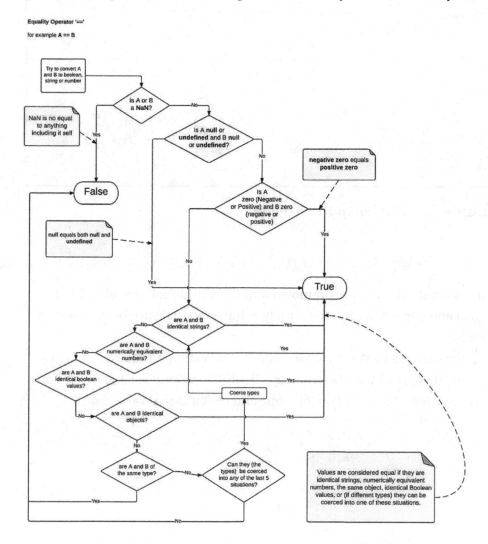

```
The Abstract Equality Comparison Algorithm
The comparison x == y, where x and y are values, produces true or false. Such a comparison is performed as follows:
1. If Type(x) is the same as Type(y), then
        1.   If Type(x) is Undefined, return true.
        2.   If Type(x) is Null, return true.
        3.   If Type(x) is Number, then
                 1.   If x is NaN, return false.
                 2.   If y is NaN, return false.
                 3.   If x is the same Number value as y, return true.
                 4.   If x is +0 and y is −0, return true.
                 5.   If x is −0 and y is +0, return true.
                 6.   Return false.
        4.   If Type(x) is String, then return true if x and y are exactly the same sequence of characters (same length and same characters in corresponding positions). Otherwise, return false.
        5.   If Type(x) is Boolean, return true if x and y are both true or both false. Otherwise, return false.
        6.   Return true if x and y refer to the same object. Otherwise, return false.
2. If x is null and y is undefined, return true.
3. If x is undefined and y is null, return true.
4. If Type(x) is Number and Type(y) is String,
   return the result of the comparison x == ToNumber(y).
5. If Type(x) is String and Type(y) is Number,
   return the result of the comparison ToNumber(x) == y.
6. If Type(x) is Boolean, return the result of the comparison ToNumber(x) == y.
7. If Type(y) is Boolean, return the result of the comparison x == ToNumber(y).
8. If Type(x) is either String or Number and Type(y) is Object,
   return the result of the comparison x == ToPrimitive(y).
9. If Type(x) is Object and Type(y) is either String or Number,
   return the result of the comparison ToPrimitive(x) == y.
10. Return false.
```

Figure 3-1. *Abstract equality comparison algorithm*

Scoping

In JavaScript, undeclared variables are promoted implicitly to global variables. To me, that seems illogical and dangerous, because surely to have a global variable you should declare it as such?

In Figure 3-2, the variable foo1 is a global variable, and variable foo2 isn't. When this code runs, you only see one alert box that says "hello." You don't see the second one because foo2 isn't set, because it went out of scope and isn't a global variable.

```
function a(){
  foo1 = 'hello';
}

function b(){
  var foo2 = 'there';
}

a();
b();

alert(foo1);
alert(foo2);
```

Figure 3-2. *Only one variable is shown in an alert*

JavaScript Strict Mode

JavaScript strict mode was released in ES5. It doesn't affect old code—in other words, using the `strict` mode command won't break JavaScript code if run in ES4, for example. Strict mode is intended to prevent unexpected errors by enforcing better programming practices.

Invocation

The `"use strict"` directive is only recognized at the *beginning* of a script or a function. This mode can run in two different scopes: file and function. If you place this directive at the beginning of your script file, all the code in that file will be run in that mode. If you place it at the beginning of your function, all the code in the function will be run in that mode.

I can't cover every aspect of strict mode but I discuss the main ones in this section.

Assigning to an Undeclared Variable or Object

Strict mode throws an error when the user assigns a value to an unassigned variable or object, preventing the creation of an unintended global variable (I talk more about this subject later in this chapter). The following throws an error in strict mode:

```
"use strict";
pie = 3.14;

"use strict";
obj = {str:10, zip:30350};
```

Deleting Variables or Objects

Strict mode doesn't allow you to use the `delete` keyword to delete variables or objects. The following throws an error in strict mode:

```
"use strict";
var pie = 3.14;
delete pie;
```

Duplicating Function Arguments

Strict mode doesn't allow a function to have more than one argument of the same name in a function. The following throws an error in strict mode:

```
"use strict";
function concat(word1, word1) {};
```

Duplicating Object Properties

Strict mode doesn't allow a function to have more than one property of the same name in an object. The following throws an error in strict mode:

```
"use strict";
var obj = {
  prop1 : 0,
  prop2 : 1,
  prop1 : 2
};
```

Read Only Properties

In ES5, users can define object properties using the function `Object.defineProperties`. This function allows the developer to define some properties as non-writeable (that is, read-only). In normal mode, the code doesn't throw an error when the code attempts to write to a read-only property. In strict mode, though, the code throws an error in this circumstance:

```
var obj = Object.defineProperties({}, {
            prop1 : {
              value : 1,
              writable : false
            }
          });

obj.prop1 = 2;
```

Non-Extensible Variables or Objects

In ES5, users can use the function `Object.preventExtensions` to prevent objects from being extended. In normal mode, the code doesn't throw an error when the code attempts to extend an object, but in strict mode, the code throws an error in this circumstance:

```
"use strict";
var obj = {prop1 : 1};
Object.preventExtensions(obj);
obj.prop2 = 2;
```

Keywords

Strict mode introduced the following reserved keywords that can't be used in your code in this mode:

- `implements`
- `interface`
- `let`
- `package`
- `private`
- `protected`
- `public`
- `static`
- `yield`

JavaScript ES6: Changes and Improvements

JavaScript ES6 is much improved over ES5. I'm not going to cover all the improvements between ES5 and ES6—just the major ones. Covering all the improvements would take several chapters. Note that if you want to play around with ES6 but aren't sure what to do, visit `www.es6fiddle.net` and try it out.

Constants

Constants are for variables that can't be reassigned new values:

```
const TAX = 0.06;
```

Block Scoped Variables and Functions

Before ES6, JavaScript had two big pitfalls with variables. First, in JavaScript, undeclared variables are promoted implicitly to global variables. As I mentioned before, in my opinion that seems illogical and dangerous. The strict mode in JavaScript throws an error if the script attempts to assign to an undeclared variable, as in the following example:

```
"use strict";
mark = true; // no 'var mark' to be found anywhere....
```

Also, when you declare variables with the var statement, this scopes the variables to the nearest whole function. The following example has two x variables assigned: one inside the function but outside the if block, and another inside the function and inside the if block. Notice how the code runs as if there's only one x variable. That's because it's scoped to the entire function. It retains the same value even if it leaves the scope of the if statement:

```
function varTest() {
  var x = 31;
  if (true) {
    var x = 71;  // same variable!
    console.log(x);  // 71
  }
  console.log(x);  // 71
}
```

Now ES6 allows developers to declare variables and functions within block scope. ES6 has a new let statement that's used to declare variables. It's similar to the var statement except that the variable is scoped to the nearest enclosing block, as in {' and '}.

The next example shows how the *inner* variable x is scoped to the nearest block in the if statement. When the code exits the if statement, the inner x variable goes out of scope. Thus, when the console log is printed in the statement below the if, it shows the value of the *outer* x variable instead:

```
function letTest() {
  let x = 31;
  if (true) {
    let x = 71;  // different variable
    console.log(x);  // 71
  }
  console.log(x);  // 31
}
```

ES6 also lets you define functions that are scoped within a block. These functions go out of scope immediately when the block terminates. For example, the following code works fine on Plunker with ES5, but throws "Uncaught ReferenceError: log is not defined" when run on Es6fiddle.net:

```
if (1 == 1){
    function log(){
       console.log("logging");
    }
    log();
}
log();
```

Arrow Functions

Arrow functions are a new ES6 syntax for writing JavaScript functions (see Figure 3-3). An *arrow* function is an anonymous function that you can write inline in your source code (usually to pass in to another function). You don't need to declare arrow functions by using the function keyword. One very important thing to remember about arrow functions is that that the value of the this variable is preserved inside the function.

```
// ES5
var multiply = function(x, y) {
    return x * y;
};

// ES6
var multiply = (x, y) => { return x * y };
```

Figure 3-3. *Arrow function*

Functions Arguments Can Now Have Default Values

You can specify default values in case some of the arguments are undefined.

For example, the following

```
function multiply(a = 10, b = 20){
  return a * b;
}
console.log(multiply(1,2));
console.log(multiply(1));
console.log(multiply());
```

results in the following output:

```
2
20
200
```

Functions Now Accept Rest Parameters

This parameter syntax enables us to represent an indefinite number of arguments as an array.

For example, the following

```
function multiply(...a){
  var result = 1;
  for (let arg in a){
    result = result * a[arg];
  }
```

```
  return result;
}
console.log(multiply(5,6));
console.log(multiply(5,6,2));
```

results in the following output:

```
30
60
```

String Interpolation

String interpolation enables variables to be data-bound into text strings. Note that the interpolation only works with the new quote character ` used for template literals. *Template literals* allow the user to use multi-line strings and string interpolation. String interpolation doesn't work with strings enclosed in the usual quotes " and '.

For example, the following:

```
var person = {name: "julie", city: "atlanta"};
console.log(person.name);
// works
console.log(`${person.name} lives in ${person.city}`);
// doesnt work
console.log("${person.name} lives in ${person.city}");
console.log('${person.name} lives in ${person.city}');
```

produces this output:

```
julie
julie lives in atlanta
${person.name} lives in ${person.city}
${person.name} lives in ${person.city}
```

Modules

Modular programming is a software design technique that emphasizes separating the functionality of a program into independent, interchangeable modules such that each contains everything necessary to execute only one aspect of the desired functionality.

Currently, most web browsers run JavaScript version ECMA 5, which wasn't written to work with modular programming. However, ECMA 6 is designed to work with modules, and its specification was agreed on June 2015. ES6 JavaScript lets you write your code into modules and use them like LEGO blocks.

For example, you could have an Internationalization Utility module that contains a lot of code for internationalization, including code to load resource bundles for different locales and so on. However you only need other code to access one method of this code, a method called getI18N(`locale, key`), which would return text for a locale and a key. JavaScript modules give you the ability to do that, letting you code a "black box" of code that's only accessible through public interfaces—in this case, an exported function.

One File

In ES6, you write each module in its own JavaScript file—one .js file. There's exactly one module per file and one file per module. You have two ways of exporting things from a module to make them usable from the outside, and both ways use the `export` keyword. You can mix the two ways of exporting things in the same module, but it's simpler if you don't. Just pick one. Once you've exported code, you can use it elsewhere by importing it.

Exporting Method 1: Named Exports

If you want your module to export more than one thing (for example, a constant, function, object, and so on), use named imports. *Named imports* enable you to export code with names.

Module `mymath.js`:

```
export const sqrt = Math.sqrt;
export function square(x) {
    return x * x;
}
export function diag(x, y) {
    return sqrt(square(x) + square(y));
}
```

Importing and using module code:

```
import { square, diag } from 'mymath';
console.log(square(11));
console.log(diag(4, 3));
```

Note how the export doesn't need a semicolon and that the names must match the original names in the module.

Exporting Method 2: Default Exports

Each module can only have one default export. This is useful if you only want your module to export one thing.

Module mymath.js:

```
export default function square(x) {
    return x * x;
}
```

Importing and using module code:

```
import sq from 'mymath';
sq();
```

Note again how the export doesn't need a semicolon and that the name sq doesn't match the function in the module. Using default exports allows you to use "nicknames" because it knows the object it's going to use, because there's only one.

Note   If you need to write modern code (ES6 or above) that can be deployed onto browsers running ES5, you can use transpilation to convert the code.

TypeScript

ES6 is a big step up from ES5, but it's still missing some pieces that are provided by modern structured languages like Java and C#—for example, strong typing, decorators, enumerations, and so on.

Don't worry. There's already something out there that builds on ES6, taking it a step further. It's called TypeScript. We'll write modern code in ES6 and TypeScript and use transpilation to convert it into compatible code to be deployed on the major web browsers.

TypeScript was written by Microsoft and is a very modern, structured language similar to Java and C#. Google, working in partnership with Microsoft on TypeScript, used it to write Angular itself. That makes using TypeScript with Angular a very good idea!

Summary

This chapter discussed many of the pitfalls of JavaScript and noted that most current web browsers still run ES5, not ES6. I mentioned that although ES6 is an improvement on ES5, TypeScript extends it and improves upon it, providing typing and many other features. TypeScript is the subject of the next chapter.

CHAPTER 4

TypeScript

TypeScript is a superset of JavaScript (written by Microsoft) that primarily provides optional static typing, classes, and interfaces. It's open source and is being developed on GitHub. The compiler is implemented in TypeScript and can work on any JavaScript host.

Being a strict superset of JavaScript means a JavaScript program is also a valid TypeScript program, and a TypeScript program can seamlessly consume JavaScript. TypeScript compiles to compatible JavaScript. TypeScript is quite similar to Java/.NET, with some differences—for example, constructors and interfaces.

You don't need to download or install TypeScript. When you use the Angular CLI (covered in Chapter 7), it will set up TypeScript for your project automatically.

In a nutshell, you can think of TypeScript like this:

TypeScript = JavaScript + Types + Classes + Modules + More

The most important of these additions is *types*, discussed in this chapter. Types enable IDEs to provide a richer environment for spotting common errors as you type the code.

Note Browsers can't run TypeScript directly—not yet anyway. TypeScript code is compiled down to JavaScript.

Microsoft's website for learning TypeScript is www.typescriptlang.org, the Playground of which is shown in Figure 4-1.

© Mark Clow 2018
M. Clow, *Angular 5 Projects*, https://doi.org/10.1007/978-1-4842-3279-8_4

Figure 4-1. *Playground area of* www.typescriptlang.org

Note that you can enter TypeScript on the left side and see it converted to JavaScript on the right side.

The rest of this chapter focuses on the main differences between the JavaScript and TypeScript languages.

Strong Typing

TypeScript provides strong typing and typing is useful because it enables the developer to specify his or her intention of how the variable is going to be used (what type of information it will store). This enables the compiler to verify that this is the case. If your code isn't using variables in a valid manner as expected, it won't compile.

Equality comparison is easier with TypeScript than with ECMA5 JavaScript because you can easily detect whether the two items compared are of the same type. If they're not, an error is produced. After type checking is completed, equality checking is easier because both items are of the same type. Having types in your code gives IDEs more information to work with. For example, if an IDE knows a variable is a string, it can narrow down the autocomplete selection to strings only.

TypeScript offers the following basic types:

- Boolean
- Number
- String
- Array
- Enum
- Any
- Void

Classes

ECMAScript 5 doesn't have classes, but TypeScript and ECMAScript 6 do.

Classes have constructors in the following format:

```
class Animal {
    private name:string;
    constructor(theName: string) { this.name = theName; }
}
```

Note that the code below will do the same thing as the code above (ie assign a value to the 'name' instance variable):

```
class Animal {
    constructor(private name: string) {}
}
```

Classes can extend other classes:

```
class Animal {
    name:string;
    constructor(theName: string) { this.name = theName; }
    move(meters: number = 0) {
        alert(this.name + " moved " + meters + "m.");
    }
}
```

```
class Snake extends Animal {
    constructor(name: string) { super(name); }
    move(meters = 5) {
        alert("Slithering...");
        super.move(meters);
    }
}

class Horse extends Animal {
    constructor(name: string) { super(name); }
    move(meters = 45) {
        alert("Galloping...");
        super.move(meters);
    }
}
```

Classes can implement interfaces (see the next section). And classes can use public and private modifiers for member variables or methods. If you don't specify public or private for a variable or a method, the compiler assumes that the member is public.

Interfaces

Think of an interface as a promise to do something (for example implement a function in a certain manner) or store certain data (such as properties, arrays). TypeScript interfaces can apply to functions:

```
interface SearchFunc {
  (source: string, subString: string): boolean;
}
var mySearch: SearchFunc;
mySearch = function(source: string, subString: string) {
  var result = source.search(subString);
  if (result == -1) {
    return false;
  }
  else {
```

```
    return true;
  }
}
```

TypeScript interfaces can also apply to properties. Interfaces can enforce properties but can also have optional properties (for example, color in the following code):

```
interface LabelledClothing {
  label: string;
  size: number;
  color? : string;
}
function printLabel(labelled: LabelledClothing) {
  console.log(labelled.label + " " + labelled.size);
}
var myObj = {size: 10, label: "Dress"};
printLabel(myObj);
```

Typescript interfaces can apply to arrays:

```
interface StringArray {
  [index: number]: string;
}
var myArray: StringArray;
myArray = ["Bob", "Fred"];
```

Classes can implement interfaces:

```
interface ClockInterface {
    currentTime: Date;
    setTime(d: Date);
}
class Clock implements ClockInterface  {
    currentTime: Date;
    setTime(d: Date) {
        this.currentTime = d;
    }
    constructor(h: number, m: number) { }
}
```

And you can have interfaces that extend other interfaces:

```typescript
interface Shape {
    color: string;
}

interface Square extends Shape {
    sideLength: number;
}

var square = <Square>{};
square.color = "blue";
square.sideLength = 10;
```

Modules

Modules are not included in ECMAScript 5, but they are in TypeScript and ECMAScript 6. The export keyword allows you to export your TypeScript objects in a module so they can be used elsewhere.

There are two main types of TypeScript modules: internal modules and external modules. In Angular, most of the time you'll be working with external modules.

Internal Modules

Internal modules are TypeScript's own approach to modularize code. You use the module keyword to create a module. Internal modules can span across multiple files, effectively creating a namespace. In a browser you load the modules using <script/> tags because there's no runtime module-loading mechanism. Or you can compile TypeScript files into a JavaScript file that you include with one <script/> tag.

You declare internal modules like this:

```typescript
module mymod {

  export function doSomething() {
    // this function can be accessed from outside the module
  }

  export class ExportedClass {
```

```
    // this class can be accessed from outside the module
  }
  class AnotherClass {
    // this class can only be accessed from inside the module
  }
}
```

To consume internal modules, you can address them using their fully qualified name:

```
var exportedClassInstance = new mymod.ExportedClass();
```

Or you can import them:

```
import ExportedClass = mymod.ExportedClass;
var exportedClassInstance = new ExportedClass();
```

External Modules

These are the types of modules most commonly used when developing in Angular. External modules use a runtime module-loading mechanism. We'll go into module loading mechanisms in chapter 9.

To use external modules, you decide whether to use AMD or CommonJS (your two choices of module systems) and then compile your sources with the –module compiler flag with values amd or commonjs.

In computing, a *namespace* is a set of symbols used to organize objects of various kinds. With external modules, your file's name and path will create the namespace, which identifies the item.

Here's an example for a file called projectdir/ExportedClass.ts:

```
class ExportedClass {
  // code ....
}
export = ExportedClass;
```

To consume external modules:

```
import ExportedClass = require("projectdir/ExportedClass");
var exportedClassInstance = new ExportedClass();
```

Enumerations and Generics

Enumerations are used to setup lists of constant values. They will be familiar to Java and .NET developers:

```
enum Color {Red, Green, Blue};
var c: Color = Color.Green;
```

As will generics:

```
interface LabelledClothing {
  label: string;
  size: number;
}
var arr: Array<LabelledClothing> = new Array<LabelledClothing>();
```

Constructors

TypeScript uses the `constructor` keyword to declare constructors, rather than the class name. Another difference is that TypeScript automatically assigns constructor arguments as properties. You don't need to assign instance variables in your constructor—that's already done for you.

This:

```
class Person {
    constructor(private firstName: string, private lastName: string) {
    }
}
```

equals this:

```
class Person {
    private firstName: string;
    private lastName: string;

    constructor(firstName: string, lastName: string) {
        this.firstName = firstName;
        this.lastName = lastName;
    }
}
```

Functions

Arrow functions don't exist in ECMAScript 5, but they do in TypeScript and ECMAScript 6. An *arrow function* is a function that you can write inline in your source code (usually to pass in to another function). Figures 4-2 through 4-4 show arrow functions.

```
var calculateInterest = function (amount, interestRate, duration) {
    return amount * interestRate * duration / 12;
}
```

Figure 4-2. *Regular function*

```
var calculateInterest2 = (amount, interestRat, duration) => {
    return amount * interestRate * duration / 12;
}
```

Figure 4-3. *The function in Figure 4-2 could be written into an arrow function in this manner*

```
var calculateInterest3 = (amount, interestRate, duration) => amount *
interestRate * duration / 12;
```

Figure 4-4. *The functions in the preceding two figures could be written in shorter form, like this*

Note   The syntax is the not the main reason why developers use arrow functions in TypeScript. The main reason is that the value of the `this` variable is preserved inside arrow functions. This can be of great benefit to the developer because regular JavaScript functions have a mechanism called *boxing* that wraps or changes the `this` object before entering the context of the called function. Inside an anonymous function, the `this` object represents the global window. In other functions, it represents something else. Many developers use arrow functions when they absolutely want to ensure that the `this` variable is what they expect.

Figure 4-5 shows an example of a regular function.

```
function Person(age) {
    this.age = age
    this.growOld = function(){
        this.age++;
    }
}
var person = new Person(1);
setTimeout(person.growOld,1000);

setTimeout(function(){ console.log(person.age); },2000); // 1, should have been 2
```

Figure 4-5. *A regular function*

After running the code in Figure 4-5, `person.age` has value 1. It should have value 2 because the `this` variable inside the `Person` function doesn't actually represent the `Person` function.

Figure 4-6 shows an example of an arrow function.

```
function Person(age) {
    this.age = age
    this.growOld = () => {
        this.age++;
    }
}
var person = new Person(1);
setTimeout(person.growOld,1000);

setTimeout(function(){ console.log(person.age); },2000); // 2
```

Figure 4-6. *An arrow function*

After running the code in Figure 4-6, `person.age` has value 2, which is correct. That's because the `this` variable inside the `Person` function represents the `Person` function as expected.

The ellipsis operator (denoted by . . .) allows a method to accept a list of arguments as an array, as in the following example:

```
function sum(...numbers: number[]) {
    var aggregateNumber = 0;
    for (var i = 0; i < numbers.length; i++)
        aggregateNumber += numbers[i];
    return aggregateNumber;
}

console.log(sum(1, 5, 10, 15, 20));
```

Getters and Setters

If you're targeting browsers with ECMAScript 5, this scripting version supports the Object.defineProperty() feature. If you use TypeScript getters and setters, then you can define and directly access properties with the . notation. If you're used to C#, then you're already quite used to this:

```
class foo {
  private _bar:boolean = false;

  get bar():boolean {
    return this._bar;
  }
  set bar(theBar:boolean) {
    this._bar = theBar;
  }
}

...

var myBar = myFoo.bar;
myFoo.bar = true;
```

Types

You can have variable types in TypeScript, but it's optional. The reason it's optional is so that TypeScript is backwards-compatible, meaning it can run all your JavaScript code. When you declare a variable in Typescript, you can specify the variable type by adding : [type] after its name.

For example, we declare a mark variable of the type number:

```
var mark: number = 123;
```

If we edit the code to assign a string to this variable, we get the syntax error highlighting shown in Figure 4-7. Note that this doesn't happen in Plunker—only in an editor like Visual Studio Code.

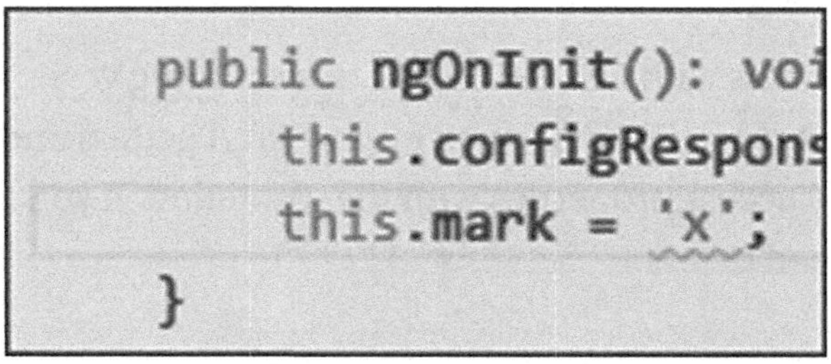

Figure 4-7. *Syntax error highlighting*

If we save this (bad) code and compile the TypeScript, we get the following error:

```
Type 'string' is not assignable to type 'number'.
```

Primitive Types

TypeScript offers the following primitive types:

- Any
- Void
- Number
- String
- Boolean

Primitive types aren't inherited from the Object class and aren't extendable (you can't subclass them). Primitive types are typically named with a lowercase first letter—for example, number.

Object Types

Object types are types that aren't primitives. They're inherited from the Object class and are extendable. Object types are typically named with an uppercase first letterfor example, Number.

Objects of this type have access to their prototype so that you can add additional functionality to the object:

```
String.prototype.Foo = function() {
    // DO THIS...
}
```

Object types also let you use the instanceof to check class:

```
myString instanceof String
```

Union Types

Sometimes you want a variable to be one of multiple types—for example, *a* string *or a* number. You can use the union (|) type for this. The following variable can be a string or a number, and the code is valid:

```
var name: string|number;

...

constructor(){
    this.name = 'abc';
    this.name = 22;
}
```

Here's another example:

```
var action = ActionNew | ActionSave | ActionDelete ;
...

if (action instanceof ActionNew){
        ...do something...
}
```

Union types can also to apply to function arguments and results:

```
function format(value: string, padding: string | number) { // ... }

function getFormatted(anyValue:any): string | number { // ... }
```

Alias Types

You can also use the type keyword to define type aliases:

```
type Location = string|number;
var loc: Location;
```

Tuple Types

A *tuple* is a finite ordered list of elements—for example: name, address, numeric zip code. TypeScript allows you to access this data using variables that use classes or tuples. The tuple type allows you to define a variable as a sequence of types:

```
var contactInfo: [string, string, number];

contactInfo = ['Mark', '12 Welton Road', 30122];
```

Compilation Options

You can configure TypeScript to your tastes: where the source code is located, how strict the compilation is, what compilation checks you want (or don't want), where the generated transpiled code is located etc. You can configure TypeScript by specifying the configuration options in a JSON-formatted file. Normally this file is called 'tsconfig.json' and you will find such a file when you generate your Angular project using the CLI. I have sometimes edited this file to make irrelevant compile checks go way if you are going something unusual. For example if you are using some regular JavaScript code within a TypeScript class.

Summary

You should now have a basic knowledge of how TypeScript improves upon JavaScript. TypeScript helps you as a developer to be more declarative and specific with your code, allowing you to declare variables with specified types and enabling more compile-time checking. It also helps you use annotations to provide information to the compiler about the Angular objects you're writing. TypeScript has really made Angular 2 and 4 easier to use.

We're going to be coding very soon, but first we'll need to set up our code editor. Chapter 6 covers editors.

CHAPTER 5

Visual Studio Code

Many editors are available that will work with TypeScript, including Visual Studio, Visual Studio Code, WebStorm, WebEssentials, Eclipse, and many more.

Different people like different editors, and different developers can work with different editors in the same project without causing many issues. There is no "right" or "wrong" editor.

I'm going to cover Visual Studio Code because it works very well and is free. I recommend you install this editor by going to `https://code.visualstudio.com` and clicking the Download link. If you end up not liking Visual Studio Code, you can easily remove it and choose a different one.

I chose Visual Studio Code because it's an open source source code editor developed by Microsoft and available for Windows, Linux, and macOS. It includes support for debugging, embedded Git control, syntax highlighting, intelligent code completion, snippets, and code refactoring. It was written by the same people who wrote TypeScript, so we know it will work well with it. It also works well with JavaScript, PHP, and more. And it's relatively compact.

Sometimes I switch over to Webstorm as it can be better at refactoring code. However 90 percent of the time Visual Studio Code works just fine.

Getting Started with Visual Studio Code

If you haven't already done so, go to `https://code.visualstudio.com`, download Visual Studio Code, and install it. Figure 5-1 shows the Download page.

© Mark Clow 2018
M. Clow, *Angular 5 Projects*, https://doi.org/10.1007/978-1-4842-3279-8_5

Figure 5-1. *Download page for Visual Studio Code*

Once the program is installed, to start the shell double-click on the Visual Studio Code icon to open it. Click File ➤ Open Folder and then select your project's root folder.

Navigate to the root folder of your project. Enter the command code . (code space period).

Seeing Files, Commands, and Hot Keys

Pressing Ctrl+P lists the files underneath the text box at the top, as shown in Figure 5-2. When you type, it filters the list.

dashboard.js|

dashboard.controller.**js** /src/client/app/dashboard	recently opened (2)
dashboard.controller.**js**.map /src/client/app/dashboard	
◻ **dashboard**.route.**js**.map /src/client/app/dashboard	file and symbol results (10)
◻ **dashboard**.module.**js**.map /src/client/app/dashboard	
◻ **dashboard**.route.**js**.html /report/coverage/report-lcov/lcov-report/app/dashboard	
◻ **dashboard**.route.**js**.html /report/coverage/report-html/app/dashboard	
◻ **dashboard**.route.spec.**js** /src/client/app/dashboard	
◻ **dashboard**.module.**js**.html /report/coverage/report-html/app/dashboard	
◻ **dashboard**.module.**js**.html /report/coverage/report-lcov/lcov-report/app/dashboard	
◻ **dashboard**.controller.**js**.html /report/coverage/report-html/app/dashboard	
◻ **dashboard**.controller.**js**.html /report/coverage/report-lcov/lcov-report/app/dashboard	
◻ **dashboard**.controller.spec.**js** /src/client/app/dashboard	

Figure 5-2. *Filtering the list of files*

Pressing Ctrl+Shift+P lists the commands at the top underneath the text box at the top, as shown in Figure 5-2. When you type, it filters the list.

>close|

Close Notification Messages	Escape, Shift+Escape
Close Window	Ctrl+W, Ctrl+Shift+W
File: Close Folder	Ctrl+K F
View: Close All Editors	Ctrl+K Ctrl+W
View: Close All Editors in Group	Ctrl+K W
View: Close Editor	Ctrl+F4, Ctrl+W
View: Close Editors in Other Groups	
View: Close Editors to the Left	
View: Close Editors to the Right	
View: Close Other Editors	
View: Reopen Closed Editor	Ctrl+Shift+T

Figure 5-3. *Filtering the list of commands*

Starting a Build

Edit the file tasks.json in the root folder of your project (see Figure 5-4). This configuration file specifies the build command we're going to use in the example project. It runs `npm run build` on the command line to invoke the build. See Chapter 10 for more information on Webpack and the build process.

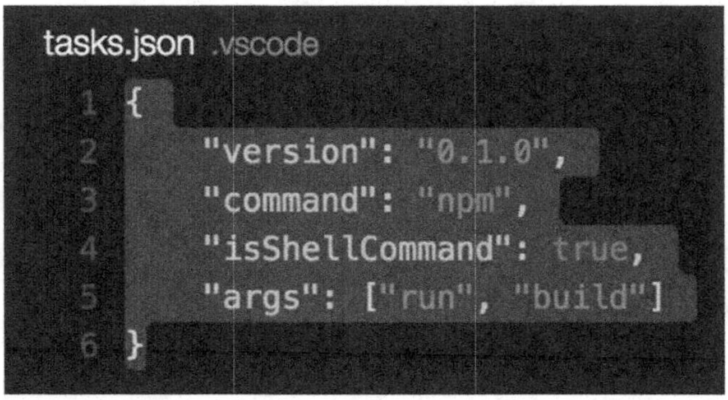

Figure 5-4. *Editing tasks.json*

To start a build, press Ctrl+Shift+B. Build output will be displayed in the Output pane. It normally takes between 10–30 seconds to run. See Figure 5-5.

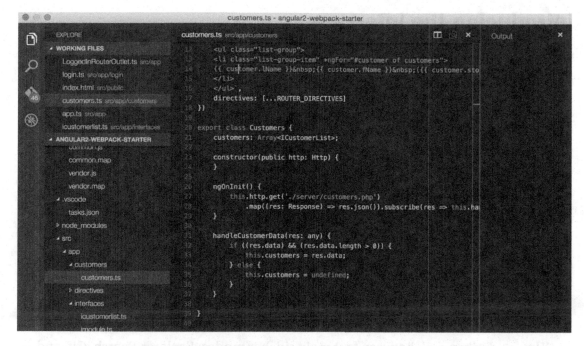

Figure 5-5. *Build output will appear in the Output pane*

To View build errors, press Ctrl+Shift+M. Errors are listed at the top of the screen (see Figure 5-6). Click an error to navigate to the source of the error.

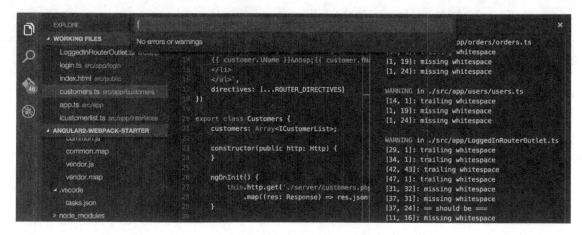

Figure 5-6. *Any errors would be listed at the top of the screen*

Introducing the Interface

Visual Studio Code shows a sidebar to the left offering different modes (Figure 5-7) and an editing area to the right.

Figure 5-7.   *The Visual Studio sidebar has four modes: Explorer, Search, Git, and Debug (from top to bottom).*

You can show and hide the sidebar using the Ctrl+B keyboard shortcut.

You can easily switch between four main sidebar modes: Explorer, Search, Git, and Debug. There are different ways to switch modes:

- Click the sidebar icons.

- Click View and choose your mode.

- Use the hotkeys (given in the following sections).

Explorer

The Explorer pane (Figure 5-8) is the first pane after the sidebar. It's split into two sections: Working Files (above) and Project Files (below—in this case, called Temp). Click a file in the file list to display it on the right side for editing.

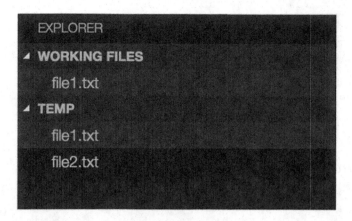

Figure 5-8. *Explorer pane*

To activate or focus the Explorer pane, click the Files icon in the sidebar, click View ➤ Explorer, or press Ctrl+E.

Working Files

When you edit files, they appear in Working Files. If you're only editing a few project files at once, it is handy having these files listed at the top in the Working Files section. When you hover over the "Working Files" heading, it shows an X to allow you to clear the list if you want.

Project Files

Project Files is a list of all the files in the project, as well as the folders.

Search

Search (Figure 5-9) works just like it does in most programs (see Figure 5-9). To activate or focus the Search pane, click the magnifier icon in the sidebar, click View ➤ Search, or press Ctrl+Shift+F.

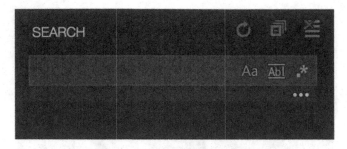

Figure 5-9. *Search*

Git

To activate or focus the Git pane, click the Git icon in the sidebar, click View ➤ Git, or press Gtrl+Shift+G. See Figure 5-10.

- 'View' menu option 'Git'.

- Control – Shift – G

Figure 5-10. *Git*

Debug

To activate or focus the Debug pane, click the Debug icon in the sidebar, click View ➤ Debug, or press Ctrl+Shift+D. See Figure 5-11.

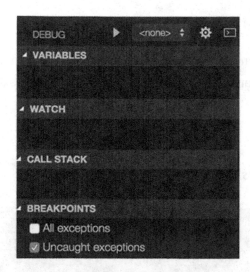

Figure 5-11. *Debug*

The debugging is more useful for debugging server-side code than for browser-side code, so it may not be of too much use to use in regard to Angular. You can debug browser code using this debugger if you enable remote debugging on your browser and attach to it, but it is probably easier just to use the available (and excellent) browser debuggers like the ones in Google Chrome.

To debug your server-side code you must first set up a debug launch task. This enables you to set up your debugging launch configuration, which you use to start the server-side code and start debugging it.

To debug, do the following:

1. Click the Debug icon in the sidebar or use another option already mentioned.

2. Click the Gear icon to open the Debug Configuration settings (in .settings/launch.json).

3. Pick your debugging configuration (next to the Gear icon) and click play to launch it.

Extensions

To activate or focus the Extensions pane, click the Extensions icon on the left (Figure 5-12), click View ➤ Extensions, or press Ctrl+Shift+X. Figure 5-13 shows the Extensions pane.

Figure 5-12. *Extensions icon*

Figure 5-13. *Extensions pane*

It's very easy to install extensions into Visual Studio Code. The Angular 5 project I work on has a build process that includes *linting*, which checks code to ensure that it follows style guidelines. Often the build will fail if the user adds too much whitespace. This becomes annoying, and it's a good idea to install the linter extension into Code so that it highlights linting issues as they occur (with a warning at the bottom left).

To view commands having to do with extensions, enter the following:

```
extensions
```

This displays the list of available extensions commands shown in Figure 5-14.

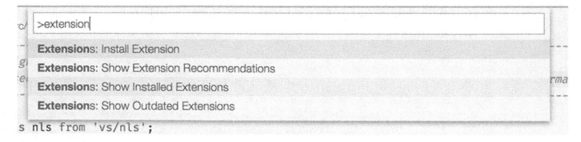

Figure 5-14. *Extensions commands*

To install an extension into Code, enter the following command and follow the instructions:

```
ext install
```

To set up the TypeScript linter in Code, enter the following command and follow the instructions (see Figure 5-15):

```
ext install tslin
```

Figure 5-15. *Installing the TypeScript linter*

A FEW OTHER HANDY THINGS TO NOTE

Being a rich editing environment, Virtual Studio Code offers IntelliSense code selection and completion. If a language service knows possible completions, the IntelliSense suggestions will pop up as you type. You can always manually trigger it by pressing Ctrl+spacebar. For saving your work, the normal File Menu Save commands apply, as does the Ctrl+S shortcut.

Visual Studio Code allows you to navigate in and out of code freely. For example, you can press Ctrl and click to "drill into" code, such as into a method. This is great when you need to look at something in detail, but you need to be able to go back to where you were. This is where navigating backward and forward comes in. To navigate backward, press Ctrl+- or click View ➤ Navigate backward. To navigate forward, press Ctrl+Shift+- or click View ➤ Navigate Forward.

Summary

Hopefully by now you've installed Visual Studio Code and checked it out. Note that the screens shown in version you installed may look a bit different from the screenshots in this chapter. The program is frequently updated.

Also remember that you're not "locked into" any particular editor. I chose Visual Studio Code to use with this book because it's simple to use and easy to get going with. If you want to use another editor with the code examples from this book, go right ahead.

Now you've installed an editor, we can move ahead with our development environment and get ready to start coding. When you develop code with Angular, you end up using a great deal of third-party code—that is, code written by other people. You try not to write it all from scratch!

So, your project will have dependencies on other people's code. The purpose of Node is to manage these dependencies, so we'll talk about Node in the next chapter.

CHAPTER 6

Node

We need to get coding soon, but we're going to need a project. To create a project, we're going to need to use the CLI (Angular's command line interface, covered in the next chapter). And the CLI needs Node to work. So, we need to discuss Node before we can start coding.

Node is a JavaScript runtime you install on your computer. It's a platform for development tools and servers (or anything else). Node is straightforward to use, and there are hundreds of modules already written for it—which means lots of code you can reuse.

Node uses the V8 JavaScript engine code written by Google for the Chrome browser, in combination with additional modules to do file I/O and other useful stuff not done in a browser. Node does nothing by itself—it's a platform on which you can run many useful JavaScript code modules, including web servers, transpilers, and more.

Node also provides dependency management with Node Package Manager, which we will cover in this chapter. It will enable you to manage your project's dependencies on 3rd party JavaScript libraries. It is essential that you get to grips with operating npm. Node Package Manager also enables you to publish your Angular code as a module, as well as use other peoples.

You're going to need Node. To download it, go to nodejs.org/download and install the core Node software for your computer. Figure 6-1 shows the Node website.

© Mark Clow 2018
M. Clow, *Angular 5 Projects*, https://doi.org/10.1007/978-1-4842-3279-8_6

Node.js® is a JavaScript runtime built on Chrome's V8 JavaScript engine. Node.js uses an event-driven, non-blocking I/O model that makes it lightweight and efficient. Node.js' package ecosystem, npm, is the largest ecosystem of open source libraries in the world.

Important security releases, please update now!

Download for macOS (x64)

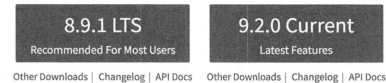

8.9.1 LTS	9.2.0 Current
Recommended For Most Users	Latest Features

Other Downloads | Changelog | API Docs   Other Downloads | Changelog | API Docs

Or have a look at the LTS schedule.

Figure 6-1.   *The Node website*

You have the option of downloading and installing the most recommended release or the latest release. Obviously, the former is more stable—that's why it's recommended.

Setting Up and Running Node

The following command sets up Node in your project. It asks you some questions and then generates the package.json file (covered shortly). Run this command in the root folder of your project:

```
npm init
```

Note   that the 'npm' command is used to invoke the node package manager.

Once you have Node installed, you'll have command-line access to the command node. Entering this command without arguments will allow you to type in JavaScript and hit Enter to run it:

```
$ node
> console.log('Hello World');
Hello World
```

The more useful way to use the command node is to enter this command plus a filename as an argument. This will execute the contents of the file as JavaScript. In this case, we we'll create the file hello.js:

```
setTimeout(function() {
    console.log('Hello World!');
}, 2000);
```

Now we can run it:

```
node hello.js
```

The program waits two seconds and then writes "Hello World" to the console.

Node Package Manager (npm)

Now that we know how to run JavaScript code through Node, we need to see about installing these useful modules. You would think that this would be simple, but it's not because many node modules depend on other node modules to work. So, when you install a node module, Node needs to ensure that any node modules that are dependencies are also installed. That's why the Node Package Manager (npm) was invented for you—to add, update, and delete node modules to your project and also manage these interdependencies.

For this purpose, Node provides a command-line access to the command npm. This command has many different arguments allowing you to install modules, update them, or uninstall them.

The website http://docs.npmjs.com is a great resource for detailed documentation on npm. And www.npmjs.com is a great resource for available node packages.

Node Module Installation Levels

There are two levels of node module installation:

- *Global*: If you're installing something that you want to use on the command line, install it globally by adding -g to the npm install on the command line:

  ```
  npm install -g typescript
  ```

- *Local*: If you're installing something that you want to use *in* your program (not from the command line), use the local level. To install a module locally, leave out the -g from the npm install on the command line:

  ```
  npm install express
  ```

Running npm install [Module Name] to Install the Module

This works great if you're doing something simple, such as adding a single additional Node module to your project. For example, one of the most useful modules is Express, a capable web server. To install Express, we could enter the following on the command line:

```
npm install express
```

This won't update your node dependency file package.json (more on this later). If you need this module to be saved as a project dependency in that file, add the --save or --save-dev argument to the command:

- *The save argument* --save: This adds the Node module that you're about to install as a Node module that's required for your project in production. Your package.json file is modified to include this dependency.

  ```
  npm install express --save
  ```

- The save argument --save-dev: This adds the Node module that you're about to install as a Node module that's required for your project in development only (that is, it's not needed for production). Once again your package.json file is modified to include this dependency.

  ```
  npm install express --save-dev
  ```

Updating Node Modules

Sometimes your dependencies change. You want to add an additional module, but adding that module requires others to be of a later version number. Node provides the following command to check whether your modules are outdated:

`npm outdated`

There are two different ways of updating modules in Node.

- You can nun the command `npm update` specifying the module to be updated. Also add the `--save` option if you want your package.json file updated with the later version. If the `-g` flag is specified, this command will update globally installed packages.

- You can edit the package.json file, update the module dependency, and then run `npm update`. This will update your modules to match the specifications in this file.

CHECKING YOUR NODE VERSION

If you already have Node installed, you can check its version by running the following command:

`npm -v`

Uninstalling Node Modules

You can nun the command `npm uninstall`, specifying the module to be uninstalled. Also add the `--save` option if you want your package.json file updated with the module removed from the dependency list. If the `-g` flag is specified, this command will remove globally installed packages.

The package.json File

Node is designed to be run from the command line within a project folder. It allows developers to store information pertinent to their project in a package.json file, which should reside in the root folder of your project. This file specifies many useful things about your project:

- The name and version of your project.

- What Node modules your project depends on (and what versions of these modules you need).

- What Node modules are required for your project in production.

- What Node modules are required for your project in development (that is, not needed for production).

Updating package.json

You can update this 'packages.json' file in two ways:

- By using node commands (on the command line) that install/ update/delete Node modules and update this file.

- By editing this file yourself. Then you run Node commands to install/ update/delete Node modules to match this file.

Version Numbers

The package.json file allows developers to specify Node modules that the project requires. When you specify the dependencies in this file, you also specify the versions of these dependencies—for example, 1.0.1. Node allows you to be flexible and specify the version number you require in many different ways, as summarized in Table 6-1.

Table 6-1. *Ways of Specifying Version Numbers*

1.2.1	Must match version 1.2.1
>1.2.1	Must be later than version 1.2.1
>=1.2.1	Must be version 1.2.1 or later
<1.2.1	Must be before version 1.2.1
<=1.2.1	Must be before or equal to version 1.2.1
~1.2.1	Must be approximately equivalent to version 1.2.1
^1.2.1	Must be compatible with version 1.2.1
1.2.x	Must be any version starting with 1.2.
*	Any version

The Folder node_modules

When you install a Node module, it's downloaded and placed into the subfolder node_modules within your project folder. Often you get a lot more than you bargained for, because the Node module you installed has many dependencies, so you end up with a huge node_modules folder with dozens of module subdirectories inside. Sometimes it takes a long time for npm to download and install the project Node modules. Also beware of copying this folder from one place to another because this can take what seems like forever. If you are copying a project from one computer to another, delete the 'node_modules' folder first then run 'npm install' on the target computer later.

There are two different ways of installing modules into Node. You can nun the command `npm install` specifying the module (to install it) or you can edit the package. json file and then run `npm install`.

Editing the package.json File and Running npm install

Manually editing your package.json file is the best way to install multiple modules when your project depends on multiple modules. First of all, you have to set up a package.json file, which contains an overview of your application, in the root folder of your project. There are a lot of available fields, but in the following example package.json file you see the minimum. The dependencies section describes the name and version of the modules you'd like to install. In this case, we'll also depend on the Express module:

```
{
  "name" : "MyStaticServer",
  "version" : "0.0.1",
  "dependencies" : {
    "express" : "3.3.x"
  }
}
```

To install the dependencies outlined in the package.json file, enter the following on the command line in the root folder of your project:

```
npm install
```

INSTALLING THE LATEST ANGULAR

Go to your project folder and issue the following command:

```
npm install @angular/{common,compiler,compiler-cli,core,
forms,http,platform-browser,platform-browser-dynamic,platform-
server,router,animations}@latest typescript@latest --save
```

Summary

Now that you know what Node is and how you can use it to manage your project's dependencies on third-party code, it's time to start coding with the Angular CLI (the command line interface). Let's get to it in the next chapter!

CHAPTER 7

Starting to Code with the CLI

When I first started developing in Angular 2, I found there was a sharp learning curve at first. It was very hard to get a project going because there was no standard Angular 2 project blueprint that would simply take care of building and running the project. You had to set up your dependencies in Node (more on that later), set up your build process, and set up a deployment process. That made Angular 2 tough at first, because you had to learn the concepts and the syntax at the same time.

Enter the CLI. The Angular CLI (command line interface) was developed to allow developers to get going with Angular fast. And it's great—it can generate projects that are well structured and well designed. I can't emphasize enough what a wonderful tool it's turned out to be how. No wonder it's been so quickly adopted.

The Angular CLI is an open source project. You can look at its code at `https://github.com/angular/angular-cli/`. The The official Angular CLI documentation is available online at `https://cli.angular.io/`. You can check out the QuickStart page at `https://angular.io/docs/ts/latest/cli-quickstart.html`.

The purpose of this chapter is to get you creating a project using the CLI. It's not going to go into great detail on the CLI yet, because that's not yet necessary—there will be much more on the CLI in later chapters. However, if you want lots of information right now, I recommend the excellent article at `www.sitepoint.com/ultimate-angular-cli-reference/`.

The Angular CLI, true to its name, uses a command line interface. You use the `ng` command in the terminal, and it goes to work. Using the command line may remind you of the "bad old days," when you had to remember a bunch of commands, but when you look at what the CLI does, you'll forget all about that:

- It lets you create new Angular applications.

- It lets you run a development server with live reloading of changes.

© Mark Clow 2018

M. Clow, *Angular 5 Projects*, https://doi.org/10.1007/978-1-4842-3279-8_7

- It lets you add more code to your Angular application

- It runs your application's tests.

- It builds your application for deployment.

- It deploys your application.

To get the CLI running, as mentioned in the preceding chapter, you first need to install Node.js version 4.0.0 or greater. If you haven't done so, go back and read about how to do that.

To install the CLI, enter the following command in a terminal, which will kick off all kinds of Node downloads:

```
npm install -g angular-cli
```

Note that the -g parameter installs Angular CLI as a global package. This will put the ng command on the path, making it usable in any directory.

You can check your version of CLI by running the following command:

```
ng --version
```

To update the CLI version, you should uninstall it and reinstall it with the following commands:

```
npm uninstall -g angular-cli
npm cache clean
npm install -g angular-cli
```

Create a Start Project

Finally, we're going to do some coding! Well, not really. Not quite yet. Let's just create the basic project and run it. Follow these steps:

1.   Open a terminal window.

2.   Navigate to a suitable folder—for example, Documents.

3.   Enter the following command, which will create a new Angular app in a folder called start and will spew out lots of files that it creates:

     ```
     ng new start
     ```

4. Navigate to the start folder.

    `cd start`

5. Enter the following command to start the app:

    `ng serve`

6. Open your web browser and browse to localhost:4200. You should
    see the text "welcome to app!" as shown in Figure 7-1. That means
    your app is running.

Figure 7-1. *The app is working*

Now you can make changes to the files in your project, and the project should
automatically—as long as you're running `ng serve`—recompile the code and refresh
the application in the web browser. This makes for a highly productive development
environment.

Now let's take a look at this project and what's in it. Launch Visual Studio Code and
open the folder start. Table 7-1 shows what's inside and how it's structured.

Table 7-1. *What's in the Root Folder?*

File or Folder	What It Is
e2e	Folder for testing files (more on testing, Karma, and Protractor later in this book)
node_modules	Folder for project node dependencies
src	Folder for project source code
.editorConfig	Editor configuration file
.gitignore	Git ignore file
angular-cli.json	CLI configuration file. You change your CLI options in this file
karma-conf.json	Karma configuration file (more on testing, Karma, and Protractor later in this book)
package.json	Node dependencies configuration file
protractor-conf.js	Protractor configuration file (more on testing, Karma, and Protractor later in this book)
README.md	Readme informational file, contains Information on CLI commands
tslint.json	Lint configuration file

Table 7-2 shows the source code. This is the really important stuff—the source code that was generated by the CLI for your project. Here's the starting point for your coding.

Table 7-2. *CLI-Generated project code*

File or Folder	What It Is
app	Folder for your application source code files, currently contains source code for an application component (more on this later)
assets	Folder for your application image and CSS files
environments	Folder for configuration files for environments—for example, configurations for development and production
favicon.ico	Application icon
index.html	The HTML page for the Angular single page application
main.ts	Code to start the application (more on this later)
styles.css	Global style definitions
test.ts	Code to run the application tests
tsconfig.json	Typescript/compiler configuration file

Modify the Start Project

Let's modify the start project and see what happens. Follow these steps:

1. Open a terminal window.

2. Navigate to the start folder and ensure that the ng start command is running and that navigating to localhost:8080 produces the "welcome to app!" web page as expected. Leave the ng start command running.

3. Edit the file src/app/app.component.ts by changing it to the following:

```
import { Component } from '@angular/core';

@Component({
  selector: 'app-root',
  templateUrl: './app.component.html',
  styleUrls: ['./app.component.css']
})
export class AppComponent {
  title = 'app works! and has been modified....';
}
```

4. Go back to your web browser. It should now display what you see in Figure 7-2.

Figure 7-2. *The app has been modified*

Note how the app automatically recompiled and reloaded as soon as you clicked Save in your editor. That's because the CLI project includes Watchman, which watches for changed files, rebuilds, and reloads your app when you change it. I'll say more about Watchman shortly.

Start Project: Compile Errors

Let's introduce a compile error into the project and see what happens.

Edit the file src/app/app.component.ts and change it to the following (remember to omit the quotes from "app works":

```
import { Component } from '@angular/core';

@Component({
  selector: 'app-root',
  templateUrl: './app.component.html',
  styleUrls: ['./app.component.css']
})
export class AppComponent {
  title = app works;
}
```

Note how the app doesn't change or reload, and that you get the error messages in the terminal window. You also get error messages in the browser console. In Chrome, you view the browser console by selecting More Tools and then Developer Tools in the menu.

Start Project: Runtime Errors

Let's introduce a runtime error into the project and see what happens:

1. Edit the file src/app/app.component.ts and change it back to the original code:

   ```
   import { Component } from '@angular/core';

   @Component({
     selector: 'app-root',
   ```

```
  templateUrl: './app.component.html',
  styleUrls: ['./app.component.css']
})
export class AppComponent {
  title = 'app works!';
}
```

2. Edit the file src/app/app.component.html and change it to the
   following (to create an error):

```
<h1>
  {{title.test.test}}
</h1>
```

The app goes blank. If you check the terminal, it says "webpack: Compiled
successfully." So, the compile worked. However, the page didn't load because we
(purposefully) introduced a runtime error (one that only occurs when the app runs). To
find the error, go to the browser console (see Figure 7-3). In Google Chrome, you view
the browser console by opening the 'Hamburger' menu, selecting More Tools and then
Developer Tools in the menu.

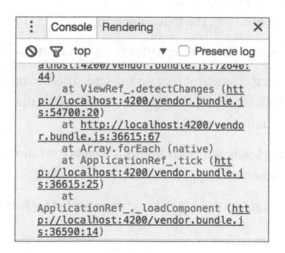

Figure 7-3. *The app has been modified*

File Watcher and Web Server

As mentioned earlier, if you leave ng serve running, this watches our files (performing a compile and redeploy when necessary) and runs a local web server on localhost:4200. When you change something and click Save, the watcher does the following:

- Creates a Webpack build, including transpilation to compatible JavaScript and bundling code (more on Webpack later in this book)

- Generates a new index.html file, adding script references as required to reference the JavaScript files bundled by Webpack

- Performs a new deployment onto the local web server

- Refreshes the web page

Bootstrapping

Bootstrapping usually refers to a self-starting process that's supposed to proceed without external input. In this case, it refers to how an Angular application starts up. This section takes a look at how the starter project bootstraps.

When we go to localhost:4200, the following happens:

1. The web browser opens the file index.html by default.

2. The browser loads the script files on the end. This includes main. bundle.js, which is a transpiled version of the typescript file main. ts. This is our main app entry point.

3. Main.bundle.js loads some modules then calls the following Angular system code:

    platformBrowserSpecific().bootstrapModule(AppModule)

4. AppModule is loaded—it's the root Angular module used to bootstrap the application. This is an Angular module, not a JavaScript module—they're different things (I cover Angular modules later in the book). If you look at AppModule.ts you'll see that it contains the following line to tell the module to bootstrap with the AppComponent:

```
@NgModule({

    ...

  bootstrap: [AppComponent]
})
```

5. The AppModule bootstraps with the AppComponent, injecting the component into the space between the start and end tags app-root:

```
<app-root>Loading...</app-root>
```

Useful CLI Options

We often use the CLI in this book and here are some of the CLI options we use in our example:

`--flat`

Generates a cli project with a flat file structure, not generating each component in its own directory.

`--inline-template`

Generates components with inline templates (more on those later). Component template markup will be generated within the component rather than in a separate file.

`--inline-style`

Generates components with inline styles (more on those later). Component styles will be generated within the component rather than in a separate file.

`--spec false`

Generates component without the unit testing 'spec' files that are normally generated for you by default.

One very useful new CLI option has been added since I wrote the examples:

```
--minimal
```

Generates a minimal cli project with inline templates, styles and without tests.

Ahead of Time Compilation

As mentioned in chapter 2, Angular is now moving more towards the aot model, in which your code is compiled in advance rather than when required. These compiler updates in 5 advance the move to aot, which will make your app run faster as it will be performing less compilation when running the app.

If you are working on a CLI project and you wish to perform aot compilation in advance, you can add the '—aot' option to your CLI commands. For example, you can run your app with aot compilation on with the following command:

```
ng serve -aot
```

This can be very useful in finding errors in advance in your templates. If your component is acting strangely and you cannot figure out why, try compiling or running your app with aot compilation on! This has helped me out on many occasions! Using the '—aot' option when running ng serve would have caught in advance the Runtime error that we introduced into the template 3 pages ago:

```
<h1>
  {{title.test.test}}
</h1>
```

Summary

This chapter introduced you to the Angular CLI. There is so much more you can do with it than just creating a starter project:

- Add different types of objects to your project

- Test your code

- Build your code

- Deploy your code

- Much more

We'll be using the CLI in all our coding examples, so don't worry: I'll be covering it much more and we'll be doing many more things with it.

The next chapter is very important: it introduces components, the building blocks of Angular user interfaces.

CHAPTER 8

Introducing Components

An Angular component is similar to an AngularJS Controller. A *component* is basically markup, meta-data, and a class (containing data and code) that combined together create a UI widget. Components are the main tools we use to build an interactive UI with. All Angular applications have a root component, often called the *application* component.

Angular provides ways for components to pass data to each other and to respond to each other's events. We'll get into component inputs and outputs in Chapter 12.

You can write a component and use it as a child component in several other components—they were designed to be self-contained and loosely coupled for this purpose. Each component contains valuable data about itself:

- What data it needs as input

- What events it may emit to the outside

- How to draw itself

- What its dependencies are

Normally when you develop components, you have one component in each of three files because there are three parts to a component: the template, the class, and the style. This is how the CLI works by default. For example, when you create an app in the CLI using the command ng new [project name], the CLI generates three files for the app component (more if you include .spec.ts testing files):

- *app.component.css*: Style

- *app.component.html*: Template

- *app.component.ts*: Class

© Mark Clow 2018

M. Clow, *Angular 5 Projects*, https://doi.org/10.1007/978-1-4842-3279-8_8

However, that's not your only option. Here are more options:

- *Include the style in the .ts class file*: This is called an *inline style* and it saves you having to have a style file for the component. As mentioned in the previous chapter, use the CLI `--inline-style` argument to generate components with inline styles.

- *Include the template in the .ts class file*: This is called an *inline template* and it saves you having to have a template file for the component. As mentioned in the previous chapter, use the CLI `--inline-template` argument to generate components with inline styles.

- *Include multiple component classes in the same file*: You can combine multiple components in the same file, like this:

```
import { Component } from '@angular/core';

@Component({
  selector: 'Paragraph',
  template: `
<p><ng-content></ng-content></p>
  `,
  styles: ['p { border: 1px solid #c0c0c0; padding: 10px }']
})
export class Paragraph {
}

@Component({
  selector: 'app-root',
  template: `
<p>
<Paragraph>Lorem ipsum dolor sit amet, consectetur adipiscing elit.
</Paragraph>
<Paragraph>Praesent eget ornare neque, vel consectetur eros. </Paragraph>
</p>
  `,
```

```
    styles: ['p { border: 1px solid black }']
})
export class AppComponent {
    title = 'welcome to app!';
}
```

You may find code examples with multiple components in the same file. This was done on purpose so that you could copy and paste more code into fewer files.

When you use components in your App, you need to ensure that each component is declared in modules. Chapter 9 introduces modules in more detail. The following is an example of a module declaring two components: AppComponent and Paragraph:

```
import { AppComponent, Paragraph } from './app.component';

@NgModule({
    declarations: [
        AppComponent,
        Paragraph
    ],
    imports: [
        BrowserModule,
        FormsModule,
        HttpModule
    ],
    providers: [],
    bootstrap: [AppComponent]
})
export class AppModule { }
```

Anatomy of a Component

Annotations provide metadata to combine all the parts together into a component. A *template* is usually HTML markup that's used to render the component in the browser—the View in Model-View-Controller (MVC). It can contain tags for nested components. A *class* has annotations to add metadata and contains data (was $scope)—the Model in MVC. It contains code for behavior—the Controller in MVC.

@Component Annotation

The annotation is located near the top of the class and is the most important element of it. It's a function that marks the class as a component and accepts an object. It uses the object to provide metadata to Angular about the component and how to run it. Annotations are also known as decorators.

If you use the CLI to generate a project and you examine the generated component app.component.ts, you'll see the following @Component annotation:

```
@Component({
  selector: 'app-root',
  templateUrl: './app.component.html',
  styleUrls: ['./app.component.css']
})
```

Table 8-1 shows the basic elements you can add to the @Component annotation.

Table 8-1. *Basic Elements for the @Component Annotation*

Annotation Element	Notes
selector	What markup tag, element this component corresponds to.
template/ templateUrl	Specifies the template, which contains the markup for the component. You have two options: you can use template to specify the template inline in a block of quotes. This works great for simple templates. Or you can use templateUrl to specify the relative path to an external template file. This is better for larger or more complicated template. If the template is longer than 10 lines, I usually put it in an external template file.
styles/ styleUrls	Specifies the CSS information for the template markup. You have two options: you can use styles to specify an array of styles inline. This works great for just a couple of style definitions. Or you can use styleUrls to specify an array of relative paths to style definition files. This is better when you use a variety of styles. If there are more than 5 styles used in the component, I usually put them in an external style file.

The selector syntax is like a JQuery selector, as shown in Table 8-2.

Table 8-2. selector Syntax

Type	Example	Example of Selected Markup	Notes
Name	welcome	\<welcome>\</welcome>	This is the most common way of using the selector. Just make sure that this tag is unique and will never be used by HTML. It's often a good idea to use a common prefix for your project and all the components therein. For example, a rewards program project could have the prefix rp_.
ID	#welcome	\<div id='welcome'> \</div>	
CSS class	.welcome	'\<div class='welcome'> \</div>	

Selectors and DSL

In Angular you create can components and directives that map to specific tags (or attributes). For example, if you're creating an application to sell cars, you could use tags and attributes like this: \<CarSearch>\</CarSearch>, \<CarList>\</CarList>, \<CarDetail>\</CarDetail>, and so on. In effect, with Angular components and directives we're creating a DSL (domain-specific language) for our application. A DSL is a computer language specialized to a particular application domain. DSLs are very powerful because they allow the code to be specific to the domain of the application (its use) and represent in language form the business entities represented.

Other Elements

Table 8-3 shows other, more advanced elements that you can add to the @Component annotation. We will go into detail on many of these later on.

Table 8-3. *Advanced Elements*

Annotation Element	Notes
animations	List of animations of this component
changeDetection	Change detection strategy used by this component
encapsulation	Style encapsulation strategy used by this component
entryComponents	List of components that are dynamically inserted into the view of this component
exportAs	Name under which the component instance is exported in a template
hosts	Map of class property to host element bindings for events, properties, and attributes
Inputs	List of class property names to data-bind as component inputs
interpolation	Custom interpolation markers used in this component's template
moduleId	ES/CommonJS module ID of the file in which this component is defined
outputs	List of class property names that expose output events that others can subscribe to
providers	List of providers available to this component and its children
queries	Configure queries that can be injected into the component
viewProviders	List of providers available to this component and its view children

Component Templates

The template contains the markup code to display the component in a web browser. Information about a component's template is provided by the annotation.

Template Location

The template markup can be included in the same file as the Component class, or it can be in a separate file:

Here's the template markup included inline in the @Component annotation:

```
@Component({
  selector: 'app-root',
```

```
template: `
<div class='app'>
[app]
<app-customer-list>
</app-customer-list>
</div>
`,
styles: ['.app {background-color:#d5f4e6;margin:10px;padding:10px;}']
})
```

And here's the template markup contained in a separate file:

```
@Component({
  selector: 'app-root',
  templateUrl: './app.component.html',
  styleUrls: ['./app.component.css']
})
```

Script Tags

The `<script>` tag isn't allowed in a component template. It's forbidden in order to eliminate the risk of script injection attacks. In practice, `<script>` is ignored, and a warning appears in the browser console.

In other words, never do this:

```
import { Component } from '@angular/core';

@Component({
  selector: 'app-root',
  template: `
<h1>
  {{title}}
</h1>
<script>
  alert('app works');
</script>
`,
  styles: []
```

```
})
export class AppComponent {
  title = 'welcome to app!';
}
```

Elvis Operator

This operator is also known as the 'safe navigation operator'.

Angular often has issues with null values, especially with template expressions. Quite often you will have an template which suddenly stops working because you add code that refers to an uninitialized variable. For example, say we have object x that is null, and we have the following code:

```
Total {{x.totalAmt}}
```

That will cause JavaScript and Zone issues (more on Zone later), and your component will suddenly not render. I wish I had a dollar for every time this has happened to me.

Lucky for us, the "Elvis" operator helps us. Simply put, the Elvis operator is a question mark in the template expression next to the variable that may be null. As soon as that variable is found to be null, the Elvis operator tells the code to exit, leaving a blank. This stops the evaluation of the property and bypasses the JavaScript issue:

```
Total {{x?.totalAmt}}
```

Sometimes you need multiple Elvis operators in a template expression:

```
Total {{x?.amt?.total}}
```

Component Styles

The styles contain the CSS rules required to change the component's style. Information about the component's template is provided by the style annotation. You can specify the component's style in the component or in an external file. When you create an Angular CLI project, its style files are specified in the .angular-cli.json file.

The styles can be included in the same file as the Component class, or they can be in a separate file.

Here's the style markup included inline in the @Component annotation:

```
@Component({
  selector: 'app-root',
```

```
template: `
<div class='app'>
[app]
<app-customer-list>
</app-customer-list>
</div>
`,
styles: ['.app {background-color:#d5f4e6;margin:10px;padding:10px;}']
})
```

And here's the style markup contained in a separate file:

```
@Component({
  selector: 'app-root',
  templateUrl: './app.component.html',
  styleUrls: ['./app.component.css']
})
```

Component Class

This TypeScript class contains both the data and the code for the component. The data is contained in variables, which can be bound to the HTML markup in the template. The code can respond to user events (such as clicking a button) or can invoke itself to start doing things.

Don't worry, this is only an introduction—we'll go into component classes in more detail in Chapter 12.

MVC: MODEL VIEW CONTROLLER

MVC is a way of writing programs, mostly for implementing user interfaces on computers. It divides a given software application into three interconnected parts: the Model (the data), the View (what the user sees), and the Controller (the commands to update the Model). In the context of Angular, it could be said that the Model is the data inside the Component class, the View is the component template, and the Controller could be code in the Component class.

Introducing Data Binding

Data binding is what made Angular so popular—the synchronization of elements of the component UI widget to the data in your component classes, and vice versa, managed by Angular for you. You set up variables in your component classes to store data and edit the HTML in your component template to add binding to that data. Now your HTML is no longer static—it changes with your data! If you want your components to interact with the user, you must use data binding in them.

In terms of MVC, at runtime Angular uses change detection to ensure that the components View always reflects the components Model. With data binding you can control the user interface of your components by changing variables, and you can accept user input, allowing them to change the value of some variables. Data binding can control every aspect of the user interface: hiding things, closing things, showing results, accepting user input, and more. It's incredibly powerful and easy to use.

Example: Data Binding in a Login Component

Let's say you have a login form with two fields, as in Figure 8-1. Each field has a text box in the HTML in the component template, and each field has a corresponding instance variable in the Component class. The text boxes and the instance variables are bound to each other. If someone enters a username, the username instance variable is updated with the new value. When the developer codes the Submit button, they get the username and password from the instance variables, rather than having to extract them from the HTML.

Figure 8-1. *Login form with two fields*

Example: Data Binding and Customer Data Input

You could have a form that enables you to input customer information using fields. Each field has a text box in the HTML in the component template, and each field has a corresponding instance variable in the Component class. Angular data binding enables you to have the instance variables updated automatically when the user inputs information into HTML fields. It also enables you to have the HTML fields updated automatically when you change the value of the instance variables, as well as having the instance variables updated automatically when the user types into the text boxes. When the developer wants to default the value of the input fields, all they need to do is set the instance variable values. The HTML textboxes will update automatically.

There are two main types of databinding—one-way and two-way:

1. *One-way data binding*: This can occur when the template (the View) is automatically kept up-to-date with the latest values in the class instance variables (the Model). Updates flow in only one direction. One-way data binding can also occur when the class instance variables (the Model) are automatically kept up-to-date with values input from the template (the View). Updates still flow in only one direction.

2. *Two-way data binding*: This is when the class instance variables (the Model) and the template (the View) keep each other up-to-date. Updates flow in both directions, as shown in Figure 8-2.

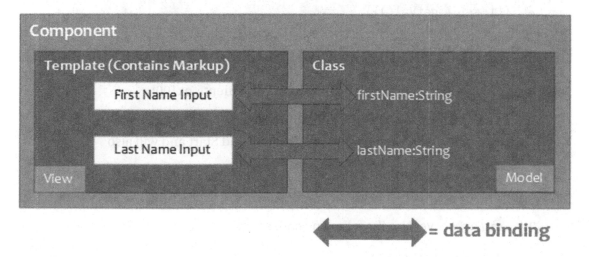

Figure 8-2. *Two-way data binding*

One-Way Data Binding

This section focuses on various aspects of one-way data binding in Angular.

One-Way Data Binding with {{ and }}

Those double curly braces are also known as *moustaches* or *interpolation*. The double curly braces are used for one-way binding a template expression, making a calculation from available data in the Model and including it in the View. The expression produces a value, and it's included in the View (the markup from the component template). The Model—that is, the data in the Component class—is never updated.

A *template expression* is usually a simple JavaScript expression. Usually the template expression is just the name of a property in the Model (that is, an instance variable in the Component class). Angular replaces that property name with the string value of the property (the string value of the instance variable).

Sometimes the template expression gets more complicated. Angular attempts to evaluate that expression (which can contain math, property names, method calls, and more) and converts the evaluation into a string. Then it replaces the contents and the curly braces with the result.

Here are some examples of curly braces and template expressions:

- `{{2+2}}`
- `{{firstName}}`
- `{{1 + 1 + getVal()}}`

One-Way Data Binding: Example Code components-ex100

The following discussion will be about example components-ex100:

1. *Build the app using the CLI*: Enter the following command, which will create a new Angular app in a folder called Start and will also create and spew out lots of files:

   `ng new components-ex100 --inline-template --inline-style`

2. *Start* `ng serve`: Use the following code:

   ```
   cd components-ex100
   ng serve
   ```

3. *Open app*: Launch your web browser and browse to localhost:4200. You should see the text "welcome to app!" as shown in Figure 8-3. That means your project is running.

Figure 8-3. *Your project is running*

4. *Edit component*: Edit the file src/app/app.component.ts and change it to the following:

```
import { Component } from '@angular/core';

@Component({
  selector: 'app-root',
  template: `
  <h1>
    {{title}}
  </h1>
  <p>
    Length: {{title.length}}
  </p>
  <p>
    Reversed: {{getReversed(title)}}
  </p>
  `,
  styles: []
})
export class AppComponent {
  title = 'welcome to app!';
```

```
getReversed(str: string){
  let reversed = '';
  for (let i=str.length-1;i>=0;i--){
    reversed += str.substring(i,i+1);
  }
  return reversed;
}
}
```

Your app should be working at localhost:4200. Note how the template uses two expressions: one to show the length of the title and another to reverse the title using a method in the class.

app works!

Length: 10

Reversed: !skrow ppa

One-Way Data Binding with [and] or *

The square braces can be used for one-way binding. With these you can bind a template expression, making a calculation from available data in the Model and including it in the data binding target.

You can also use the prefix * instead of the double square braces:

```
[Data Binding Target] = "Template Expression"
```

Or:

```
*Data Binding Target = "Template Expression"
```

The data binding target is something in the DOM (including element properties, component properties, and directive properties) that can be bound to the result of the expression to the right side of the target, as shown in Table 8-4.

Table 8-4. *Data Binding Target Markup*

Markup	Description
`<img [src] = "imageUrl">`	Sets image source to property `imageUrl` in the Model.
`<div [ngClass] = "{selected: isSelected}"> </div>`	Sets CSS class according to property `isSelected` in the Model.
`<car-detail [car]="selectedCar"> </car-detail>`	Sets the `car` attribute of the `car-detail` to property `selectedCar` in the Model. The `car-detail` could be a component, and this would pass information from the current template to that component using the `car` attribute.
`<button [style.color] = "isSpecial ? 'red' : 'green'">`	Sets the `button` color according to property `isSpecial` in the Model.

A *template expression* is used to calculate a value from available data in the Model.

One-Way Data Binding: Example Code components-ex200

The following discussion will be about example components-ex200:

1. *Build the app using the CLI*: Enter the following command:

   ```
   ng new components-ex200 --inline-template --inline-style
   ```

2. *Start* ng serve: Use the following code:

   ```
   cd components-ex200
   ng serve
   ```

3. *Open app*: Launch your web browser and browse to localhost:4200. You should see the text "welcome to app!"

4. *Edit component*: Edit the file src/app/app.component.ts and change it to the following:

   ```
   import { Component } from '@angular/core';

   @Component({
   ```

103

```
    selector: 'app-root',
    template: `
    <h1>Doesnt work:</h1>
    <img src="starUrl">
    <h1>Works:</h1>
    <img [src]="starUrl">
    `,
    styles: []
})
export class AppComponent {
  starUrl = 'https://developer.mozilla.org/samples/cssref/images/
  starsolid.gif';
}
```

Your app should be working at localhost:4200. Note the following (and see Figure 8-4):

- The first image tag fails because it doesn't wrap src. It takes the startUrl literally rather than calculating it as an expression from an instance variable.

- The second image tag works because it wraps src in square brackets, meaning this is an expression that requires calculating the value of the startUrl instance variable.

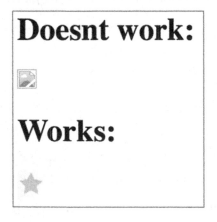

Figure 8-4. *Author please add caption*

Sometimes you need to dynamically create attributes in the HTML elements generated by your template. This is useful if you want to have data inside your HTML, which you can extract later using JavaScript code. For example:

```
<li
  id="12345"
  data-make="bmw"
  data-model="m3"
  data-parent="cars">
...
</li>
```

In this case, the id tag is used to identify the element (very useful for JavaScript and CSS), and there are various data elements that store information.

In Angular you can use the [attr.***name***] syntax to set attributes in the generated HTML.

One-Way Data Binding: Example Code components-ex250

This component will list some cars and let you click the View button to view an article about the car, as shown in Figure 8-5.

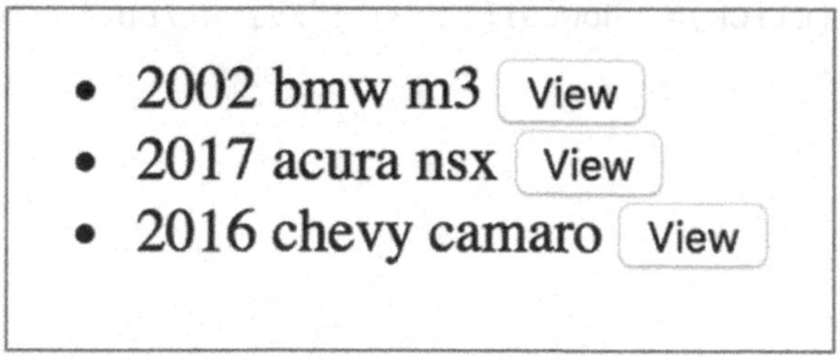

Figure 8-5. *Component that lists cars*

The interesting thing about the component is that it stores attribute data in each <li> element. This will be about example components-ex250:

1. *Build the app using the CLI*: Enter the following command:

```
ng new components-ex250 --inline-template --inline-style
```

2. *Start* ng serve: Use the following code:

```
cd components-ex250
ng serve
```

3. *Open app*: Open your web browser and browse to localhost:4200.
   You should see the text "welcome to app!" That means your
   project is running.

4. *Edit component*: Edit the file src/app/app.component.ts and
   change it to the following:

```
import { Component } from '@angular/core';
import { Car } from './car';
@Component({
  selector: 'app-root',
  template: `
    <ul>
      <li *ngFor="let car of _cars">
        <span [attr.id]="car.id" [attr.data-desc]="car.make + '
        ' + car.model" [attr.data-article]="car.article">
          {{car.year}} {{car.
          make}} {{car.model}} <button
          (click)="showCar($event)">View</button></span>
      </li>
    </ul>
  `,
  styles: []
})
export class AppComponent {
  _cars = [
    new Car('car1', 2002, 'bmw', 'm3',
    'https://en.wikipedia.org/wiki/BMW_M3'),
    new Car('car2', 2017, 'acura', 'nsx',
    'https://en.wikipedia.org/wiki/Honda_NSX'),
    new Car('car3', 2016, 'chevy', 'camaro',
    'https://en.wikipedia.org/wiki/Chevrolet_Camaro')
  ];
```

```
showCar(event){
  const desc = event.target.parentElement.dataset.desc;
  if (window.confirm('If you click "ok" you would be
  redirected to an article about the ' +
      desc + '. Cancel will load this website '))
    {
    window.location.href=event.target.parentElement.
    dataset.article;
    };
  }
}
```

5. *Create class*: Create the file src/app/car.ts and change it to the
    following:

```
export class Car {
    constructor(
        private _id: string,
        private _year: number,
        private _make: string,
        private _model: string,
        private _article: string){
    }

    public get id() : string {
        return this._id;
    }

    public get year() : number {
        return this._year;
    }

    public get make() : string {
        return this._make;
    }

    public get model() : string {
        return this._model;
    }
```

```
        public get article() : string {
            return this._article;
        }

    }
```

You've reached the end of the exercise. Note the following:

- How the desc data attribute is generated:

  ```
  [attr.data-desc]="car.make + ' ' + car.model"
  ```

- How the JavaScript is used to get the desc data attribute:

  ```
  const desc = event.target.parentElement.dataset.desc;
  ```

Two-Way Data Binding

This section focuses on two-way data binding.

Two-Way Data Binding with [(and)]

[()] is also known as *banana in a box*. You've already seen this, actually. The [(and)] format is used for two-way binding a property—in other words, reading it and writing it from the Model. The format is like this:

```
[(Data Binding Target)] = "Property"
```

"Data Binding Target" is something in the DOM (including Component and Directive tags) that can be bound to the property of the expression to the right side of the target. For the input box, the data binding target is ngModel, which corresponds to the text in the input box.

This is a property in the Model (an instance variable in the Component class).

Two-Way Data Binding: Example Code components-ex300

This is a component that changes foreground and background colors when the user changes their input, as shown in Figure 8-6:

1. *Build the app using the CLI*: Enter the following command:

   ```
   ng new components-ex300 --inline-template --inline-style
   ```

2. *Start* ng serve: Use the following code:

```
cd components-ex300
ng serve
```

3. *Open app*: Open your web browser and browse to localhost:4200.
    You should see the text "welcome to app!" That means your
    project is running.

4. *Edit module*: Edit the file src/app/app.module.ts and change it to
    the following:

```
import { BrowserModule } from '@angular/platform-browser';
import { NgModule } from '@angular/core';

import { AppComponent } from './app.component';
import { FormsModule } from '@angular/forms';

@NgModule({
  declarations: [
    AppComponent
  ],
  imports: [
    BrowserModule,
    FormsModule
  ],
  providers: [],
  bootstrap: [AppComponent]
})
export class AppModule { }
```

5. *Edit component*: Edit the file src/app/app.component.ts and
    change it to the following:

```
import { Component } from '@angular/core';

@Component({
  selector: 'app-root',
  template: `
```

```
<p>
Foreground: <input [(ngModel)]="fg" />
</p>
<p>
Background: <input [(ngModel)]="bg" />
</p>
<div [ngStyle]="{'color': fg, 'background-color': bg,
'padding': '5px'}">
Test
</div>
`,
styles: []
})
export class AppComponent {
  fg = "#ffffff";
  bg = "#000000";
}
```

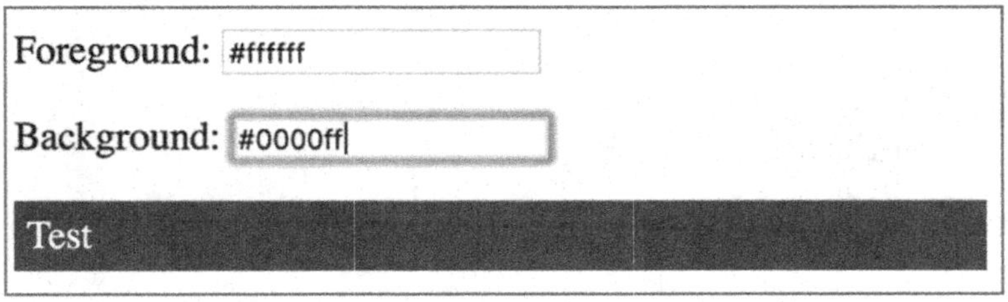

Figure 8-6. *Changing foreground and background colors*

Your app should be working at localhost:4200. When the user changes the color value, this updates the Model, which then updates the template's HTML:

- Binding occurs from the input field to the Model (when the user changes the color values). When the input field changes, the Model updates to match.

- Binding occurs from the Model to the template's HTML. When the Model updates, the template's HTML updates to match.

Event Handling

A user interface needs to respond to user input. That's why we have event handling in our component templates. We specify a target event and which statement should happen when that event occurs. The format goes like this:

```
(Target Event) = "Template Statement"
```

"Target Event" is the name of the event in-between the brackets. "Template Statement" is an instruction on what to do when the target event occurs. Normally this is a call to a method in the Component class that does something—normally, modify instance variables that are bound to the template, causing a change in the UI. The event information is available in the $event variable, which may or may not be utilized. For example, if you're watching for input in a text box, you could pass the value of the text in the text box to the method using information from $event. You'll see this in the next example.

Event Handling: Example Code components-ex400

This component accepts input in a textbox, captures the input event, and displays the input in both upper and lower-case, as shown in Figure 8-7:

1. *Build the app using the CLI*: Enter the following command:

   ```
   ng new components-ex400 --inline-template --inline-style
   ```

2. *Start* ng serve: Use the following code:

   ```
   cd components-ex400
   ng serve
   ```

3. *Open app*: Launch a web browser and navigate to localhost:4200. You should see "welcome to app!"

4. *Edit class*: Edit app.component.ts and change it to the following:

   ```
   import { Component, AfterViewInit, ViewChild } from
   '@angular/core';

   @Component({
   ```

111

```
    selector: 'app-root',
    template: `
    <input #input type="text" (input)="textInput($event)"
value=""/>
    <hr>
    Upper-Case: {{upperCase}}
    <br/>
    Lower-Case: {{lowerCase}}
    `,
    styles: []
})
export class AppComponent implements AfterViewInit{
  upperCase: string= '';
  lowerCase: string = '';
  @ViewChild('input') inputBox;

  textInput(event){
    this.upperCase = event.target.value.toUpperCase();
    this.lowerCase = event.target.value.toLowerCase();
  }

  ngAfterViewInit() {
    this.inputBox.nativeElement.focus()
  }
}
```

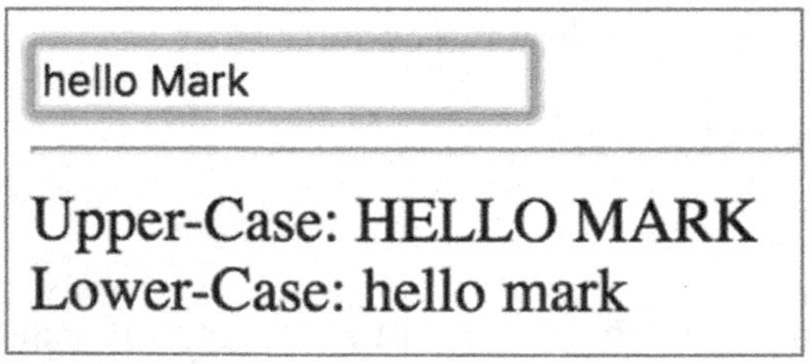

Figure 8-7. *Displaying the input*

Your app should be working at localhost:4200. Note the following:

- A template variable #input and viewChild are used to get a reference to the input box. After the view is initialized (lifecycle method ngAfterViewInit is fired), focus is set to the input box.

- The template uses the following code to listen for the `input` event, firing the method `textInput` (passing in the event object) when it occurs:

```
(input)="textInput($event)"
```

- The class has a method, `textInput`, that's fired by the `input` event. It calculates the uppercase and lowercase versions of the user's input, which it sets to instance variables that are bound (one-way) from the class to the template.

CDK

The Angular CDK (Component Development Kit) was released in 2017 with Angular 5. Its purpose is to enable developers to create high-quality Angular custom components. The CDK is contains services, directives, components, classes and modules. The CDK contains code for component accessibility, text directionality, platform detection, and dynamic component instantiation. If you really want to get into building your own library of custom reusable components then you will need to install the '@angular/cdk' node module and get started.

Summary

This chapter covers important concepts, so I strongly recommend following the examples before moving on. After reading this chapter you should have some basic knowledge of components, including what they consist of. You also know that a component consists of annotations, a template, and a class. We also talked about event handling.

Now that we can write user interface components, we'll turn our attention to modularizing our Angular code in the next chapter. Don't worry if you don't ully understand components yet—later chapters will go into more detail.

CHAPTER 9

Introducing Modules

The word *module* refers to small units of independent, reusable code. A typical module is a cohesive block of code dedicated to a single purpose. A module *exports* something of value in that code, typically one thing, such as an object.

This chapter is all about introducing the concepts of the different modules. It doesn't include many coding examples—you will be coding modules later on.

JavaScript gives you the freedom to do many things very badly—you're under no obligation to write reusable code. You can scatter your code anywhere. This has to change now that JavaScript and its environment are maturing. You need to make objects simpler by concealing their internal workings and leaving public interfaces available from the outside. You need to be able to package code up into reusable blocks that can be packaged and deployed separately from each other. You also need the ability to load them on demand, rather than loading everything up (slowly) when the app starts.

Different Types of Modules

This chapter introduces the three types of ways AngularJS, Angular, and JavaScript have modularized code:

- *The AngularJS module system included in the original version of Angular*: This enabled you to modularize your code at a course-grained level.

- *JavaScript modules now available in ES6 and TypeScript*: These enable you to modularize your code at a fine-grained level. Remember, there is one module per source code file (.ts or .js).

© Mark Clow 2018
M. Clow, *Angular 5 Projects*, https://doi.org/10.1007/978-1-4842-3279-8_9

- *The Angular module system*: This enables you to modularize your code at a course-grained level. You can bundle units of Angular code into modules. For example, if you're writing a system in Angular that contains an application for sales, an application for human resources, and an application for taxes, you could split these three applications into separate feature modules and a shared module for sharing common code, as illustrated in Figure 9-1.

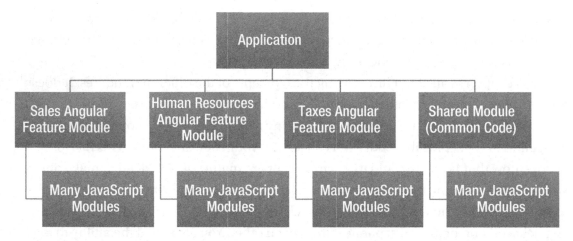

Figure 9-1. *Angular applications are made up of Angular modules and JavaScript modules*

AngularJS Module System

AngularJS had its own module system, which was simple. You had an Angular module, which could contain Angular controllers, directives, and so on.

In Figure 9-2 we're declaring module xxx, which depends on many other modules: ngCookies, ngRoute, ngResource, ngSanitize, angularSpinner, ui.bootstrap.demo, ui.bootstrap, ui.select, wj, and angularModalService. After the code, we would declare the items within this module xxx.

```
angular.module('xxx', [//'services.config',
                            'ngCookies',
                            'ngRoute',
                            'ngResource',
                            'ngSanitize',
                            'angularSpinner',
                            'ui.bootstrap.demo',
                            'ui.bootstrap',
                            'ui.select',
                            'wj',
                            'angularModalService'
])
```

Figure 9-2. Declaring module xxx

JavaScript Modules

JavaScript used to work with libraries, and these libraries were very useful for helping a developer in an area of development. For example, JQuery used to help developers with UI development. These libraries were well written but weren't implemented as modules. Rather, they were implemented as JavaScript scripts (as in .js script files) that would create JavaScript objects to do things. This was before the JavaScript module system existed.

Now ES6 and later support modules. In Javascript modules, every file is one module. You can code your own modules or use other people's modules. You can use Node to pull dependent modules into your project (into the node_modules folder).

When we code in Angular 5 in TypeScript, we use two JavaScript module keywords:

- Export: Export module code

- Import: Import module code

Exporting Code

You write your application as a collection of small modules. Your code exports objects from the module to the outside world using the export keyword. For example, the following code is used to tell TypeScript that you're exporting the class App for use elsewhere:

```
export class App {...}
```

Here's how to export a default object from a module:

```
module "foo" {
  export default function() { console.log("hello!") }
}
```

Importing Code

import statements tell TypeScript to go get module code from somewhere. The *somewhere* can be from someone else's module or from local code in the same project.

Importing Code from Someone Else's Module

When you use import statements to go get code from someone else's module, you identify the module name and the name of the item you want to import, specifying the module name after the from. This is typically the way you import code from a Node module. For example, you import the Component from Angular:

```
import { Component } from '@angular/core';
```

Here is how to import the date picker from ngx-bootstrap:

```
import { DatepickerModule } from 'ngx-bootstrap/datepicker';
```

Importing Your Project Code

When you import code from local code in the same project, you specify a relative path to that code. The following example specifies a relative path (the ./). This tells TypeScript that the code is in the same folder as the code that's going to use that module:

```
import {AppComponent} from './app.component';
```

Here are some more import syntaxes:

- Import all:

  ```
  import * as myModule from 'my-module';
  ```

- With named import, the name needs to *exactly* match the name of an object exported in the module:

  ```
  import { myMember } from 'my-module';
  ```

- For multiple named imports from a module, the names need to *exactly* match the names of objects exported in the module:

```
import { foo, bar } from 'my-module';
```

- With a default import from a module, the name doesn't need to match any object exported in the module. It can be an alias. It knows it has to import the default object from the module:

```
import myDefault from 'my-module';
```

Angular Module System

The Angular module system is how Angular bundles code into reusable modules. The Angular system code itself is modularized using this module system. Many third-parties provide additional functionality to Angular using modules, which you can easy include into your application.

Why doesn't Angular just use JavaScript modules? Why force developers into using its own module system? Well, for a start, it does use standard JavaScript modules, but they don't go far enough. They don't make it easy for Angular to declare long blocks of Angular code that consist of disparate objects tied together—for example, components, services, and pipes. In the earlier days of Angular 2, developers didn't have the option of Angular modules, and developers used module loaders to load and start applications (System.js). To me, it didn't work well in practice. It was hard to learn, easy to break, and too complicated.

I worked on Angular2 when it was in beta and liked the product, but I hated how complicated it was with module loading, having to learn System.js et al. I came back to it later to find that you could quickly and simply use the Angular CLI to build a modularized application that used Webpack for deployment. I welcome the Angular module system and think it works elegantly with the CLI and Webpack.

Modules in the Start Project

You've already used the Angular module system, even if you didn't realize it. If you open the Start project you created using the CLI, you'll see that you already have a file app. module.ts. Note that modules should have .module in their names. Let's open it up and take a look:

```
import { BrowserModule } from '@angular/platform-browser';
import { NgModule } from '@angular/core';
import { FormsModule } from '@angular/forms';
import { HttpModule } from '@angular/http';

import { AppComponent } from './app.component';

@NgModule({
  declarations: [
    AppComponent
  ],
  imports: [
    BrowserModule,
    FormsModule,
    HttpModule
  ],
  providers: [],
  bootstrap: [AppComponent]
})
export class AppModule { }
```

Let's look at some of the elements here:

- @NgModule *annotation*: This annotation is the most important part of this class. It's a function that accepts an object and uses the object to provide metadata to Angular about the module: how to compile it and how to run it. So, the @NgModule is Angular's declarative way for you to tell Angular how to put the pieces together. Note that the @NgModule itself needs to be imported from @angular/core at the top.

- `declarations`: This should be an array of the Angular components, directives, and pipes used by your module and nothing else—no ES6 classes or anything else. When you add a component using the CLI command `ng generate component`, it imports the component and adds it to this list of declarations. If you add a component and use it without declaring it here, you'll receive an error message in the browser console.

- `import`: This should be an array of Angular modules required by the application here. These modules must be defined using `@NgModule`. Angular itself has many system modules that you'll find useful, and the CLI includes several of these for you by default, including the browser module, the forms module, and the http module.

- `providers`: This should be an array of Angular `provider` objects required by the application. These `provider` objects are services classes and values that are injected into your classes for you using dependency injection. If you had a common service object used by the components to talk to the server, you would add it here as a provider.

- `bootstrap`: You can use modules to contain the code for your application. To run, your application needs to know how to start and with what component it should start (the root). This is where you specify the root component, which will be created and mounted into the HTML when the application starts. This root component is often called AppComponent.

Root Module

Your Angular application can contain multiple modules. But it always has a starting point, a module that it uses to bootstrap itself. This is the root module, often called the AppModule.

Routing Module

We'll go into routing later on, but routing is very important to an Angular application. It allows the user to map components to URLs and navigate the user interface. When we use the CLI to build an Angular application, it builds a separate module for your application's routing, usually in the file app-routing.ts. This may seem superfluous, but it very neatly packages the Angular routing objects together with your app's routing setup together into one module, which handles all routing for your app.

Feature Modules

Domain-driven design (DDD) is an approach to software development the address complex needs by connecting the implementation to an evolving model. DDD often has to deal with modeling very large, complex business requirements, and its approach to this is to break these requirements into contexts. *Bounded contexts* are areas of business requirements that can be logically separated, as illustrated in Figure 9-3.

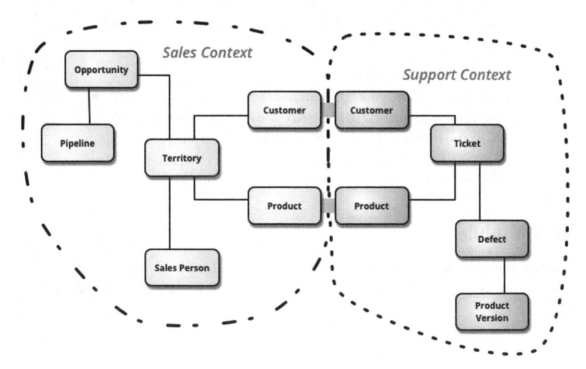

Figure 9-3. *Bounded contexts*

As you can see, in Figure 9-3 there are two contexts: Sales and Support. Each could be a separate part of your Angular application. In fact, each could be contained in its own separate module, called a *feature module*. Each module can contain specific code to meet specific requirements not required anywhere else. For example, the Sales module could contain an Angular UI to manage the sales pipeline, and this would not be used anywhere else. So, a feature module often contains code that isn't intended to be used outside that module.

When required, the root module can include as many feature modules as required. The feature module can even be loaded on demand when the user (for example) clicks the Sales menu.

Shared Modules

You can think of feature modules as blocks of code that aren't shared. *Shared* modules are the opposite—they contain the most commonly used code that's modularized so it can be reused as much as possible. When required, the root module can include as many shared modules as required.

Angular Module System: Example modules-ex100

This example is a very basic exercise of how you can use root modules, feature modules, and shared modules together.

The example has a component with two links at the top: Sales and Support. You can click each link to navigate through the app, between the two components. Each of these two components, Sales and Support, is a separate feature module.

This example has a root module, App, the feature modules (already mentioned), and a component from a shared module called Shared, as illustrated in Figure 9-4.

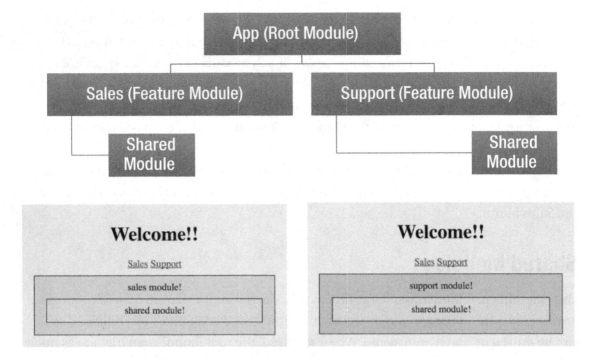

Figure 9-4. *Example of Angular module system*

Let's go through the example:

1. *Build the app using the CLI*: Use the following command:

   ```
   ng new modules-ex100
   ```

2. *Start* ng serve: Use the following code:

   ```
   cd modules-ex100
   ng serve
   ```

3. *Open app*: Launch a web browser and navigate to localhost:4200. You should see "welcome to app!"

4. *Generate modules*: Let's use the CLI to generate additional modules:

   ```
   ng generate module shared
   ng generate module routing --routing
   ng generate module sales
   ng generate module support
   ```

5. *Generate components*: Let's use the CLI to generate additional components:

```
ng generate component sales
ng generate component support
ng generate component shared
```

6. *Edit component styles*: Edit the file sales.component.css and change it to the following:

```css
div {
    background-color: #bdcebe;
    border: 1px solid #000000;
    padding: 10px;
    margin: 10px;
}
```

Edit the file support.component.css and change it to the following:

```css
div {
    background-color: #eca1a6;
    border: 1px solid #000000;
    padding: 10px;
    margin: 10px;
}
```

Edit the file shared.component.css and change it to the following:

```css
div {
    background-color: #d6cbd3;
    border: 1px solid #000000;
    padding: 10px;
    margin: 10px;
}
```

Edit the file app.component.css and change it to the following:

```
div {
    background-color: #e3eaa7;
    border: 10px;
    padding: 10px;
}
```

7. *Edit component templates*: Edit the file sales.component.html and change it to the following:

```
<div>
  sales module!
  <app-shared></app-shared>
</div>
```

Edit the file support.component.html and change it to the following:

```
<div>
  support module!
  <app-shared></app-shared>
</div>
```

Edit the file shared.component.html and change it to the following:

```
<div>
  shared module!
</div>
```

Edit the file app.component.html and change it to the following:

```
<div style="text-align:center">
  <h1>
    Welcome!!
  </h1>
  <a [routerLink]="['sales']">Sales</a>
  <a [routerLink]="['support']">Support</a>
  <router-outlet></router-outlet>
</div>
```

8. *Edit routing module*: Edit the file routing.module.ts and change it to the following:

```
import { NgModule } from '@angular/core';
import { CommonModule } from '@angular/common';
import { Routes, RouterModule } from '@angular/router';
import { SalesComponent } from '../sales/sales.component';
import { SupportComponent } from '../support/support.component';

const routes: Routes = [
  {
    path: 'sales',
    component: SalesComponent
  },
  {
    path: 'support',
    component: SupportComponent
  },
  {
    path: '**',
    component: SalesComponent
  }
];

@NgModule({
  imports: [RouterModule.forRoot(routes)],
  exports: [RouterModule],
  providers: []
})
export class RoutingModule { }
```

9. *Edit Sales module*: Edit the file sales.module.ts and change it to the following:

```
import { NgModule } from '@angular/core';
import { CommonModule } from '@angular/common';
import { SalesComponent } from './sales.component';
```

```
@NgModule({
  imports: [
    CommonModule
  ],
  declarations: [SalesComponent]
})
export class SalesModule { }
```

10. *Edit Shared module*: Edit the file shared.module.ts and change it
     to the following:

```
import { NgModule } from '@angular/core';
import { CommonModule } from '@angular/common';
import { SharedComponent } from './shared.component';

@NgModule({
  imports: [
    CommonModule
  ],
  exports: [
    SharedComponent
  ],
  declarations: [SharedComponent]
})
export class SharedModule { }
```

11. *Edit Support module*: Edit the file support.module.ts and change it
     to the following:

```
import { NgModule } from '@angular/core';
import { CommonModule } from '@angular/common';
import { SupportComponent } from './support.component';

@NgModule({
  imports: [
    CommonModule
  ],
```

```
    declarations: [SupportComponent]
})
export class SupportModule { }
```

12. *Edit App module*: Edit the file app.module.ts and change it to the following:

```
import { BrowserModule } from '@angular/platform-browser';
import { NgModule } from '@angular/core';

import { AppComponent } from './app.component';
import { RoutingModule } from './routing/routing.module';
import { SalesComponent } from './sales/sales.component';
import { SupportComponent } from './support/support.component';
import { SharedModule } from './shared/shared.module';

@NgModule({
  declarations: [
    AppComponent,
    SalesComponent,
    SupportComponent
  ],
  imports: [
    BrowserModule,
    RoutingModule,
    SharedModule
  ],
  providers: [],
  bootstrap: [AppComponent]
})
export class AppModule { }
```

Your app should be working at localhost:4200. Note the following:

- The Routing module provides the code for the app routing. The root app imports this module, and all the routing code is ready and usable.

- The Shared module provides the shared component. The root app only has to import this module to get access to its component.

- The Sales and Support modules don't have to import the Shared module or the Shared component, even though it's used in the Sales and Support components.

- The Sales and Support modules don't import anything other than the Angular Common module. This Common module has nothing to do with our code. It's Angular's way of providing the code for basic Angular directives like `NgIf`, `NgFor`, and so on.

Deployment: Separate Modules

The ability to have feature modules, shared modules, and so on accessible from one root module sounds great, but the problem is that you may need to update the feature modules separately, especially if you have a separate team working on each feature. For example, the "Sales" people may have different release dates than the "Support" people. Unfortunately, the example under examination is deployed in one group of Webpack modules.

If you want Sales to be deployable separately from Support, then each should be its own single page application in its own folder. That makes life much easier when it's time to deploy.

Deployment: Using Node to Manage Dependencies on Common Code

Another issue with deployment is the common code. Sales may need a different version of the common code than Support. One may use new common objects, and the other may not. That makes it a good time to consider using Node to manage each project's dependency on common code.

You can create Node modules from Angular projects. Remember, Angular has modules that are deployed through Node modules. That's a little beyond the scope of this book, but I've done this myself, thanks to the following superb article: `https://medium.com/@cyrilletuzi/how-to-build-and-publish-an-angular-module-7ad19c0b4464`.

You'll need to set up some code from a public code repository for this to work, such as GitHub. Here's a very simple example that I put up on GitHub: `https://github.com/markclowisg/sharedcomponents`.

Useful Node Commands

When working with Angular and Node together, you may also want to consider using the node package manager commands `npm link` and `npm scope`:

- `npm link`: This is very useful when it comes time to build your Node modules. It lets you set up a link so that dependent projects can use your Node code without it having to be continually rebuilt and redeployed to your repository. It's much easier to do everything locally and copy up to your repository later on.

- `npm scope`: This is useful when you have several npm common code projects and you want to group them under a name prefix. Angular does this with its `@angular` npm package prefix. You may want to consider this. If you work for company "abc" and you have two common npm packages for components and services, you may want to use scopes so they can be `@abc/components` and `@abc/services`.

Summary

This chapter covered a wide range of subjects to do with modularization. It introduced you to the concept of modularization and how it's implemented in JavaScript and Angular.

If you found this chapter overwhelming, don't worry. You could skip the "Deployment" section and come back to it later. Modularization may seem complicated and somewhat obtuse, but it has value and can make your projects more maintainable.

The next chapter covers Webpack, which the Angular CLI uses to bundle up your code into deployable files.

CHAPTER 10

Introducing Webpack

Nowadays you can do a lot more stuff in modern browsers, and this is going to increase even more in the future. Thanks to technologies like Angular 5, there will be fewer page reloads and more JavaScript code in each page, a lot of code on the client side. You need a way to deploy all this code efficiently so that it loads quickly.

Your complex client-side application may contain modules, some of which may load synchronously, some asynchronously. So how do we package it all and deploy it most efficiently – we use Webpack!

Webpack and the Angular CLI

The Angular CLI uses Webpack to transpile, compile, and deploy project code. It also uses the webpack-dev-server as its web server by default. Later in this chapter you I talk about Webpack configuration and webpack.config.js. You'll look for it in your project and notice that it's missing. That's on purpose because the people who wrote the Angular CLI wanted to hide as many configuration details as possible to make things simpler, and this includes the Webpack configuration.

The following Angular CLI command makes the Webpack configuration file available:

```
ng eject
```

However, take care with this command because there may be some unexpected side-effects. See https://github.com/angular/angular-cli/wiki/eject and http://stackoverflow.com/questions/39187556/angular-cli-where-is-webpack-config-js-file-new-2017-feb-ng-eject for more on this subject.

Webpack is a module bundler. It takes modules with dependencies and generates static assets representing those modules. Figure 10-1 illustrates.

© Mark Clow 2018
M. Clow, *Angular 5 Projects*, https://doi.org/10.1007/978-1-4842-3279-8_10

```
"dependencies": {
    "@angular/animations": "^5.0.0",
    "@angular/common": "^5.0.0",
    "@angular/compiler": "^5.0.0",
    "@angular/core": "^5.0.0",
    "@angular/forms": "^5.0.0",
    "@angular/http": "^5.0.0",
```

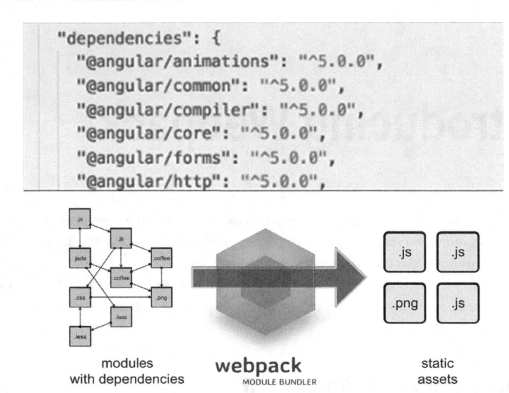

Figure 10-1. *Webpack generates static assets representing modules*

Modules and Dependencies

If you use Node for your development, Webpack will read your Node configuration file packages.json and automatically include your dependencies as static assets in the build. That takes the pain out of configuring module loading and deployment—you don't have to figure anything out. I've used Webpack on every Angular 5 project I've ever worked on because it makes life easier.

Webpack is good for large projects because it allows for development and production modes. Development mode can utilize non-minimized assets like JavaScript, enabling your application to be debugged in this mode. Production mode can use minimized assets so it has a lighter footprint.

Your code base can be split into multiple *chunks*, and those chunks can be loaded on demand, reducing the initial loading time of your application. Result: quicker loading times. As a developer, you also have control over configuring these chunks (more on this later).

The development process goes like this:

1. Code your project.

2. Run Webpack as part of your build process (or have it run for you by the CLI).

3. After the build, your static assets are ready to deploy on the server.

Installing and Configuring Webpack

You don't need to install Webpack if you're using the CLI. Webpack runs under Node. But if you want to experiment with Webpack separately, you can use the following command to install it (from the root folder of your project):

```
npm install webpack -g
```

If you run the `ng eject` command mentioned earlier, your Webpack options will be contained in the webpack.config.js file in the root folder of your project. In this file you'll find the following:

- *Output path*: You can specify where the bundled assets are put—the output path.

- *Entry points*: Your app can start in different places using different code. Webpack will pack the code for deployment so that it can start with these different codes but share common packaged chunks.

- *Loaders*: A loader is a Node function that takes a type of file and converts files of this type into a new source for bundling (see Figure 10-2). Loaders are Node packages used by Webpack.

```
loaders: [
  // Support for .ts files.
  {
    test: /\.ts$/,
    loader: 'ts-loader',
    query: {
      'ignoreDiagnostics': [
        2403, // 2403 -> Subsequent variable declarations
        2300, // 2300 -> Duplicate identifier
        2374, // 2374 -> Duplicate number index signature
        2375  // 2375 -> Duplicate string index signature
      ]
    },
    exclude: [ /\.(spec|e2e)\.ts$/, /node_modules\/(?!(ng2-.+))/ ]
  },
```

Figure 10-2. *Loaders*

- *Plugins*: I use the CommonsChunk plugin in the book's example
  project to split our code into deployable chunks that can be loaded
  separately. The CommonsChunk plugin checks which chunks of
  code (modules) you use the most and puts them in a file. This gives
  you a common file that has the CSS and JavaScript needed by every
  page in your application.

```
plugins: [
  new CommonsChunkPlugin({ name: 'vendor', filename: 'vendor.js', minChunks: Infinity }),
  new CommonsChunkPlugin({ name: 'common', filename: 'common.js', minChunks: 2, chunks: ['app', 'vendor'] })
  // include uglify in production
],
```

The code in Figure 10-3 is used to create the following:

- app.js

- app.map

- common.js

- common.map

- vendor.js

- vendor.map

Summary

This short chapter introduced you to the basics of Webpack. Webpack offers developers a surprising amount of control, and we could spend a great deal of time going into its configurability.

But we need to continue learning Angular. Chapter 11 introduces another very important element: directives.

CHAPTER 11

Introducing Directives

Directives are markers on a DOM element (such as an attribute) that tell Angular to attach a specified behavior to an existing element.

Directives have been around since AngularJS. They're quite complex to use, though they're a lot easier to use in Angular, especially when it comes to passing data into directives. Directives used to be the main way of creating custom tags in an AngularJS application; now that's been replaced by directives and components.

Angular itself provides many directives to help you in your coding. You can also code your own.

As Chapter 8 stated, components have three main elements:

- The annotation provides Angular with metadata to combine all the parts together into a component.

- The template contains markup (usually HTML) that's used to render the component in the browser.

- The class contains the data and code for the component. The code implements the desired behavior of the component.

As you can see, the template is used to generate the markup for the display of the component. This markup may include tags (or other selectors) for other Angular components, thus allowing the composition of components from other components. This markup may also include directives to implement certain behaviors.

For example, you may have a component that displays the promotion details of a promotion request. However, someone wanting to view the promotion request may not have the rights to view the information, meaning some elements should be hidden. You could use the Angular `ngIf` directive to evaluate the user's rights and hide or show elements based on them.

M. Clow, *Angular 5 Projects*, https://doi.org/10.1007/978-1-4842-3279-8_11

Types of Directives

Now we know that directives are used by the component templates, but they may affect the output of templates in different ways. Some directives may completely change the structure of the output of the template. These directives can change the DOM layout by adding and removing view DOM elements. Let's call these *structural* directives. And some directives may simply change the appearance of items output by the template. Let's call these *non-structural* directives.

Angular includes several structural directives for you to use in the template:

- NgIf

- NgFor

- NgSwitch, NgSwitchWhen, NgSwitchDefault

Angular also includes several non-structural directives for use in the template:

- NgClass

- NgStyle

- NgControlName

- NgModel

ngIf

This is a directive that you add to an element in the markup, usually to a container element like a div. If the template expression for the ngIf is true, then the content inside the element is included in the view DOM after the bindings have been completed. If the template expression for the ngIf is false, then the content inside the element is excluded from the view DOM after the bindings have been completed. So, the ngIf directive is used to include or exclude an element of the UI, including the element's child elements. Markup excluded by ngIf wont be invisible, it just wont be in the DOM at all.

In this example (directives-ex100), we toggle between showing a name and an address, as shown in Figure 11-1.

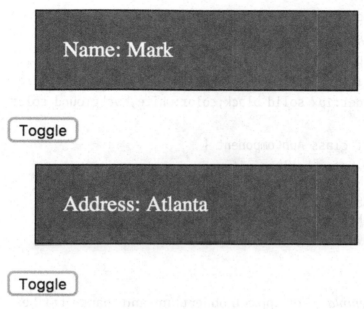

Figure 11-1. *Toggling between name and address*

Let's use ngIf to hide and show elements:

1. *Build the app using the CLI*: Use the following command:

   ```
   ng new directives-ex100
   ```

2. *Start* ng serve: Use the following code:

   ```
   cd directives-ex100
   ng serve
   ```

3. *Open app*: Open web browser and navigate to localhost:4200. You should see "welcome to app!"

4. *Edit class*: Edit app.component.ts and change it to the following:

```
import { Component } from '@angular/core';

@Component({
  selector: 'app-root',
  templateUrl: './app.component.html',
  styles: ['div.box { width: 200px;padding:20px;margin:20px;
  border:1px solid black;color:white;background-color:green }']
})
export class AppComponent {
  showName: boolean = true;

  toggle(){
    this.showName = !this.showName;
  }
}
```

5. *Edit template*: Edit app.component.html and change it to the following:

```
<div *ngIf="this.showName" class="box">
  Name: Mark
</div>
<div *ngIf="!this.showName" class="box">
  Address: Atlanta
</div>
<button (click)="this.toggle()">Toggle</button>
```

ngFor

This is a directive for processing each item of an iterable object, outputting a markup for each one. This is known as a structural directive because it can change the DOM layout by adding and removing view DOM elements.

ndFor is useful for generating repeating content, such as a list of customers, elements of a dropdown, and so on.

Each item processed of the iterable has variables available in its template context, as shown in Table 11-1.

Table 11-1. *ngFor Variables*

Variable	Description
Item itself	Example: ngFor="#name of names". In this case, the item has the variable name.
Index	Current loop iteration for each template context.
last	Boolean value indicating whether the item is the last one in the iteration.
even	Boolean value indicating whether this item has an even index.
odd	Boolean value indicating whether this item has an odd index.

This will be example directives-ex200, as shown in Figure 11-2.

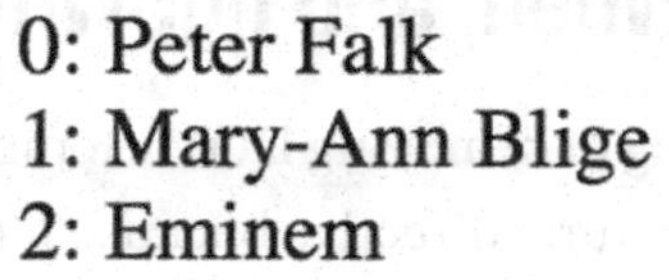

0: Peter Falk
1: Mary-Ann Blige
2: Eminem

Figure 11-2. *ngFor showing a list*

Let's use ngFor to show a list:

1. *Build the app using the CLI*: Use the following command:

   ng new directives-ex200

2. *Start* ng serve:

   cd directives-ex200
   ng serve

3. *Open app*: Open a web browser and navigate to localhost:4200.
   You should see "welcome to app!"

4. *Edit class*: Edit app.component.ts and change it to the following:

   ```
   import { Component } from '@angular/core';

   @Component({
     selector: 'app-root',
     templateUrl: './app.component.html',
     styleUrls: ['./app.component.css']
   })
   ```

143

```
export class AppComponent {
  names = [
    'Peter Falk', 'Mary-Ann Blige', 'Eminem'];
}
```

5. *Edit template*: Edit app.component.html and change it to the
    following:

    ```
    <div *ngFor="let name of names; let i = index;">
      <div>{{i}}: {{name}}</div>
    </div>
    ```

ngSwitch, ngSwitchWhen, and ngSwitchDefault

ngSwitch is a directive for adding or removing DOM elements when they match switch
expressions. It's known as a structural directive because it can change the DOM layout
by adding and removing view DOM elements.

This will be example directives-ex300, as shown in Figure 11-3.

Figure 11-3. ngSwitch hiding and showing elements

Let's use ngSwitch to hide and show elements according to your selection:

1. *Build the app using the CLI*: Use the following command:

   ```
   ng new directives-ex300
   ```

2. *Start* ng serve: Use the following code:

   ```
   cd directives-ex300
   ng serve
   ```

3. *Open app*: Open a web browser and navigate to localhost:4200. You should see "welcome to app!"

4. *Edit class*: Edit app.component.ts and change it to the following:

   ```
   import { Component } from '@angular/core';

   @Component({
     selector: 'app-root',
     templateUrl: './app.component.html',
     styles: ['.block1 {background-color:#d5f4e6;margin:10px;
     padding:10px;}',
     '.block2 {background-color:#d5f4ff;margin:10px;padding:10px;}',
     '.block3 {background-color:#d5cce6;margin:10px;padding:10px;}']
   })
   export class AppComponent {
     selection = 'name';
     options = ['name','address','other'];
   }
   ```

5. *Edit template*: Edit app.component.html and change it to the following:

   ```
   <select [(ngModel)]="selection">
     <option *ngFor="let option of options">{{option}}</option>
   </select>
   <div [ngSwitch]="selection">
     <div class="block1" *ngSwitchCase="options[0]">name</div>
     <div class="block2" *ngSwitchCase="options[1]">address</div>
     <div class="block3" *ngSwitchDefault>other</div>
   </div>
   ```

145

6. *Edit module*: Edit app.module.ts and change it to the following:

```
import { BrowserModule } from '@angular/platform-browser';
import { NgModule } from '@angular/core';
import { FormsModule } from '@angular/forms'
import { AppComponent } from './app.component';

@NgModule({
  declarations: [
    AppComponent
  ],
  imports: [
    BrowserModule, FormsModule
  ],
  providers: [],
  bootstrap: [AppComponent]
})
export class AppModule { }
```

ngClass

We can the change the appearance of DOM elements by adding or removing classes using this directive. Its argument is an object that contains pairs of the following:

- A CSS class name

- An expression

The CSS class name is added to the target DOM element if the expression is true—otherwise it's omitted. It is not just useful for setting a CSS class. It's probably easier to use something like the following code:

```
<div [class]="classNames">Customer {{name}}.</div>
```

In the next example, ngClass lets the user click an animal in an animal list to select it. The selected animal is highlighted in red. This will be example directives-ex400, as shown in Figure 11-4.

cat

dog

zebra

giraffe

Figure 11-4. ngClass highlighting in a list

Let's do example directives-ex400:

1. *Build the app using the CLI*: Use the following command:

ng new directives-ex400

2. *Start* ng serve: Use the following code:

cd directives-ex400
ng serve

3. *Open app*: Open a web browser and navigate to localhost:4200. You should see "welcome to app!"

4. *Edit class*: Edit app.component.ts and change it to the following:

```
import { Component } from '@angular/core';
@Component({
  selector: 'app-root',
  templateUrl: './app.component.html',
  styles: [
    '.selected { color: white; background-color:red; padding: 10px;
    margin: 10px }',
    '.unselected { background-color: white; padding: 10px;
    margin: 10px}'
  ]
})
export class AppComponent {
  selectedAnimal = 'cat';
  animals = ['cat', 'dog', 'zebra', 'giraffe'];
```

147

```
    onAnimalClicked(event:Event){
      const clickedAnimal = event.srcElement.innerHTML.trim();
      this.selectedAnimal = clickedAnimal;
    }
  }
```

5. *Edit template*: Edit app.component.html and change it to the
    following:

```
<div *ngFor="let animal of animals">
  <div [ngClass]="{'selected': animal === selectedAnimal,
'unselected' : animal !== selectedAnimal}"
    (click)="onAnimalClicked($event)">{{animal}}</div>
</div>
```

Your app should be working at localhost:4200.

ngStyle

This is a directive for setting the CSS styles of an element. If you only want to set one
style, it's probably easier to use something like the following code:

```
<div [style.fontSize]="selected ? 'x-large' : 'smaller'" >
  Some text.
</div>
```

But if you want to set multiple styles, ngStyle is the way to go. This directive expects
an expression that evaluates to an object containing style properties. This expression can
be inline code like this:

```
[ngStyle]="{'color': 'blue', 'font-size': '24px', 'font-weight': 'bold'}"
```

Or a function call like this:

```
[ngStyle]="setStyles(animal)"
```

... later on in the class ...

```
setStyles(animal:String){
    let styles = {
```

```
    'width' : '50px'
  }
  return styles;
}
```

It lets the user click on an animal in an animal list to select it. The selected animal is highlighted in red, as shown in Figure 11-5.

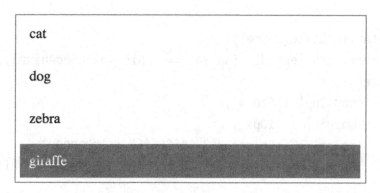

```
cat

dog

zebra

giraffe
```

Figure 11-5. *ngStyle highlighting in a list*

Let's do example directives-ex500:

1. *Build the app using the CLI*: Use the following command:

   ```
   ng new directives-ex500
   ```

2. *Start* ng serve: Use the following code:

   ```
   cd directives-ex500
   ng serve
   ```

3. *Open app*: Open a web browser and navigate to localhost:4200. You should see "welcome to app!"

4. *Edit class*: Edit app.component.ts and change it to the following:

   ```
   import { Component } from '@angular/core';
   @Component({
     selector: 'app-root',
     templateUrl: './app.component.html'
   })
   ```

```
export class AppComponent {
  selectedAnimal = 'cat';
  animals = ['cat', 'dog', 'zebra', 'giraffe'];

  onAnimalClicked(event:Event){
    const clickedAnimal = event.srcElement.innerHTML.trim();
    this.selectedAnimal = clickedAnimal;
  }

  getAnimalStyle(animal){
    const isSelected = (animal === this.selectedAnimal);
    return {
      'padding' : '10px',
      'margin' : '10px',
      'color' : isSelected ? '#ffffff' : '#000000',
      'background-color' : isSelected ? '#ff0000' : '#ffffff',
    }
  }
}
```

5. *Edit template*: Edit app.component.html and change it to the
    following:

```
<div *ngFor="let animal of animals">
  <div [ngStyle]="getAnimalStyle(animal)" (click)="onAnimalClicked
($event)">{{animal}}</div>
</div>
```

Your app should be working at localhost:4200.

Note   Angular also uses other directives for form handling. I cover those in a later
chapter.

Creating Directives

Directives and components are both Angular objects that correspond to elements in the markup and can modify the resulting user interface. They both have selectors. The *selector* is used to identify the component or directive that's associated with markup in the web page or a template. For components, you usually use the tag name—for example `CustomerList`. For directives, you usually use a tag attribute name, which utilizes square brackets—for example, `[tooltip]`.

Directives and components both have annotations. Directives have the `@Directive` annotation, and Components have the `@Component` annotation. They also both have classes, and the classes can use dependency injection in the same manner through the constructor.

However, deirectives and components aren't completely the same. A component requires a view, for example, whereas a directive doesn't. Directives don't have a template. There's no bundled HTML markup that's used to render the element.

Directives add behavior to an existing DOM element. For example, you could add a directive for a tooltip. You create the directive, you add the directive selector to the HTML or the templates that use it, and it delivers the functionality (you will need to add imports as well).

Creating a directive is similar to creating a component:

1. Import the `Directive` decorator.

2. Add the `@Directive` annotation, including a CSS attribute selector (in square brackets) that identifies the directive as an attribute. You can also add other elements to the `@Directive` annotation, including input properties and host mappings.

3. Specify the name of the public input property for binding (if required).

4. Write the `Directive` class. This class will use constructor injection and will probably manipulate the injected element and renderer.

5. Apply the decorator to the components or directives that are going to use it.

As mentioned earlier, directives are markers on a DOM element (such as an attribute) that tell Angular to attach a specified behavior to an existing element. That means we need a way to access the DOM element that the directive is being applied to, as well as ways to modify the DOM element.

Angular provides us with two very useful objects: the `ElementRef` and the `Renderer`.

- The `ElementRef` object gives you direct access to the DOM element for the directive through the `nativeElement` property. Be cautious with the use of the `ElementRef` object. Permitting direct access to the DOM can make your application more vulnerable to XSS attacks.

- The `Renderer` object gives us many helper methods to enable us to modify the DOM element.

We can inject both into our class. The following code accepts the `ElementRef` (which lets you access the DOM element using its `nativeElement` property) and the `Renderer` through the constructor and makes each one a private instance variable:

```
constructor(private element: ElementRef, private renderer: Renderer) {
}
```

Creating Simple Directive: Example directives-ex600

This is a simple directive that changes the size of the HTML element to which it's added:

1. *Build the app using the CLI*: Use the following command:

   ```
   ng new directives-ex600
   ```

2. Navigate to directory; Use the following code:

   ```
   cd directives-ex600
   ```

3. *Create directive using CLI*: Use the CLI to create the files and also modify the module app.module.ts:

   ```
   ng generate directive sizer
   ```

This will generate some files, including sizer.directive.ts.

4. *Edit sizer.directive.ts*: Change it to the following:

```
import { Directive, Input, Component, ElementRef, Renderer,
|OnInit } from '@angular/core';

@Directive({
  selector: '[sizer]'
})
export class SizerDirective implements OnInit {
  @Input() sizer : string;

  constructor(private element: ElementRef, private renderer: Renderer) {
  }

  ngOnInit() {
    this.renderer.setElementStyle(this.element.nativeElement,
    'font-size', this.sizer);
  }
}
```

Note how the directive does its work in the ngOnInit method
that's fired after the directive has initialized. If you were to
move the setElementStyle code to the constructor, this would
work because the sizer input variable doesn't have its value
immediately set—it's set when the app component initializes.

5. *Edit template*: Edit app.component.html and change it to the
following:

```
<div sizer="72px">
  {{title}}
</div>
```

6. *View application*: Open a web browser and navigate to
localhost:4200. It should display "app works" in large text.

Your app should be working at localhost:4200. Note how you can use the renderer to
update the style and change the size.

Accessing the DOM Events in Directives

We may also need a way to access the DOM events for the element linked to the directive. Angular provides different ways to access these events.

Using the Directive Element host

This can be used to specify the events, actions, properties and attributes related to the host element. It can be used to bind events to code in the class:

```
@Directive({
  selector: 'input',
  host: {
    '(change)': 'onChange($event)',
    '(window:resize)': 'onResize($event)'
  }
})
class InputDirective {
  onChange(event:Event) {
    // invoked when the input element fires the 'change' event
  }
  onResize(event:Event) {
    // invoked when the window fires the 'resize' event
  }
}
```

HostListeners

Angular HostListeners are annotations that allow you to bind a method in your class to a DOM event:

```
@HostListener('mouseenter') onMouseEnter() {
  this.highlight('yellow');
}

@HostListener('mouseleave') onMouseLeave() {
  this.highlight(null);
}
```

```
private highlight(color: string) {
  this.el.nativeElement.style.backgroundColor = color;
}
```

Accessing the DOM Properties in Directives

You may want to modify the properties for the element linked to the directive. You can do this using the element ref. However, there's another way. You can use the @HostBinding directive to bind a DOM property of the element to an instance variable in your Angular directive. Then you can update the value of the variable, and the DOM property will automatically be updated to match.

For example, in the following code you could control the background color of the element by modifying the value of the backgroundColor instance variable:

```
@Directive({
    selector: '[myHighlight]',
})
class MyDirective {
  @HostBinding('style.background-color') backgroundColor:string = 'yellow';
}
```

Creating a Directive with Events: Example directives-ex700

This is an example directive that works with host events. Host events map to DOM events in the host element. They're useful when you need a directive that responds to things happening on the DOM:

1. *Build the app using the CLI*: Use the following command:

   ```
   ng new directives-ex700
   ```

2. *Navigate to directory*: Use this command:

   ```
   cd directives-ex700
   ```

3. *Create directive using CLI*: Use the CLI to create the files and modify the module app.module.ts:

```
ng generate directive hoverer
```

This will generate some files, including hoverer.directive.ts.

4. *Edit hoverer.directive.ts*: Change it to the following:

```
import { Directive, Input, ElementRef, Renderer } from '@angular/core';

@Directive({
  selector: '[hoverer]',
  host: {
    '(mouseenter)': 'onMouseEnter()',
    '(mouseleave)': 'onMouseLeave()'
  }
})

export class HovererDirective {
  @Input() hoverer;

  constructor(
    private elementRef:ElementRef,
    private renderer:Renderer) { }

  onMouseEnter(){
    this.renderer.setElementStyle(
      this.elementRef.nativeElement, 'color', this.hoverer);
  }

  onMouseLeave(){
    this.renderer.setElementStyle(
      this.elementRef.nativeElement, 'color', 'black');
  }
}
```

5. *Edit template*: Edit app.component.html and change it to the following:

```
<h1 hoverer="red">{{title}}</h1>
```

6. *View Application*: Open a web browser and navigate to
    localhost:4200. It should turn red when you hover over
    "welcome to app!"

Your app should be working at localhost:4200.

Summary

After studing this chapter, you should know how to write directives and understand how they're different from components.

Directives are very useful when reused to add common behavior to user interfaces. They're often placed into shared modules so they can be reused across applications. For example, you could write a directive to enable or disable buttons across an entire application based on the user's settings (or some other state). This directive could be specified by an element attribute. You would add the directive to the shared module (or the main module) and then modify the application's templates to include the directive's attrıbute on the buttons.

We're done with directives for the moment. The next chapter gets back to components and looks at them in more detail.

CHAPTER 12

More Components

The purpose of this chapter is to enhance your knowledge of components further with more advanced topics.

Components and Child Components

As you know, a component is a building block in a user interface. An Angular application always has an Application (or root) component. This component (like other components) has a tag in the HTML, and Angular bootstraps into that component. This Application component (like other components) can contain other (child) components.

So, components can contain other components. This is known as composition. As I put it in an earlier chapter, components are like LEGO bricks for the UI. *Composition* is the art of composing an application using these LEGO bricks together. I'll introduce composition with an example.

When you write a single page application, the convention is that you have a hierarchy of components—a composition. Figure 12-1 shows an example.

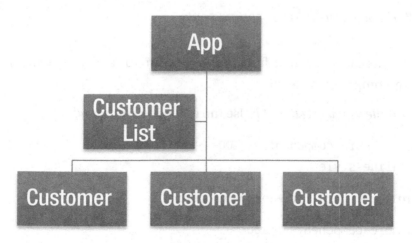

Figure 12-1. *Hierarchy of components*

M. Clow, *Angular 5 Projects*, https://doi.org/10.1007/978-1-4842-3279-8_12

When you're coding with a composition, you must take great care to store the data (known as *state*) in the correct place so it's never repeated (stored twice). Pete Hunt at Facebook wrote a superb article about this at `https://facebook.github.io/react/docs/thinking-in-react.html`. The article is about React, but the same rules apply to Angular.

Data Flowing Downwards

Data should flow downwards from higher-level components to lower-level components. When you create a component that receives data from outside, you must explicitly tell Angular to expect that data as input, using the @Input decorator. You place the @Input decorator next to the instance variable to which the data will be injected from outside.

When you pass data into a component from the outside, you pass that data into the component using input properties.

Sometimes you may want the name of the input property to be different from the name of the instance variable to which it will be injected. That's when you need to use an `alias`, which allows you to specify the input property name. The `alias` may be specified inside parentheses in the @Input decorator. Figure 12-2 shows an example.

```
bmw : m3
porsche : 911
bmw : m3
```

Figure 12-2. Passing data to car components

This component will pass data from the application to car components. This will be example more-components-ex100:

1. *Build the app using the CLI*: Use the following command:

   ```
   ng new more-components-ex100 --inline-template
   --inline-style
   ```

2. *Start* ng serve: Use the following code:

   ```
   cd more-components-ex100
   ng serve
   ```

3. *Open app*: Open a web browser and navigate to localhost:4200. You should see "welcome to app!"

4. *Edit app class*: Edit app.component.ts and change it to the following:

```
import { Component } from '@angular/core';
import { ICar } from './icar';

@Component({
  selector: 'app-root',
  template: `
  <car *ngFor="let car of cars" [theCar]="car"></car>
  `,
  styles: []
})
export class AppComponent {
  cars:Array<ICar> = [
    {make: 'bmw', model: 'm3'},
    {make: 'porsche', model: '911'},
    {make: 'bmw', model: 'm3'}
  ];
}
```

5. *Create* ICar *interface*: Use the following command:

```
ng generate interface ICar
```

6. *Edit ICar Interface*: Edit icar.ts and change it to the following:

```
export interface ICar {
  make: string,
  model: string
}
```

7. *Create* Car *class*: Use the following code:

```
ng generate component Car --inline-template
--inline-style --flat
```

8.   *Edit* Car *class*: Edit car.component.ts and change it to the following:

```
import { Component, Input } from '@angular/core';
import { ICar } from './icar';

@Component({
  selector: 'car',
  template: `
    <p>
      {{car.make}} : {{car.model}}
    </p>
  `,
  styles: []
})
export class CarComponent {
  @Input('theCar') car: ICar;
}
```

Your app should be working at localhost:4200. Note the following:

- The Application component has a list of three cars. We use the ngFor directive to iterate over the list of cars, generating a Car component for each one. We use the theCar input property to pass the car to the Car component.

- We have a Car component to display each car. In the Car component, we use the theCar aliased input property to accept the car instance variable from the outside.

Warning   You can pass objects that contain fields through the @Input() properties and through the inputs element of the @Component annotation. For example, you could perform an HTTP request to get a customer object that contains a name and address then pass it into a child component through an attribute to display it. This works well, but bear in mind that the attribute you're passing in may be null until the server returns the response. So the child component may attempt to display elements like the name and address of a null object, which can cause Angular to throw exceptions and *not* display the data when it has come back from the server. This has caught me out several times. The solution to this is to use the Elvis operator.

Events Flowing Upwards

Sometimes you need to compose parent components that contain child components and control them. Parent components need to have code that responds to things happening (events) on child components. Events should flow upwards, emitted upwards from lower-level components and responded to by higher-level components.

Here's how to set up a child component to pass custom events up to parent components:

1.   Import the `EventEmitter` class.

2.   Specify the custom events that your component will emit by using the `events` element of the `@Component` directive. You must remember to do this!

3.   Create an event emitter in your class as an instance variable.

4.   Call the event emitter method `emit` when you want to emit an event.

Here's how to set up a parent component to receive custom events from child components:

1.   Add the component with the custom events to your other component. Remember to import it and specify it in the `directive` element of the `@Component` annotation.

2.   Add the component with the custom event to the markup in the template of the other component. Edit the markup in the template to respond to the custom event using the event name in round brackets and the template statement it will fire—for example: `(wordInput)="wordInputEvent($event)"`. Notice that this uses the same syntax as non-custom events.

Emitting Output through @Output()

You create an `@Output()` instance variable of type `EventEmitter` in the child component/directive. You modify the child component/directive to use this instance variable to emit events when required. You modify the parent component to bind an event attribute of the same name in its template with a template statement. Angular will emit the event from the child component/directive to the parent and will invoke the template statement. Figure 12-3 shows an example.

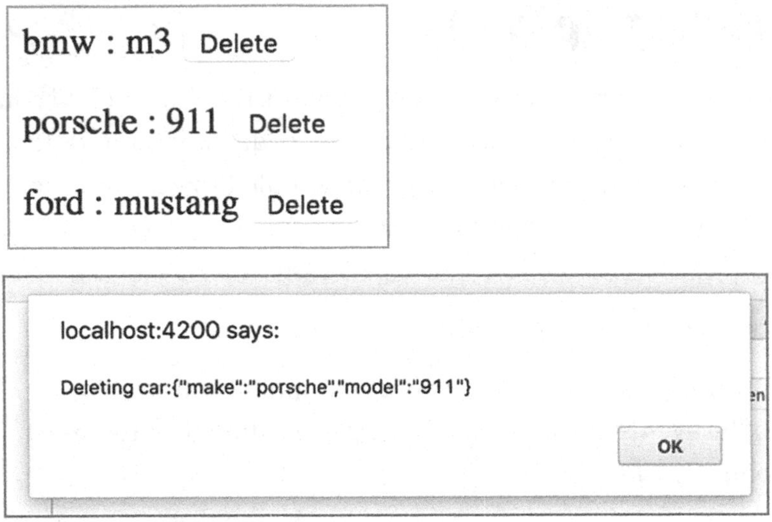

Figure 12-3. *Emitting output*

Figure 12-3 shows how events can flow upward from one component to another. This will be example more-components-ex200:

1. *Build the app using the CLI*: Use the following command:

   ```
   ng new more-components-ex200 --inline-template
   --inline-style
   ```

2. *Start* ng serve: Use the following code:

   ```
   cd more-components-ex200
   ng serve
   ```

3. *Open app*: Open web browser and navigate to localhost:4200. You should see "welcome to app!"

4. Edit app class: Edit app.component.ts and change it to the following:

   ```
   import { Component } from '@angular/core';
   import { ICar } from './icar';

   @Component({
     selector: 'app-root',
     template: `
   ```

```
    <car *ngFor="let car of cars"
    (carDelete)="deleteCar(car)" [theCar]="car">
    </car>
    `,
    styles: []
})
export class AppComponent {
  cars:Array<ICar> = [
    {make: 'bmw', model: 'm3'},
    {make: 'porsche', model: '911'},
    {make: 'ford', model: 'mustang'}
  ];

  deleteCar(car: ICar){
    alert('Deleting car:' + JSON.stringify(car));
  }
}
```

5. *Create* ICar *interface*: Use the following code:

```
ng generate interface ICar
```

6. *Edit* ICar *interface*: Edit icar.ts and change it to the following:

```
export interface ICar {
    make: string,
    model: string
}
```

7. *Create* Car *class*: Use the following code:

```
ng generate component Car --inline-template
--inline-style --flat
```

8. *Edit* Car *class*: Edit car.component.ts and change it to the following:

```
import { Component, Input, Output, EventEmitter } from
'@angular/core';
```

165

```
import { ICar } from './icar';

@Component({
  selector: 'car',
  template: `
    <p>
      {{car.make}} : {{car.model}}
      <button (click)="delete(car)">Delete</button>
    </p>
  `,
  styles: []
})
export class CarComponent {
  @Input('theCar') car: ICar;
  @Output() carDelete = new EventEmitter();

  delete(car: ICar){
    this.carDelete.emit(car);
  }
}
```

Your app should be working at localhost:4200. Note the following:

- The Application component has a list of three Cars. It listens for the carDelete event, firing the deleteCar method when it occurs.

- We have a Car component to display each car. It contains a delete button and emits a carDelete event when the user clicks it.

Composition: Example

Let's use the Angular CLI to create a crude example of a component that contains other components. We'll write an app that contains a customer list which contains three customers, as shown in Figure 12-4.

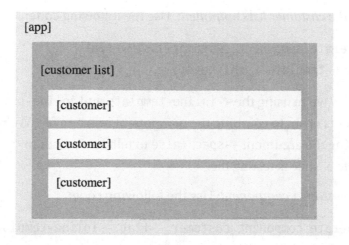

Figure 12-4. *Customer list with three customers*

This will be example more-components-ex300:

1. *Build the app using the CLI*: Use the following command:

   ```
   ng new more-components-ex300 --inline-template
   --inline-style
   ```

   Notice the `--inline-template` and `--inline-style` arguments.
   These tell the CLI to combine the template and style into the
   component's class, making the component definition one file
   instead of three—much easier when you have small templates
   with few styles. When you get to code much larger components,
   you may want to rethink this.

   When you use this command (and the following commands),
   you can add the `--spec` argument to tell the CLI not to create a
   .spec.ts file for the app and the components. I just left the `spec` file
   generation alone.

2. *Start* `ng serve`: Use the following code:

   ```
   cd more-components-ex300
   ng serve
   ```

3. *Open app*: Open a web browser and navigate to localhost:4200.
   You should see "welcome to app!"

4. *Create the customer list component*: Use the following code:

```
ng generate component customer-list --flat
--inline-template --inline-style
```

Note how we're using the `--inline-template` and `inline-style` arguments again to combine the component into one file. We're also using the argument `--spec false` to tell the CLI not to generate a .spec.ts testing file.

5. *Create customer component*: Use the following code:

```
ng generate component customer --flat --inline-template
--inline-style
```

Again we're using the `--inline-template` and `inline-style` arguments to combine the component into one file. And we're using the argument `--spec false` to tell the CLI not to generate a .spec.ts testing file.

6. *Edit the app component*: Copy and paste the following code into app.component.ts:

```
import { Component } from '@angular/core';

@Component({
  selector: 'app-root',
  template: `
  <div class='app'>
  [app]
  <app-customer-list>
  </app-customer-list>
  </div>
  `,
  styles: ['.app {background-color:#d5f4e6;margin:10px;pad
  ding:10px;}']
})

export class AppComponent {
}
```

7. *Edit the customer list component*: Copy and paste the following
   code into customer-list.component.ts:

```
import { Component, OnInit } from '@angular/core';

@Component({
  selector: 'app-customer-list',
  template: `
    <div class='customerList'>
    <p>
    [customer list]
    </p>
    <app-customer>
    </app-customer>
    <app-customer>
    </app-customer>
    <app-customer>
    </app-customer>
    </div>
    `,
  styles: ['.customerList {background-color:#80ced6;margin
  :10px;padding:10px;}']
})
export class CustomerListComponent implements OnInit {

  constructor() { }

  ngOnInit() {
  }

}
```

8. *Edit the customer component*: Copy and paste the following code
   into customer.component.ts:

```
import { Component, OnInit } from '@angular/core';
@Component({
  selector: 'app-customer',
  template: `
```

```
    <div class='customer'>
      [customer]
    </div>
    `,
    styles: ['.customer {background-color:#fefbd8;margin:10p
    x;padding:10px}']
})
export class CustomerComponent implements OnInit {

    constructor() { }

    ngOnInit() {
    }

}
```

Your app should be working at localhost:4200. You have composed an app consisting of different components. Note the following:

- Each component has a @Component directive at the top that specifies the selector. For example, the customer component:

```
@Component({
    selector: 'app-customer',
```

When you need to include that component in another component, you use the selector as a tag. For example, the customer list component uses the customer component's tag to include it in the template three times:

```
<app-customer>
</app-customer>
<app-customer>
</app-customer>
<app-customer>
</app-customer>
```

- The file app.module.ts was modified by the CLI. Each component was added as a declaration in the module (more on modules later).

Data Flowing Downwards: Example

Let's modify example more-components-ex300 to pass data down from the customer list component to the customer components, as shown in Figure 12-5.

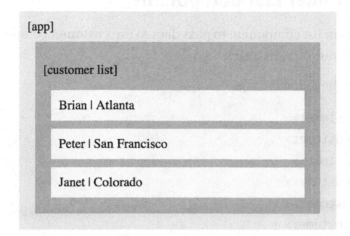

Figure 12-5. *Customer list with three customers*

This will be example more-components-ex400.

Edit the Customer Component

We edit the customer component to accept input data from the outside:

- Modify the imports to include the Input class from the Angular core:

  ```
  import { Component, OnInit, Input } from '@angular/core';
  ```

- Change the template to include string interpolation of the instance variable customer: {{customer.name}} and {{customer.city}}. This will output the contents of the name and city properties of the customer instance variable:

  ```
  template: `
    <div class='customer'>
      {{customer.name}} | {{customer.city}}
    </div>
  `,
  ```

- Declare instance variable `customer` as an input variable:

  ```
  @Input() customer;
  ```

Edit the Customer List Component

We edit the customer list component to pass data to the customer component using one-way data binding (more on this later):

- Replace the following tags

  ```
  <app-customer>
  </app-customer>
  <app-customer>
  </app-customer>
  <app-customer>
  </app-customer>
  ```

  with the following:

  ```
  <app-customer *ngFor="let customer of customerList"
  [customer]="customer">
  </app-customer>
  ```

- Declare the instance variable `customerList` and populate it with data. Add the code after `export` and before `constructor`:

  ```
  private customerList = [
    { name: 'Brian', city: 'Atlanta'},
    { name: 'Peter', city: 'San Francisco'},
    { name: 'Janet', city: 'Colorado'},
  ];
  ```

Your app should be working at localhost:4200. You modified the component list to contain customer list data and you passed this data down to the customer using one-way (downwards) data binding. Note the following:

- The customer list component sets up the customer list data as an instance variable, and the template refers to this variable.

- The customer list component uses an `ngFor` in the template. This allows the template to iterate over the customer list, creating a `customer` variable for each customer and passing it down to the customer component via a bound attribute.

- The customer component declares an instance variable called `customer`. It uses an annotation `@Input()` to tell Angular to have its value automatically set from the outside. Note that the `Input` class has to be imported at the top of the customer component's class.

- The customer component uses `{{customer.name}}` and `{{customer.city}}` in the template to output the `name` and `city` properties of the instance variable called `customer`.

Events Flowing Upwards: Example

Let's modify the preceding example to fire events from the customer component to the customer list component, as shown in Figure 12-6. This will be example ex300, and it's based on example more-components-ex500.

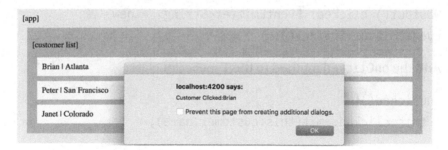

Figure 12-6. *Firing events*

This will be example ex300.

173

Edit the Customer Component

We edit the Customer component to output a clicked event when the user clicks a customer:

- Modify the import to include the Output and EventEmitter classes from the Angular core:

```
import { Component, OnInit, Input, Output, EventEmitter }
from '@angular/core';
```

- Modify the template to call the method onClicked when the user clicks a customer:

```
template: `
    <div class='customer'(click)="onClicked()">
      {{customer.name}} | {{customer.city}}
    </div>
    `,
```

- Add an instance variable for the event emitter to the TypeScript class:

```
@Output() clicked: EventEmitter<String> = new
EventEmitter<String>();
```

- Add the onClicked method to the TypeScript class:

```
onClicked(){
  this.clicked.emit(this.customer.name);
}
```

Edit the Customer List Component

We edit the customer list component to respond to the clicked event emitted by the customer component:

- Modify the template to bind to the clicked event, calling the onCustomerClicked method when the event occurs:

```
<app-customer *ngFor="let customer of customerList"
[customer]="customer" (clicked)="onCustomerClicked($event)">
```

- Add the method onCustomerClicked to receive the event data and display an alert box with the customer name:

```
onCustomerClicked(customerName:String){
   alert('Customer Clicked:' + customerName);
}
```

Your app should be working at localhost:4200. The app should now display an alert box when you click a customer. Note how the events are flowing up from multiple customer components to a single customer list component. Also note the following:

- The customer component sets up an instance variable for an event emitter that outputs an event with string data. It uses an annotation @Output() to tell Angular that other components should be able to bind to this event.

- The customer component template includes the Angular directive (click) to listen and respond to the user clicking the div. It fires a method that uses the event emitter to output the event.

- The customer list component includes an event handler to listen and respond to the custom clicked event in the customer component.

- The customer list component contains code in the onCustomerClicked method to receive the data from the event and display an alert box.

Template Reference Variables

A *template reference variable* is a reference to one or more elements within a template. You can use the ref- prefix instead of #.

Once you've declared a template reference variable, you can use it in either the template or in the code. However, you need to know that this variable isn't set by Angular until the ngAfterViewInit lifecycle method has completed (more on Angular lifecycles later in this book).

ViewChild: Example

ViewChild declares a reference to a child element in the component. When you declare your instance variable, you specify a selector in parentheses, which is used to bind the child element to the instance variable.

This example shows text (see Figure 12-7) and it looks similar to the CLI default application. This is example more-components-ex600.

Figure 12-7. ViewChild example

If you examine the code, you'll see that it uses a template variable to refer to the h1 element:

```
<h1 #title></h1>
```

And it has code to set its inner HTML after the component has finished loading the view:

```
ngAfterViewInit(){
  this.title.nativeElement.innerHTML = 'app works differently!'
}
```

Also note that the template variable is referred to by some interpolation in the template:

```
The title is {{title.innerHTML}}
```

Let's do example more-components-ex600:

1. *Build the app using the CLI*: Use the following command:

   ```
   ng new more-components-ex600 --inline-template
   ```

   Remember that --inline-template tells the CLI to use inline templates when generating the new application.

2. *Start* ng serve: Use the following code:

```
cd more-components-ex600
ng serve
```

3. *Open app*: Open a web browser and navigate to localhost:4200.
   You should see "welcome to app!"

4. *Edit class*: Edit app.component.ts and change it to the following:

```
import { Component, ElementRef, ViewChild, AfterViewInit } from
'@angular/core';

@Component({
  selector: 'app-root',
  template: `
  <h1 #title></h1>
  The title is {{title.innerHTML}}
  `,
  styleUrls: ['./app.component.css']
})
export class AppComponent implements AfterViewInit  {
  @ViewChild('title') title: ElementRef;

  ngAfterViewInit(){
    this.title.nativeElement.innerHTML = 'app works differently!'
  }
}
```

5. *View app*: You should see "app works differently!"

ViewChildren: Example

ViewChildren declares a reference to multiple child elements in the component. When you declare your instance variable, you specify a selector in parentheses, which is used to bind the child elements to the instance variable.

This selector can be the child type (that is, the class of the Child Angular element) or the template reference(s) (#name).

177

This example uses `ViewChildren` to access a list of paragraphs (see Figure 12-8). We use `ViewChildren` with a list of child reference names, separated by commas. This is example more-components-ex700.

Lorem ipsum dolor sit amet, consetetur sadipscing elitr, sed diam nonumy eirmod tempor invidunt ut labore et dolore magna aliquyam erat, sed diam voluptua.

At vero eos et accusam et justo duo dolores et ea rebum. Stet clita kasd gubergren, no sea takimata sanctus est Lorem ipsum dolor sit amet. Lorem ipsum dolor sit amet, consetetur sadipscing elitr, sed diam nonumy eirmod tempor invidunt ut labore et dolore magna aliquyam erat, sed diam voluptua.

Number of Paragraphs:2

Figure 12-8. *Accessing a list of paragraphs*

Let's do example more-components-ex700:

1. *Build the app using the CLI*: Use the following command:

   ```
   ng new more-components-ex700 --inline-template
   ```

2. *Start* ng serve: Use the following code:

   ```
   cd more-components-ex700
   ng serve
   ```

3. *Open app*: Open a web browser and navigate to localhost:4200. You should see "welcome to app!"

4. *Edit class*: Edit app.component.ts and change it to the following:

   ```
   import { Component, ViewChildren, AfterViewInit } from '@angular/core';
   ```

```
@Component({

  selector: 'app-root',
  template: `
  <p #paragraph1>Lorem ipsum dolor sit amet, consetetur
  sadipscing elitr, sed diam nonumy eirmod tempor invidunt
  ut labore et dolore magna aliquyam erat, sed diam
  voluptua. </p>
  <p #paragraph2>At vero eos et accusam et justo duo
  dolores et ea rebum. Stet clita kasd gubergren, no sea
  takimata sanctus est Lorem ipsum dolor sit amet. Lorem
  ipsum dolor sit amet, consetetur sadipscing elitr,  sed
  diam nonumy eirmod tempor invidunt ut labore et dolore
  magna aliquyam erat, sed diam voluptua.</p>
  <p *ngIf="note">{{note}}</p>
  `,
  styles: ['p { background-color: #FFE5CC; padding: 15px;
  text-align: center}']
})
export class AppComponent implements AfterViewInit{
  @ViewChildren('paragraph1, paragraph2') paragraphs;
  note: string = '';

  ngAfterViewInit(){
    setTimeout(_ => this.note = 'Number of Paragraphs:' +
    this.paragraphs.length);
  }
}
```

Your app should be working at localhost:4200. You should see two paragraphs of text, with a paragraph count beneath, as in Figure 12-8.

NgContent and Transclusion: Example

Transclusion is the inclusion and transference of content from the area inside the component's tags into the component's template. The NgContent tag is used for transclusion. It even has a selector that allows you to select which content to include. If you use a [in the selector (as in [test]), then this can be used to select content with this attribute (for example, <div test>hejwejgwegrhj</div>).

This example is very simple and doesn't use selectors. It just includes the text between the component tags. This is example more-components-ex800 (see Figure 12-9).

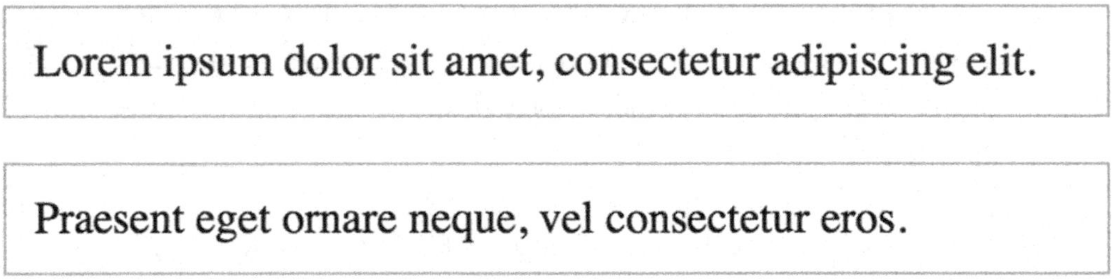

Lorem ipsum dolor sit amet, consectetur adipiscing elit.

Praesent eget ornare neque, vel consectetur eros.

Figure 12-9. *Text between component tags*

Let's do example more-components-ex800:

1. *Build the app using the CLI*: Use the following command:

   ```
   ng new more-components-ex800 --inline-template
   ```

2. *Start* ng serve: Use the following code:

   ```
   cd more-components-ex800
   ng serve
   ```

3. *Open app*: Open a web browser and navigate to localhost:4200. You should see "welcome to app!"

4. *Edit classes*: This time we're going to add two Component classes into the same file. Edit app.component.ts and change it to the following:

```
import { Component } from '@angular/core';

@Component({
  selector: 'Paragraph',
  template: `
  <p><ng-content></ng-content></p>
  `,
  styles: ['p { border: 1px solid #c0c0c0; padding:
  10px }']
})
export class Paragraph {
}

@Component({
  selector: 'app-root',
  template: `
  <p>
  <Paragraph>Lorem ipsum dolor sit amet, consectetur
  adipiscing elit. </Paragraph>
  <Paragraph>Praesent eget ornare neque, vel consectetur
  eros. </Paragraph>
  </p>
  `,
  styleUrls: ['./app.component.css']
})
export class AppComponent {
  title = "welcome to app!";
}
```

5. *Edit module*: We have two Component classes in the same file. We need to ensure that both Components are declared in the module definition—otherwise, they won't be useable. Edit app.module.ts and change it to the following:

```
import { BrowserModule } from '@angular/platform-browser';
import { NgModule } from '@angular/core';
import { FormsModule } from '@angular/forms';
import { HttpModule } from '@angular/http';
```

```
import { AppComponent, Paragraph } from './app.component';

@NgModule({
  declarations: [
    AppComponent,
    Paragraph
  ],
  imports: [
    BrowserModule,
    FormsModule,
    HttpModule
  ],
  providers: [],
  bootstrap: [AppComponent]
})
export class AppModule { }
```

You should see two paragraphs of text, as in Figure 12-9.

ContentChild: Example

You can use ngContent to transclude additional content. Transclusion refers to injecting content into a specific element in the DOM. You can use ContentChild to declare a reference to a child element in the transcluded additional content.

This example is like the previous one except it uses ContentChild to get a reference to the title element inside the transcluded content (see Figure 12-10). It then includes the inner HTML from that element. This is example more-components-ex900.

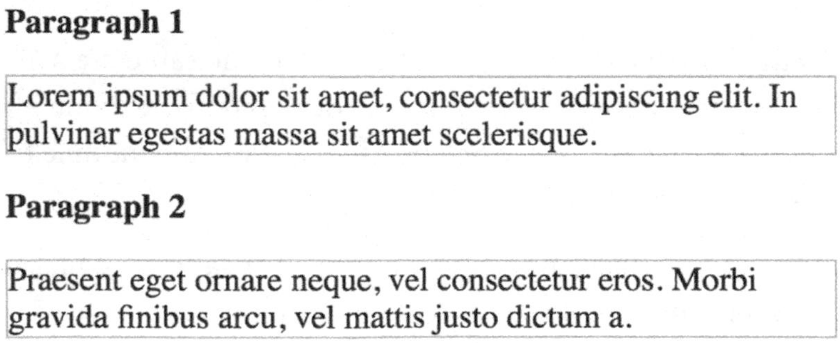

Paragraph 1

> Lorem ipsum dolor sit amet, consectetur adipiscing elit. In pulvinar egestas massa sit amet scelerisque.

Paragraph 2

> Praesent eget ornare neque, vel consectetur eros. Morbi gravida finibus arcu, vel mattis justo dictum a.

Figure 12-10. *Text between component tags*

Let's do example more-components-ex900:

1. *Build the app using the CLI*: Use the following command:

   ```
   ng new more-components-ex900 --inline-template
   ```

2. *Start* ng serve: Use the following code:

   ```
   cd more-components-ex900
   ng serve
   ```

3. *Open app*: Open a web browser and navigate to localhost:4200.
   You should see "welcome to app!"

4. *Edit classes*: Edit app.component.ts and change it to the following:

   ```
   import { Component, ContentChild } from '@angular/core';

   @Component({
     selector: 'Paragraph',
     template: `
     <div>
     <b>{{title.nativeElement.innerHTML}}</b>
     <p><ng-content></ng-content></p>
     </div>
     `,
     styles: ['p { border: 1px solid #c0c0c0 }']
   })
   export class Paragraph {
     @ContentChild('title') title;
   }

   @Component({
     selector: 'app-root',
     template: `
     <p>
     <Paragraph><title #title>Paragraph 1</title>Lorem ipsum
     dolor sit amet, consectetur adipiscing elit. In pulvinar
     egestas massa sit amet scelerisque.</Paragraph>
   ```

```
<Paragraph><title #title>Paragraph 2</title>Praesent
eget ornare neque, vel consectetur eros. Morbi gravida
finibus arcu, vel mattis justo dictum a.</Paragraph>
</p>
`,
  styleUrls: ['./app.component.css']
})
export class AppComponent {
  title = 'welcome to app!';
}
```

5. *Edit module*: We have two Component classes in the same file. We need to ensure that both Components are declared in the module definition—otherwise, they won't be useable. Edit app.module.ts and change it to the following:

```
import { BrowserModule } from '@angular/platform-browser';
import { NgModule } from '@angular/core';
import { FormsModule } from '@angular/forms';
import { HttpModule } from '@angular/http';

import { AppComponent, Paragraph } from './app.component';

@NgModule({
  declarations: [
    AppComponent,
    Paragraph
  ],
  imports: [
    BrowserModule,
    FormsModule,
    HttpModule
  ],
  providers: [],
  bootstrap: [AppComponent]
})
export class AppModule { }
```

You should see two paragraphs of text.

ContentChildren: Example

You can use `ContentChildren` to declare a reference to multiple child elements in the transcluded additional content.

This example is like the previous one exceptit uses `ContentChild` to get a reference to the `title` element inside the transcluded content (see Figure 12-11). It then includes the inner HTML from that element. This is example more-components-ex1000.

Lorem ipsum dolor sit amet, consectetur adipiscing elit.
- Albertus Falx
- Godefridus Turpilius
- Demipho Renatus

Number of people: 3

Praesent eget ornare neque, vel consectetur eros.
- Hanno Grumio
- Lycus Auxilius

Number of people: 2

Figure 12-11. *List of people and people count*

Let's do example more-components-ex1000:

1. *Build the app using the CLI*: Use the following command:

    ```
    ng new more-components-ex1000 --inline-template
    ```

2. *Start* `ng serve`: Use the following code:

    ```
    cd more-components-ex1000
    ng serve
    ```

3. *Open app*: Open a web browser and navigate to localhost:4200. You should see "welcome to app!"

4. *Edit classes*: Edit app.component.ts and change it to the following:

```
import { Component, ContentChildren } from '@angular/
core';

@Component({
  selector: 'Person',
  template: `
  <div> - <ng-content></ng-content></div>
  `,
  styles: ['']
})
export class Person {
}

@Component({
  selector: 'Paragraph',
  template: `
  <div>
  <ng-content></ng-content>
  <p *ngIf="people">Number of people: {{people.length}}
  </p>
  </div>
  `,
  styles: ['div { border: 1px solid #c0c0c0; margin:10px;
  padding:10px }', 'p { margin: 5px 0 }']
})
export class Paragraph {
  @ContentChildren(Person) people;
}

@Component({
  selector: 'app-root',
  template: `
  <Paragraph>Lorem ipsum dolor sit amet, consectetur
  adipiscing elit.
    <Person>Albertus Falx</Person>
    <Person>Godefridus Turpilius</Person>
    <Person>Demipho Renatus</Person>
```

```
    </Paragraph>
    <Paragraph>Praesent eget ornare neque, vel consectetur
    eros.
      <Person>Hanno Grumio</Person>
      <Person>Lycus Auxilius</Person>
    </Paragraph>
      `,
    styleUrls: ['./app.component.css']
})
export class AppComponent {
  title = 'welcome to app!';
}
```

5. *Edit module*: We have three Component classes in the same file. We
   need to ensure that both Components are declared in the module
   definition—otherwise, they won't be useable. Edit app.module.ts
   and change it to the following:

```
import { BrowserModule } from '@angular/platform-browser';
import { NgModule } from '@angular/core';
import { FormsModule } from '@angular/forms';
import { HttpModule } from '@angular/http';

import { AppComponent, Paragraph, Person } from './app.component';

@NgModule({
  declarations: [
    AppComponent,
    Paragraph,
    Person
  ],
  imports: [
    BrowserModule,
    FormsModule,
    HttpModule
  ],
```

```
    providers: [],
    bootstrap: [AppComponent]
})
export class AppModule { }
```

You should see two paragraphs of text. Each paragraph should have a list of people and a people count at the bottom, as in Figure 12-11.

Component Class Lifecycle

Like AngularJS, Angular manages the components for you—when it creates them, when it updates them, when it destroys them, and so forth. Each component has what are known as *lifecycle events*: birth and life events like changes and death. Sometimes you need to add extra code that's fired for you by Angular when these events occur.

Constructor vs. OnInit

Sometimes you need to set up your component and initialize it. You have two choices here: you can use the constructor or the OnInit lifecycle method. The OnInit lifecycle method is fired when the component is first initialized.

Tip   It's up to you which one you should use, but many people follow this general rule of thumb. We mostly use ngOnInit for initialization/declaration and avoid work in the constructor. The constructor should only be used to initialize class members but shouldn't do actual "work."

You may want to add some code to do something once the component has loaded and is visible. For example, place the input focus on the first field so the user can just start typing away. You might think you could add this code to the component class constructor, but that would be incorrect because the constructor is fired before the component is visible. In fact, you would probably add this code to ngAfterViewInit—after the view has been initialized.

Interfaces

To hook into a lifecycle method, your component's class should implement the required interface. The interface will then force you to implement the corresponding method.

For example, to implement a method fired after the view has initialized, you should implement the interface `AfterViewInit`, which requires the method `ngAfterViewInit`. Table 12-1 has more details.

Table 12-1. *Interfaces and Methods*

Interface	Method	Description
OnChanges	ngOnChanges	Called when an input or output binding value changes
OnInit	ngOnInit	After the first ngOnChanges
DoCheck	ngDoCheck	Developer's custom change detection
AfterContentInit	ngAfterContentInit	After component content initialized
AfterContentChecked	ngAfterContentChecked	After every check of component content
AfterViewInit	ngAfterViewInit	After component's view(s) are initialized
AfterViewChecked	ngAfterViewChecked	After every check of a component's view(s)
OnDestroy	ngOnDestroy	Just before the directive is destroyed

NgOnChanges: Example

This callback is invoked when the value of a bound property changes. It executes every time the value of an input property changes. It will receive a changes map, containing the current and previous values of the binding, wrapped in a `SimpleChange` (see Figure 12-12). This is example more-components-ex1100.

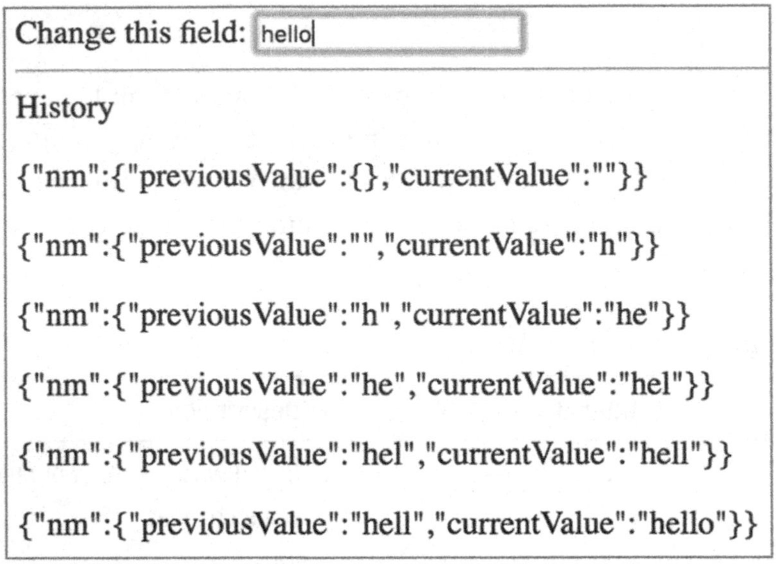

```
Change this field: hello|

History

{"nm":{"previousValue":{},"currentValue":""}}

{"nm":{"previousValue":"","currentValue":"h"}}

{"nm":{"previousValue":"h","currentValue":"he"}}

{"nm":{"previousValue":"he","currentValue":"hel"}}

{"nm":{"previousValue":"hel","currentValue":"hell"}}

{"nm":{"previousValue":"hell","currentValue":"hello"}}
```

Figure 12-12. *Component with a text box that lets you enter text*

When you make a change, the changes are recorded below. Let's do example more-components-ex1100:

1. *Build the app using the CLI*: Use the following command:

```
ng new more-components-ex1100 --inline-template
--inline-style
```

2. *Start* ng serve: Use the following code:

```
cd more-components-ex1100
ng serve
```

3. *Open app*: Open a web browser and navigate to localhost:4200. You should see "welcome to app!"

4. *Edit classes*: Edit app.component.ts and change it to the following:

```
import { Component, Input, OnChanges, SimpleChanges } from
'@angular/core';

@Component({
  selector: 'name',
  template: `
```

```
    <p *ngFor="let change of changes">
    {{change}}
    </p>
    `,
    styles: []
})
export class NameComponent implements OnChanges{
  @Input('name') nm;
  changes: Array<string> = [''];

  ngOnChanges(changes: SimpleChanges){
    this.changes.push(JSON.stringify(changes));
  }
}

@Component({
  selector: 'app-root',
  template: `
  Change this field: <input [(ngModel)]="name" />
  <hr/>
  History
  <name [name]="name"></name>
  `,
  styles: []
})
export class AppComponent{
  name: string = '';
}
```

5. *Edit module*: Edit app.module.ts and change it to the following:

```
import { BrowserModule } from '@angular/platform-browser';
import { NgModule } from '@angular/core';
import { FormsModule } from '@angular/forms';
import { HttpModule } from '@angular/http';

import { AppComponent, NameComponent } from './app.component';
```

```
@NgModule({
  declarations: [
    AppComponent,
    NameComponent
  ],
  imports: [
    BrowserModule,
    FormsModule,
    HttpModule
  ],
  providers: [],
  bootstrap: [AppComponent]
})
export class AppModule { }
```

Your app should be working at localhost:4200. Note the following:

- Both components reside in the same file, but they have to be imported and declared separately in the module.

- The app component uses two-way binding to the name instance variable. It passes the name instance variable to the Name component.

- The Name component uses the lifecycle method ngOnChanges to listen for changes to input properties (in this case, name). When this method is fired it uses JSON.stringify to dump out a string representation of the change to a list of the changes below.

NgOnInit: Example

This callback is invoked once Angular is done creating the component and has initialized it. It's called directly after the constructor and after the ngOnChange is triggered for the first time. This is a component that displays logs, as shown in Figure 12-13. This will be example more-components-ex2000.

> Thu Jun 01 2017 21:27:04 GMT-0400 (EDT)
>
> Thu Jun 01 2017 21:27:05 GMT-0400 (EDT)

Figure 12-13. *Displaying logs*

A log of when the component initializes and when the lifecycle method ngOnInit is invoked. Let's do example more-components-ex2000:

1. *Build the app using the CLI*: Use the following command:

   ```
   ng new more-components-ex1200 --inline-template --inline-style
   ```

2. *Start* ng serve: Use the following code:

   ```
   cd more-components-ex1200
   ng serve
   ```

3. *Open app*: Open a web browser and navigate to localhost:4200. You should see "welcome to app!"

4. *Edit class*: Edit app.component.ts and change it to the following:

   ```typescript
   import { Component, OnInit } from '@angular/core';

   @Component({
     selector: 'app-root',
     template: `
   <p *ngFor="let log of logs">
   {{log}}
   </p>
     `
     ,
     styles: []
   })
   export class AppComponent implements OnInit{
     logs: Array<string> = [ new Date()+''];
     constructor(){
       for (let i=0;i<1000;i++){
         console.log(i);
       }
   ```

```
  }
  ngOnInit(){
    this.logs.push(new Date()+'');
  }
}
```

Your app should be working at localhost:4200. Note the following:

- The log is initialized when the instance variable is defined.

- The constructor has some code to slow down the creation of the component.

- The log is augmented when Angular is done creating the component.

NgDoCheck: Example

This callback is invoked every time the input properties of a component or a directive are checked. We can use this lifecycle hook to extend the check with our own custom check logic.

This is a component that will let you create an array and will figure out what you change, as shown in Figure 12-14. This will be example more-components-ex1300.

Let's do more-components-ex1300:

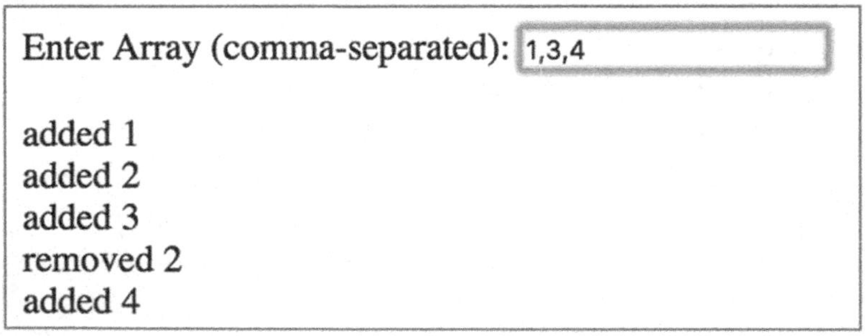

Figure 12-14. *Creating an array and figuring out what you change*

1. *Build the app using the CLI*: Use the following command:

```
ng new more-components-ex1300 --inline-template --inline-style
```

2. *Start* ng serve: Use the following code:

```
cd more-components-ex1300
ng serve
```

3. *Open app*: Open a web browser and navigate to localhost:4200. You should see "welcome to app!"

4. *Edit classes*: Edit app.component.ts and change it to the following:

```
import { Component, Input, DoCheck, IterableDiffers } from
'@angular/core';

@Component({
  selector: 'numbers',
  template: `
  {{numbers}}
  <br/>
  <p *ngFor="let change of changes">
  {{change}}
  </p>
  `,
  styles: ['p{padding:0;margin:0}']
})
export class NumbersComponent implements DoCheck {
  @Input('numbers') numbersArray: Array<string>;
  changes: Array<string> = [];
  differ;

  constructor(private differs: IterableDiffers) {
    this.differ = differs.find([]).create(null);
  }

  ngDoCheck() {
    const differences = this.differ.diff(this.
    numbersArray);
    if (differences) {
      if (differences.forEachAddedItem) {
        differences.forEachAddedItem((item) => {
```

```
            if ((item) && (item.item)){
              this.changes.push('added ' + item.item);
            }
          });
        }
        if (differences.forEachRemovedItem) {
          differences.forEachRemovedItem((item) => {
            if ((item) && (item.item)){
              this.changes.push('removed ' + item.item);
            }
          });
        }
      }
    }
  }

@Component({
  selector: 'app-root',
  template: `
  Enter Array (comma-separated): <input
  [(ngModel)]="numbers" (onModelChange)="onModelChange"/>
  <br/>
  <numbers [numbers]="numbers.split(',')"></numbers>
  `,
  styles: []
})
export class AppComponent {
  numbers = '';
}
```

5. *Edit module*: Edit app.module.ts and change it to the following:

```
import { BrowserModule } from '@angular/platform-browser';
import { NgModule } from '@angular/core';
import { FormsModule } from '@angular/forms';
import { HttpModule } from '@angular/http';
```

```
import { AppComponent, NumbersComponent } from './app.
component';

@NgModule({
  declarations: [
    AppComponent,
    NumbersComponent
  ],
  imports: [
    BrowserModule,
    FormsModule,
    HttpModule
  ],
  providers: [],
  bootstrap: [AppComponent]
})
export class AppModule {}
```

Your app should be working at localhost:4200. Note the following:

- The app component parses the `input` string into an array and passes it to the `Numbers` component.

- The `Numbers` component has an `Iterable Differ` injected via the constructor so that it can be an instance variable and used later.

- When the input changes and the `input` property to the `Numbers` component change, that component uses the `differ` to analyze the changes and add each change to the change log.

NgAfterContentInit: Example

This callback is invoked after ngOnInit: when the component or directive's content has been initialized and the bindings have been checked for the first time.

In this example, the app component declares a crew structure with members inside its content, as shown in Figure 12-15. Later on, this lifecycle callback is used to select the first crew member on the list. This will be example more-components-ex1400.

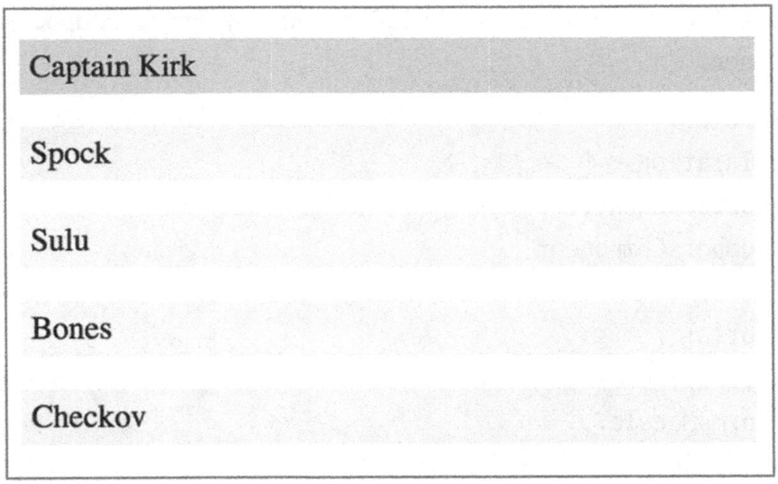

Figure 12-15. *Declaring a crew structure and selecting a member*

Time to do example more-components-ex1400:

1. *Build the app using the CLI*: Use the following command:

   ```
   ng new more-components-ex1400 --inline-template --inline-style
   ```

2. *Start* ng serve: Use the following code:

   ```
   cd more-components-ex1400
   ng serve
   ```

3. *Open app*: Open a web browser and navigate to localhost:4200. You should see "welcome to app!"

4. *Edit classes*: Edit app.component.ts and change it to the following:

   ```
   import { Component, Input, AfterContentInit,
   ContentChildren, QueryList } from '@angular/core';

   @Component({
     selector: 'member',
     template: `
     <p [style.backgroundColor]="getBackgroundColor()"><ng-
     content></ng-content></p>
     `,
     styles: ["p{padding: 5px}"]
   })
   ```

```
export class MemberComponent {
  selected = false;
  getBackgroundColor(){
    return this.selected ? "#FFCCCC" : "#CCFFFF";
  }
}

@Component({
  selector: 'crew',
  template: `
<p><ng-content></ng-content></p>
  `,
  styles: []
})
export class CrewComponent implements AfterContentInit {
  @ContentChildren(MemberComponent) members:
  QueryList<MemberComponent>;

  ngAfterContentInit() {
    this.members.first.selected = true;
  }
}

@Component({
  selector: 'app-root',
  template: `
<crew>
  <member>Captain Kirk</member>
  <member>Spock</member>
  <member>Sulu</member>
  <member>Bones</member>
  <member>Checkov</member>
</crew>
  `,
  styles: []
})
export class AppComponent {}
```

5. *Edit module*: Edit app.module.ts and change it to the following:

```
import { BrowserModule } from '@angular/platform-browser';
import { NgModule } from '@angular/core';
import { FormsModule } from '@angular/forms';
import { HttpModule } from '@angular/http';

import { AppComponent, CrewComponent, MemberComponent }
from './app.component';
@NgModule({
  declarations: [
    AppComponent,
    CrewComponent,
    MemberComponent
  ],
  imports: [
    BrowserModule,
    FormsModule,
    HttpModule
  ],
  providers: [],
  bootstrap: [AppComponent]
})
export class AppModule { }
```

Your app should be working at localhost:4200. Note the following:

- The app component declares a crew structure with members *inside its content*.

- The Crew component declares the instance variable members (which is declared using @ContentChildren) to map into the list of crew members inside its own crew tag in the content. This variable is of the type QueryList so it can be queried easier.

- The Crew content uses the lifecycle method ngAfterContentInit to access the instance variable of members once it's been set for you by Angular. This lifecycle method then sets the selected instance variable of the first member so that he or she is highlighted.

- The Member component shows the content inside the member tag and sets the component's background color according to the selected instance variable.

NgAfterContentChecked: Example

This callback is performed after every check of the component or directive's content, effectively when all the bindings of the components have been checked; even if they haven't changed. This example allows you to pick a card, as shown in Figure 12-16. This will be example more-components-ex1500.

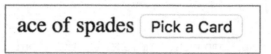

Figure 12-16. *Picking a card*

Let's do example more-components-ex1500:

1. *Build the app using the CLI*: Use the following command:

   ```
   ng new more-components-ex1500 --inline-template --inline-style
   ```

2. *Start* ng serve: Use the following code:

   ```
   cd more-components-ex1500
   ng serve
   ```

3. *Open app*: Open a web browser and navigate to localhost:4200. You should see "welcome to app!"

4. *Edit classes*: Edit app.component.ts and change it to the following:

   ```
   import { Component, ContentChild, AfterContentChecked }
   from '@angular/core';

   @Component({
     selector: 'card',
     template: `
   <ng-content></ng-content>
     `,
   ```

```
    styles: []
  })
  export class CardComponent {
  }

  @Component({
    selector: 'app-root',
    template: `
    <card>{{card}}</card>
    <button (click)="pickCard($event)">Pick a Card</button>
    `,
    styles: []
  })
  export class AppComponent implements AfterContentChecked {
    card = CARD_ACE_OF_SPADES;

    @ContentChild(CardComponent) contentChild:
    CardComponent;

    ngAfterContentChecked() {
      console.log("content inside card has been checked: " +
      this.card);
    }

    pickCard() {
      this.card = this.card === CARD_ACE_OF_SPADES ? CARD_
      TEN_OF_CLUBS : CARD_ACE_OF_SPADES;
    }
  }

  const CARD_ACE_OF_SPADES = 'ace of spades';
  const CARD_TEN_OF_CLUBS = 'ten of clubs';
```

5. *Edit module*: Edit app.module.ts and change it to the following:

```
import { BrowserModule } from '@angular/platform-browser';
import { NgModule } from '@angular/core';
import { FormsModule } from '@angular/forms';
```

```
import { HttpModule } from '@angular/http';

import { AppComponent, CardComponent } from './app.
component';

@NgModule({
  declarations: [
    AppComponent,
    CardComponent
  ],
  imports: [
    BrowserModule,
    FormsModule,
    HttpModule
  ],
  providers: [],
  bootstrap: [AppComponent]
})
export class AppModule { }
```

Your app should be working at localhost:4200. Note the following:

- The app component uses a Card component to display the current card. The current card is an instance variable, the value of which is placed inside the Card component as inner content.

- The app component has a button to allow you to flip to another card. It changes the value of the instance variable.

- The app component has a ngAfterContentChecked method that's fired automatically when the content inside the Card component changes. This is fired when the current card changes.

NgAfterViewInit: Example

This callback is invoked after a component's view and its children's views are created and have been initialized. It's useful for performing component initializations. Note that the @ViewChild and @ViewChildren instance variables are set and available at this point (unlike earlier in the component lifecycle). This example shows you how to set initial input focus, as shown in Figure 12-17. This will be example more-components-ex1600.

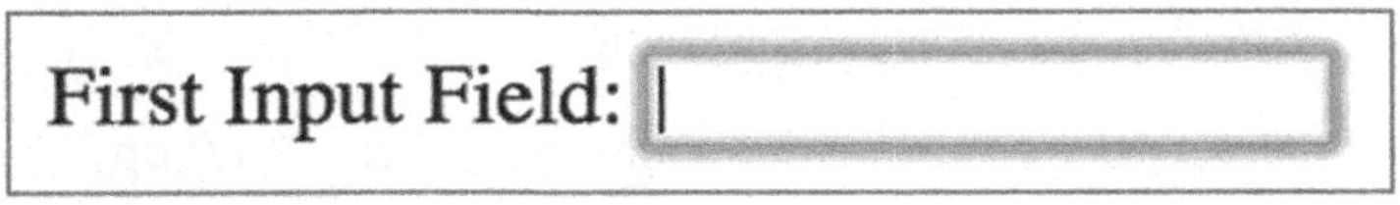

First Input Field: |

Figure 12-17. *Setting initial inpur focus*

Let's do example more-components-ex1600:

1. *Build the app using the CLI*: Use the following command:

   ```
   ng new more-components-ex1600 --inline-template --inline-
   style
   ```

2. *Start* ng serve: Use the following code:

   ```
   cd more-components-ex1600
   ng serve
   ```

3. *Open app*: Open a web browser and navigate to localhost:4200.
   You should see "welcome to app!"

4. *Edit class*: Edit app.component.ts and change it to the following:

   ```
   import { Component, AfterViewInit, ViewChild } from '@
   angular/core';

   @Component({
     selector: 'app-root',
     template: `
       First Input Field: <input #firstInput />
     `,
     styles: []
   })
   export class AppComponent implements AfterViewInit{
     @ViewChild('firstInput') firstInput;

     ngAfterViewInit(){
       // ViewChild variables are available in this method.
       // Set initial focus.
       this.firstInput.nativeElement.focus();
     }
   }
   ```

Your app should be working at localhost:4200. Note the following:

- The app component sets up the firstInput instance variable to reference the template variable declared as #firstInput.

- The app component has a ngAfterViewInit method that's fired once the view has been initialized and the firstInput instance variable is available. This method sets the initial input focus.

NgAfterViewChecked: Example

This callback is invoked after every check of the component's view. It applies to components only, when all the bindings of the children directives have been checked, even if they haven't changed. It can be useful if the component is waiting for something coming from its child components.

Don't set any variables bound to the template here. If you do, you'll receive the "Expression has changed after it was checked" error.

This example allows you to input something and displays a message saying if your input is numeric or not, as shown in Figure 12-18. This will be example more-components-ex1700.

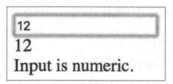

Figure 12-18. *Displaying whether input is numeric or not*

Let's do example more-components-ex1700:

1. *Build the app using the CLI*: Use the following command:

    ```
    ng new more-components-ex1700 --inline-template --inline-style
    ```

2. *Start* ng serve: Use the following code:

    ```
    cd more-components-ex1700
    ng serve
    ```

3. *Open app*: Open a web browser and navigate to localhost:4200. You should see "welcome to app!"

4. *Edit class*: Edit app.component.ts and change it to the following:

```
import { Component, ViewChild, AfterViewChecked } from
'@angular/core';

@Component({
  selector: 'app-root',
  template: `
  <input [(ngModel)]="input"/>
  <br/>
  {{input}}
  <br/>
  <div #message></div>
  `,
  styles: []
})
export class AppComponent implements AfterViewChecked {
  input: string = '';

  @ViewChild('message') message;

  ngAfterViewChecked(){
    console.log('AfterViewChecked');
    if (isNaN(parseInt(this.input))){
      this.message.nativeElement.innerHTML = "Input not
      numeric.";
    }else{
      this.message.nativeElement.innerHTML = "Input is
      numeric.";
    }
  }
}
```

5. *Edit class*: Edit app.module.ts and change it to the following:

```
import { BrowserModule } from '@angular/platform-browser';
import { NgModule } from '@angular/core';
import { AppComponent } from './app.component';
import { FormsModule } from '@angular/forms';

@NgModule({
  declarations: [
    AppComponent
  ],
  imports: [
    BrowserModule,
    FormsModule
  ],
  providers: [],
  bootstrap: [AppComponent]
})
export class AppModule { }
```

Your app should be working at localhost:4200. Note the following:

- The app component sets up the message instance variable to reference the template variable declared as #message.

- The app component has a ngAfterViewChecked method that's fired once the view's bindings have been checked. This is the method in which we check the input and set the message to indicate whether the user's input is numeric or not.

NgOnDestroy: Example

This callback is invoked when a component, directive, pipe, or service is destroyed. Add code here to destroy any references that may remain as instance variables (ithat is, clean up your references).

This example counts up using an interval timer, which it destroys when the component is destroyed, as shown in Figure 12-19. It's the perfect place to get the component ready to be disposed of—for example, to cancel background tasks. This will be example more-components-ex1800.

23615

Figure 12-19. *Counting up with an interval timer*

Now let's do example more-components-ex1800:

1. *Build the app using the CLI*: Use the following command:

   ```
   ng new more-components-ex1800 --inline-template
   --inline-style
   ```

2. *Start* ng serve: Use the following code:

   ```
   cd more-components-ex1800
   ng serve
   ```

3. *Open app*: Open a web browser and navigate to localhost:4200.
   You should see "welcome to app!"

4. *Edit class*: Edit app.component.ts and change it to the following:

   ```
   import { Component, OnInit, OnDestroy } from '@angular/
   core';

   @Component({
     selector: 'app-root',
     template: `
     <h1>
       {{count}}
     </h1>
     `,
     styles: []
   })
   export class AppComponent implements OnInit, OnDestroy{
     interval;
     count = 0;

     ngOnInit(){
       this.interval = setInterval(() => {
   ```

```
        this.count++;
      })
    }
    ngOnDestroy(){
      clearInterval(this.interval);
      delete this.interval;
    }
  }
```

Your app should be working at localhost:4200. Note the following:

- The app component has a `ngOnInit` method that's fired once it has loaded. It initializes the interval, which counts up.

- The app component has a `ngOnDestroy` method that is fired when it's being destroyed. It clears the interval, which stops the counting up.

Summary

This was an important chapter because you'll spend the majority of your time writing components. You need to know that your user interface is made up of a hierarchy of components, with each one having its own lifecycle from creation to destruction.

It is also very important to note how your data flows downwards, from high-level components down to lower-level components. And you need to know how the events flow in the opposite direction.

In the next chapter we'll discuss how you can create service objects to perform nonvisual tasks and plug these objects into your components using dependency injection.

CHAPTER 13

Dependency Injection

In software engineering, *dependency injection* is a software design pattern that implements inversion of control for resolving dependencies. A *dependency* is an object that can be used (a service). An *injection* is the passing of a dependency to a dependent object (a client) that would use it. After getting used to Angular, you will take the dependency injection for granted because it is so easy to use.

For example, this code

```
var svc = new ShippingService(new ProductLocator(),
    new PricingService(), new InventoryService(),
    new TrackingRepository(new ConfigProvider()),
    new Logger(new EmailLogger(new ConfigProvider())));
```

could be replaced by something like this:

```
var svc = container.Resolve<IShippingService>();
```

Some of the advantages of dependency injection include the following:

- Your code is cleaner and more readable.

- Objects are loosely coupled.

- Possible to eliminate, or at least reduce, a component's unnecessary dependencies.

- Reducing a component's dependencies typically makes it easier to reuse in a different context.

- Increases a component's testability.

- Moves the dependencies to the interface of components, so you don't reference the dependencies explicitly—you reference them via interfaces.

211

© Mark Clow 2018
M. Clow, *Angular 5 Projects*, https://doi.org/10.1007/978-1-4842-3279-8_13

Services and Providers

Angular's provided services are listed in Table 13-1.

Table 13-1. *Angular's Provided Services*

Service	Description
Http	For HTTP communication with the server
Form	Form handler code
Router	Page navigation code
Animation	UI animations
UI Library	For example, `NgBootstrap`

Tip   You can download other services from `www.ngmodules.org`.

You might want to write specific implementations of the following services:

- Server communication

- Security

- Auditing

- Logging

- Session

Remember that your implementations can "wrap" other services. For example, your server communication service could itself use the Angular Http service and add more functionality, implement something differently, or just have a different configuration.

When you write services, you typically write them as TypeScript classes, with one file (filename.service.ts) per class. It's a good idea to mark these classes as injectable using the `@Injectable()` annotation. `@Injectable()` marks a class as available to an injector for instantiation. Generally speaking, an injector reports an error when trying to instantiate a class that's not marked as `@Injectable()`.

Providers are used to register classes, functions, or values so that they can be used by the dependency injection. The `Injector` class uses the provider to supply information so that it can create an instance of an object to be injected into another. So, a provider is basically a source of information on how to create an instance of an object. This information includes a *token*, the identifier of an object that may need to be created. When you see `provider()` in your Angular code, you're seeing a call to an Angular function to register information on how to create an object.

There are three types of providers: class providers, factory providers, and value providers. Later in this chapter I'll introduce the class providers first because they're used the most.

Each component has its own injector that's used with the providers to create objects for the component. When components have child components, the injector creates child injectors for the child components.

When the dependency injection needs to inject an object into a component, it attempts to resolve the object in the local injector (that is, the one for the component) using the `get` method. If that can't be resolved (in other words, if the object doesn't already exist in the injector), it attempts to resolve the object in the parent component's injector and so forth, all the way to the Application component. This ensures that the nearest (local) injector's provider is used in preference to a higher-level provider. This is known as *shadowing*, and it's similar to how local variables with the same name are used in preference to global variables of the same name.

Normally Angular handles the resolution and creation of dependencies for you. However, the `Injector` class offers you methods to invoke this yourself—for example, `resolveAndCreate`.

Creating a Service: Example

This is a simple component that uses a service to provide information about cars. This will be example dependency-injection-ex100. It will provide the service in the car component, as illustrated in Figure 13-1.

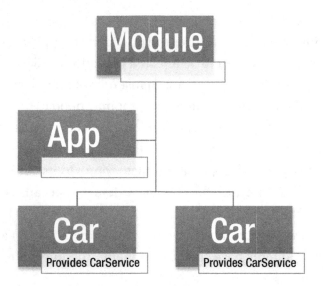

Figure 13-1. *Component using a service to provide information*

Let's try the exercise:

1. *Build the app using the CLI*: Use the following command:

   ```
   ng new dependency-injection-ex100 --inline-template --inline-style
   ```

2. *Start* ng serve: Use the following code:

   ```
   cd dependency-injection-ex100
   ng serve
   ```

3. *Open app*: Open a web browser and navigate to localhost:4200. You should see "app works!"

4. *Create service class*: Create car.service.ts and change it to the following:

   ```
   import { Injectable } from '@angular/core';

   @Injectable()
   export class CarService {
       constructor(){
           console.log('CarService: constructor');
       }
   ```

```
    // Some dummy method.
    isSuperCharged(car: string){
        return car === 'Ford GT' ? 'yes' : 'no';
    }
}
```

5. *Edit class*: Edit app.component.ts and change it to the following:

```
import { Component, OnInit, Input } from '@angular/core';
import { CarService } from './car.service';

@Component({
  selector: 'car',
  template: `
  <h3>
    {{name}} Is Supercharged: {{supercharged}}
  </h3>
  `,
  styles: [],
  providers: [CarService]
})
export class CarComponent implements OnInit{
  @Input() name;
  supercharged: string = '';
  constructor(private service: CarService){}
  ngOnInit(){
    this.supercharged = this.service.isSuperCharged(this.name);
  }
}

@Component({
  selector: 'app-root',
  template: `
  <car name="Ford GT"></car>
  <car name="Corvette Z06"></car>
  `,
  styles: []
})
```

```
export class AppComponent {
  title = 'app works!';
}
```

6. *Edit module*: Edit app.module.ts and change it to the following:

```
import { BrowserModule } from '@angular/platform-browser';
import { NgModule } from '@angular/core';
import { FormsModule } from '@angular/forms';
import { HttpModule } from '@angular/http';

import { AppComponent, CarComponent } from './app.component';

@NgModule({
  declarations: [
    AppComponent, CarComponent
  ],
  imports: [
    BrowserModule,
    FormsModule,
    HttpModule
  ],
  providers: [],
  bootstrap: [AppComponent]
})
export class AppModule { }
```

Your app should be working at localhost:4200. Note the following:

- The car service outputs a log when in the constructor. This service contains a method isSuperCharged that receives a car name as an argument and returns a yes or no accordingly, as shown in Figure 13-2.

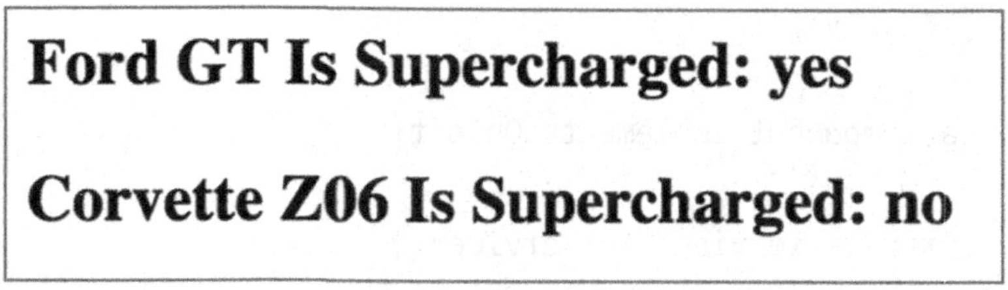

> **Ford GT Is Supercharged: yes**
>
> **Corvette Z06 Is Supercharged: no**

Figure 13-2. *Returning a yes or no*

- The app component has a car component that's used twice. The car component specifies the `car` service as a provider. The car component invokes the `service` method `isSuperCharged` in the method `ngOnInit`. `ngOnInit` is fired when the component has been initialized.

Why do multiple instances of the same service get created? Open the console and you'll see something like Figure 13-3.

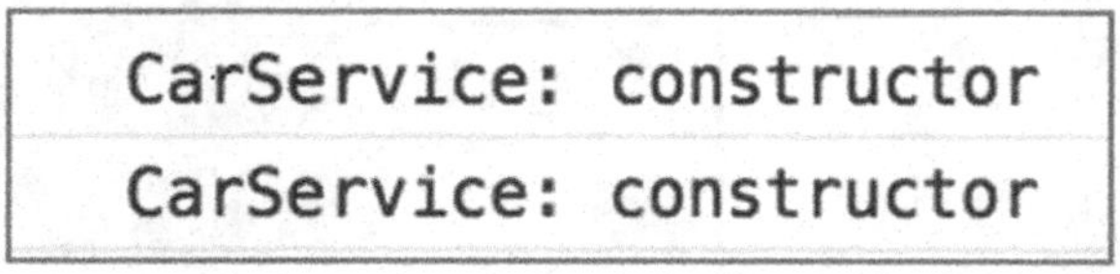

```
CarService: constructor
CarService: constructor
```

Figure 13-3. *Constructor invoked twice*

As you can see, the constructor is invoked twice, as the service is created twice. That's because the `CarService` is provided in the car component and the car component is create twice. Here's an excerpt of the car component:

```
@Component({
  selector: 'car',
  ...
```

```
  providers: [CarService]
})
export class CarComponent implements OnInit{
  ...
  constructor(private service: CarService){}
  ...
}
```

What we want is for a single instance of the service to be created, as illustrated in Figure 13-4.

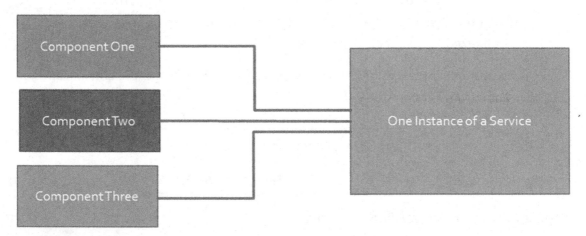

Figure 13-4.   *We want one instance of a service created*

To make that happen, we simply move the provider to the application level or a class that's only being used once. In the code example, we could specify the provider in the

What if we want to share a singleton of the service? We don't specify that we need it on the Car object, because there are multiple Cars. We need to specify that we need the service somewhere else on an *application level*.

Let's convert our app to share *one* instance of the service.

Convert App to Share One Instance of Service: Example dependency-injection-ex200

This is a simple component that uses a service to provide information about cars, as shown in Figure 13-5.

> **Ford GT Is Supercharged: yes**
>
> **Corvette Z06 Is Supercharged: no**

Figure 13-5. *Service providing information about cars*

Example dependency-injection-ex200 is the same as dependency-injection-ex100 except it provides the service in the app component so that only one instance of the CarService is created, as illustrated in Figure 13-6.

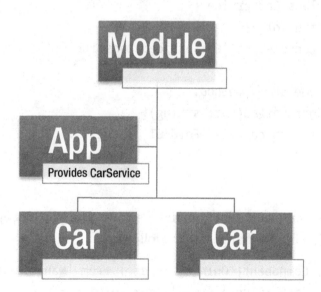

Figure 13-6. *One instance of CarService provided in the app component*

Let's do exercise dependency-injection-ex200:

1. *Build the app using the CLI*: Use the following command:

   ```
   ng new dependency-injection-ex200 --inline-template --inline-style
   ```

2. *Start* ng serve: Use the following code:

   ```
   cd dependency-injection-ex200
   ng serve
   ```

3. *Open app*: Open a web browser and navigate to localhost:4200. You should see "app works!"

4. *Create service class*: This is the same as the previous example. Edit car.service.ts and change it to the following:

   ```
   import { Injectable } from '@angular/core';

   @Injectable()
   export class CarService {
       constructor(){
           console.log('CarService: constructor');
       }
       // Some dummy method.
       isSuperCharged(car: string){
           return car === 'Ford GT' ? 'yes' : 'no';
       }
   }
   ```

5. *Edit class*: This is different from the previous example. Edit app. component.ts and change it to the following:

   ```
   import { Component, OnInit, Input } from '@angular/core';
   import { CarService } from './car.service';

   @Component({
     selector: 'car',
     template: `
     <h3>
   ```

```
        {{name}} Is Supercharged: {{supercharged}}
      </h3>
      `,
      styles: [],
      providers: []
})
export class CarComponent implements OnInit{
  @Input() name;
  supercharged: string = '';
  constructor(private service: CarService){}
  ngOnInit(){
    this.supercharged = this.service.isSuperCharged(this.name);
  }
}

@Component({
    selector: 'app-root',
    template: `
    <car name="Ford GT"></car>
    <car name="Corvette Z06"></car>
    `,
    styles: [],
    providers: [CarService]
})
export class AppComponent {
    title = 'app works!';
}
```

6. *Edit module*: This is the same as the previous example. Edit app.
   module.ts and change it to the following:

```
import { BrowserModule } from '@angular/platform-browser';
import { NgModule } from '@angular/core';
import { FormsModule } from '@angular/forms';
import { HttpModule } from '@angular/http';

import { AppComponent, CarComponent } from './app.component';

@NgModule({
```

221

```
      declarations: [
        AppComponent, CarComponent
      ],
      imports: [
        BrowserModule,
        FormsModule,
        HttpModule
      ],
      providers: [],
      bootstrap: [AppComponent]
    })
    export class AppModule { }
```

Your app should be working at localhost:4200. Note that the CarService constructor is only logged once in the console. That's because it only needs to be created once in the app component and can be used by all subcomponents.

Convert App to Share One Instance of Service: Example dependency-injection-ex300

This is a simple component that uses a service to provide information about cars, as shown in Figure 13-7.

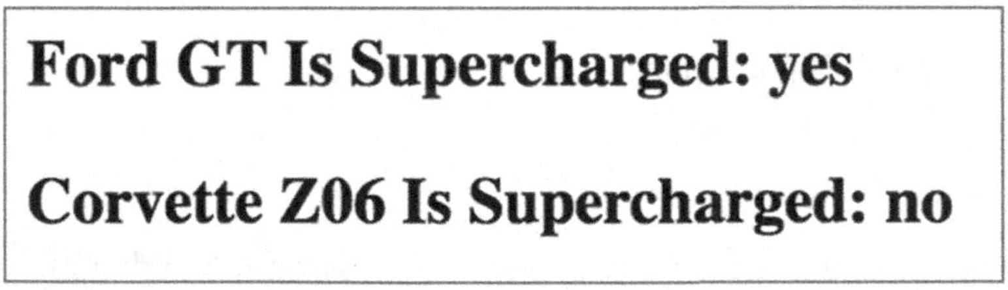

Ford GT Is Supercharged: yes

Corvette Z06 Is Supercharged: no

Figure 13-7. Service providing information about cars

Example dependency-injection-ex300 is the same as dependency-injection-ex200 except it provides the service in the module so that only one instance of the CarService is created and can be used anywhere in the app, as illustrated in Figure 13-8.

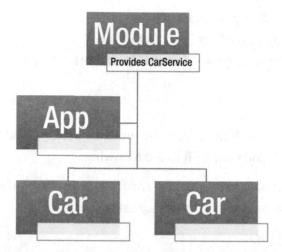

Figure 13-8. *One instance of* `CarService` *provided in the module*

Let's do exercise dependency-injection-ex300:

1. *Build the app using the CLI*: Use the following command:

   ```
   ng new dependency-injection-ex300 --inline-template --inline-style
   ```

2. *Start* ng serve: Use the following code:

   ```
   cd dependency-injection-ex300
   ng serve
   ```

3. *Open app*: Open a web browser and navigate to localhost:4200.
   You should see "app works!"

4. *Create service class*: This is the same as the previous example. Edit
   car.service.ts and change it to the following:

   ```
   import { Injectable } from '@angular/core';

   @Injectable()
   export class CarService {
       constructor(){
           console.log('CarService: constructor');
       }
   ```

```
    // Some dummy method.
    isSuperCharged(car: string){
        return car === 'Ford GT' ? 'yes' : 'no';
    }
}
```

5. *Edit class*: This is different from the previous example. Edit app.
   component.ts and change it to the following:

```
import { Component, OnInit, Input } from '@angular/core';
import { CarService } from './car.service';

@Component({
  selector: 'car',
  template: `
  <h3>
    {{name}} Is Supercharged: {{supercharged}}
  </h3>
  `,
  styles: []
})
export class CarComponent implements OnInit{
  @Input() name;
  supercharged: string = '';
  constructor(private service: CarService){}
  ngOnInit(){
    this.supercharged = this.service.isSuperCharged(this.name);
  }
}

@Component({
  selector: 'app-root',
  template: `
  <car name="Ford GT"></car>
  <car name="Corvette Z06"></car>
  `,
  styles: []
})
```

```
export class AppComponent {
  title = 'app works!';
}
```

6. *Edit module*: This is different to the previous example. Edit app. module.ts and change it to the following:

```
import { BrowserModule } from '@angular/platform-browser';
import { NgModule } from '@angular/core';
import { FormsModule } from '@angular/forms';

import { HttpModule } from '@angular/http';
import { AppComponent, CarComponent } from './app.component';

import { CarService } from './car.service';

@NgModule({
  declarations: [
    AppComponent, CarComponent
  ],
  imports: [
    BrowserModule,
    FormsModule,
    HttpModule
  ],
  providers: [CarService],
  bootstrap: [AppComponent]
})
export class AppModule { }
```

Your app should be working at localhost:4200. Note that the `CarService` constructor is only logged once in the console. That's because it only needs to be created once in the App module and can be used by all subcomponents.

Class Providers: Example dependency-injection-ex350

As mentioned earlier, there are three types of providers: class providers, factory providers, and value providers. Class providers allow us to tell the provider which class to use for a dependency.

Figure 13-9 shows a component that relies on a Watch service.

Seiko Time:Mon Jun 12 2017 21:29:40 GMT-0400 (EDT)

Figure 13-9. *Component relying on a Watch service*

Let's do example dependency-injection-ex350:

1. *Build the app using the CLI*: Use the following command:

   ```
   ng new dependency-injection-ex350 --inline-template --inline-style
   ```

2. *Start* ng serve: Use the following code:

   ```
   cd dependency-injection-ex350
   ng serve
   ```

3. *Open app*: Open a web browser and navigate to localhost:4200. You should see "app works!"

4. *Edit class*: Edit app.component.ts and change it to the following:

   ```
   import { Component } from '@angular/core';
   class Watch {
     getTime(): string {
       return new Date() + "";
     }
   }
   ```

```
class Seiko extends Watch {
  getTime(): string{
    return "Seiko Time:" + super.getTime();
  }
}

@Component({
  selector: 'app-root',
  template: `
  <h1>
    {{watch.getTime()}}
  </h1>
  `,
  styles: [],
  providers: [{
    provide: Watch,
    useClass: Seiko
  }]
})
export class AppComponent {
  constructor(private watch:Watch){}
}
```

Your app should be working at localhost:4200. Note that when we use the `Provider` element of the `@Component` annotation to create the dependency, we specify that subclass of the `Watch` (a Seiko).

Factory Providers: Example dependency-injection-ex400

Factory providers use a function to provide Angular with an instance of an object. This is useful when you need to dynamically change the object that you want created, based on some data.

This is a simple component that uses a logging service:

1. *Build the app using the CLI*: Use the following command:

```
ng new dependency-injection-ex400 --inline-template --inline-style
```

2. *Start* ng serve: Use the following code:

```
cd dependency-injection-ex400
ng serve
```

3. *Open app*: Open a web browser and navigate to localhost:4200. You should see "app works!"

4. *Create service class*: This is the same as the previous example. Create logging.service.ts and change it to the following:

```
import { Injectable } from '@angular/core';

@Injectable()
export class LoggingService {
    constructor(private dateAndTime: boolean){
        console.log('LoggingService: constructor');
    }
    log(message){
        console.log((this.dateAndTime ? new Date() + ': ' : '') +
        message);
    }
}
```

5. *Edit class*: Edit app.component.ts and change it to the following:

```
import { Component } from '@angular/core';
import { LoggingService } from './logging.service';

@Component({
  selector: 'app-root',
  template: `
  <h1>
    {{title}}
  </h1>
  `,
```

```
      styles: [],
      providers: [provideLoggingService()]
    })
    export class AppComponent {
      constructor(private logging: LoggingService){
        logging.log('test log');
      }
      title = 'app works!';
    }
    export const LOGGING_USE_DATE = false;
    export function provideLoggingService() {
      return {
        provide: LoggingService,
        useFactory: () => new LoggingService(LOGGING_USE_DATE)
      }
    }
```

Your app should be working at localhost:4200. Note that this logging service has the option of including the logging date and time. You can set this using the constructor to the logging service. A factory provider is used to provide an instance of the logging service.

Figure 13-10 shows the date included in logging:

```
export const LOGGING_USE_DATE = true;
export function provideLoggingService() {
  return {
    provide: LoggingService,
    useFactory: () => new LoggingService(LOGGING_USE_DATE)
  }
}
```

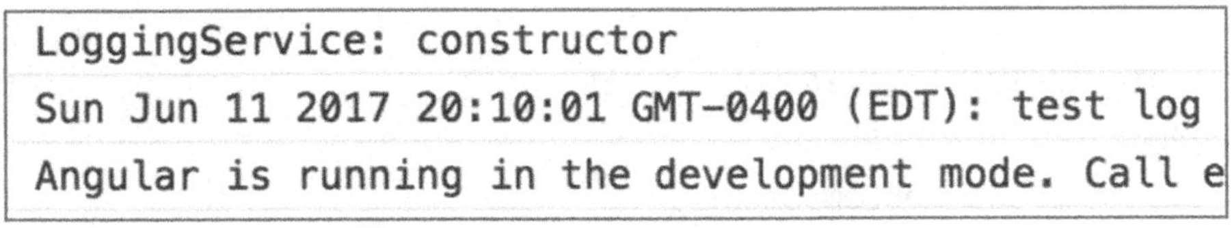

```
LoggingService: constructor
Sun Jun 11 2017 20:10:01 GMT-0400 (EDT): test log
Angular is running in the development mode. Call e
```

Figure 13-10. *Date included in logging*

Figure 13-10 shows the date not included in logging:

```
export const LOGGING_USE_DATE = false;
export function provideLoggingService() {
  return {
    provide: LoggingService,
    useFactory: () => new LoggingService(LOGGING_USE_DATE)
  }
}
```

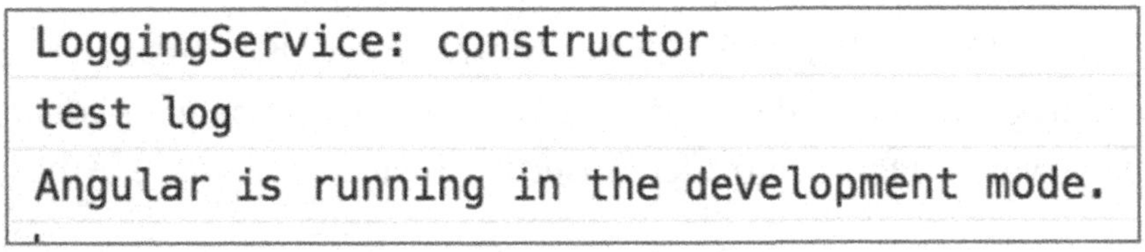

```
LoggingService: constructor
test log
Angular is running in the development mode.
```

Figure 13-11. *Date not included in logging*

Factory Providers: Example dependency-injection-ex500

This is a simple component that displays a playing card, as shown in Figure 13-12.

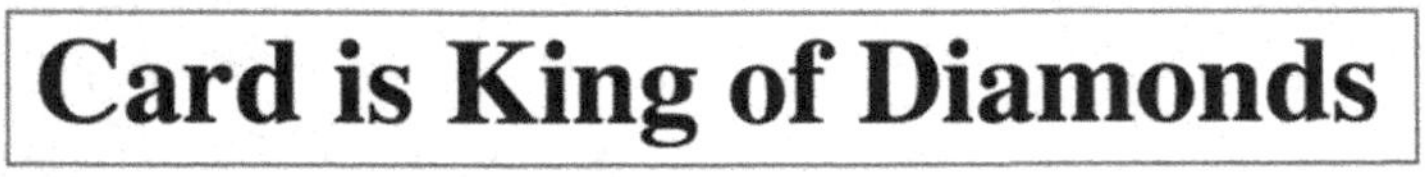

Card is King of Diamonds

Figure 13-12. *Displaying a playing card*

Let's do example dependency-injection-ex500:

1. *Build the app using the CLI*: Use the following command:

   ```
   ng new dependency-injection-ex500 --inline-template --inline-style
   ```

2. *Start* ng serve: Use the following code:

   ```
   cd dependency-injection-ex500
   ng serve
   ```

3. *Open app*: Open a web browser and navigate to localhost:4200.
   You should see "app works!"

4. *Create* Card *class*: This is the same as the previous example. Edit
   card.ts and change it to the following:

   ```
   import { Injectable } from '@angular/core';

   @Injectable()
   export class Card {
       constructor(public suite: string, public rank: string) {}
       toString(): string {
           return "Card is " + this.rank + " of " + this.suite;
       }
   }
   ```

5. *Edit class*: Edit app.component.ts and change it to the following:

   ```
   import { Component } from '@angular/core';
   import { Card } from './card';
   @Component({
     selector: 'app-root',
     template: `
   <h1>
     {{title}}
   </h1>
   `
     ,
     styles: [],
     providers: [{
       provide: Card,
   ```

```
  useFactory: () => {
    const suite: number = Math.floor(Math.random() * 4);
    const suiteName: string =
      suite == 0 ? "Clubs" :
      suite == 1 ? "Diamonds" :
      suite == 2 ? "Hearts" : "Spades";
    const rank: number = Math.floor(Math.random() * 15);
    const rankName: string =
      rank == 0 ? "Ace" :
      rank == 1 ? "Joker" :
      rank == 2 ? "King" :
      rank == 3 ? "Queen" :
      (rank - 3).toString();
    return new Card(suiteName, rankName);
  }
}]
})

export class AppComponent {
  title = 'app works!';
  constructor(card:Card){
    this.title = card.toString();
  }
}
```

Value Providers: Example dependency-injection-ex600

You've seen code and examples for class providers and factory providers. Now let's look at value providers. Value providers simply provide a value of an object, as shown in Figure 13-13.

Language is: en

Figure 13-13. *Value of an object*

Let's go through example dependency-injection-ex600:

1. *Build the app using the CLI*: Use the following command:

    ```
    ng new dependency-injection-ex600 --inline-template --inline-style
    ```

2. *Start* ng serve: Use the following code:

    ```
    cd dependency-injection-ex600
    ng serve
    ```

3. *Open app*: Open a web browser and navigate to localhost:4200. You should see "app works!"

4. *Edit class*: Edit app.component.ts and change it to the following:

    ```
    import { Component, Injector } from '@angular/core';

    @Component({
      selector: 'app-root',
      template: `
    <h1>
      {{title}}
    </h1>
    `,
      styles: [],
      providers: [{
        provide: 'language',
        useValue: 'en'
      }]
    })
    ```

```
export class AppComponent {
  title: string = '';
  constructor(private injector: Injector){
    this.title = 'Language is: ' + injector.get('language');
  }
}
```

Injector API

You don't need to know the Injector API in great detail yet. If you feel overwhelmed at this point in the chapter, feel free to skip to the next chapter and come back to this later on.

However, if you want even more control over creating dependencies, you can access the Injector object directly. The Injector is a class in the Angular core package. It's a dependency injection container used for instantiating objects and resolving dependencies.

If the classes you're attempting to resolve and create (using the Injector) have dependencies themselves, the Injector automatically attempts to resolve and create those for you. You can also use the additional options in the Provider class when you use it.

Here's an example:

```
import { Injector } from '@angular/core';

const injector = Injector.resolveAndCreate([Car, Engine, Tires, Doors]);

const car = injector.get(Car);
```

And another example:

```
import { Injector } from '@angular/core';

const injector = Injector.resolveAndCreate(
  [
    provide(Car, useClass: Car)),
    provide(Engine, useClass: Engine)),
```

```
    provide(Tires, useClass: Tires)),
    provide(Doors, useClass: Doors))
  ]
);

const car = injector.get(Car);
```

Summary

This chapter covered a lot of ground, from the concept of dependency injection all the way to the `Injector` itself. At this point you don't need to know everything about the Injector API.

What you do need to know is the basics of dependency injection in Angular—how you can set up your providers and use contructor injection. I hope you followed the examples and that they help you understand how the dependency injection works.

Using services with dependency injection is something you will use all the time. Most of the time your application will use one instance of each service. Having a single instance of each service can be very useful because you can then use these services to hold state information (for example a customer list) accessed by multiple components. Also sometimes you will use single-instance services as a 'communication' bridge between components.

In the next chapter we'll start covering third-party widget libraries. Why spend precious time developing a bespoke look and feel when huge companies offer libraries of well-tested and beautifully designed UI widgets for you?

CHAPTER 14

Angular and UI Widgets

Angular is the core of many new JavaScript apps. However, you need to couple Angular with a front-end UI framework, such as Bootstrap or Material Design. I cover Bootstrap first in this chapter because it's currently the more common of the two, and then I talk about Material Design.

Using a UI Widget Library with Angular

You can use a UI widget library in two ways:

- *The pre-Angular way*: Use HTML markup and JavaScript in the normal manner.

- *The Angular way*: Use custom markup directives. You utilize a third-party module of custom components and directives that generate UI widget HTML markup.

Pre-Angular Way

You can create components using HTML and JavaScript that style components in the same manner as you would in JQuery or another earlier JavaScript library.

HTML is, of course, a markup language and the most common document format of the web. A markup language annotates a document. Some markup languages, including HTML, have specifications that determine how to display the structured data—it tells the computer how to display something. In Angular, we write dynamic user interfaces, and Angular components use HTML markup to tell the computer how to display things.

The markup is in the template, which is specified in the @Component annotation of the component. It's also sometimes specified in the @View annotation (more on that later).

M. Clow, *Angular 5 Projects*, https://doi.org/10.1007/978-1-4842-3279-8_14

The Angular Way

You can create components using a module of pre-built and styled Angular components and directives, delivered as a module so you can reuse them. This is a module of component objects (like the ones you've written in earlier chapters) and directives that enable you to use tags to create a bootstrap UI. This requires you to use someone else's code, but it saves you time by providing pre-built components and the directives to use them with. Chapter 11 covered directives.

In this chapter (and others) I'm using the ng2-bootstrap module (`http://valor-software.github.io/ng2-bootstrap/`), which is a Bootstrap implementation for Angular.

Pre-Angular vs. Angular with NgBootstrap

Figure 14-1 shows a common UI element: a tab. We'll write the HTML markup for the same tab with and without the ng2-bootstrap module.

Figure 14-1.   *Common UI element: a tab*

Here's the pre-Angular way using HTML, CSS, and JavaScript:

```
<div class="tabbable tabs-left" style="margin-top: 100px;">
  <ul class="nav nav-tabs">
    <li class="active"><a href="#pane1" data-toggle="tab" rel="popover"
    id="tab">Homee</a></li>
    <li><a href="#pane2" data-toggle="tab" title="blah blah"
    id="tab1">Profile</a></li>
    <li><a href="#pane3" data-toggle="tab" id="tab2">Messages</a></li>
    <li><a href="#pane4" data-toggle="tab">Settings</a></li>
  </ul>
```

```
<div class="tab-content">
  <div id="pane1" class="tab-pane active">...</div>
  <div id="pane2" class="tab-pane">...</div>
  <div id="pane3" class="tab-pane">...</div>
  <div id="pane4" class="tab-pane">...</div>
</div>
</div>
```

And here's the Angular way with the ng2-bootstrap module:

```
<ngb-tabset>
  <ngb-tab title="Home">
    <ng-template ngbTabContent>
      ...
    </ng-template>
  </ngb-tab>
  <ngb-tab title="Profile">
    <ng-template ngbTabContent>
      ...
    </ng-template>
  </ngb-tab>
  <ngb-tab title="Messages">
    <ng-template ngbTabContent>
      ...
    </ng-template>
  </ngb-tab>
  <ngb-tab title="Settings">
    <ng-template ngbTabContent>
      ...
    </ng-template>
  </ngb-tab>
</ngb-tabset>
```

The module makes the code smaller. Note it calls tabs ngb-tabs instead of divs.

Bootstrap

Bootstrap is an open source group of tools that has HTML and CSS design templates for interface elements like forms, buttons, typography, and navigation, plus optional JavaScript extensions. Bootstrap makes developing dynamic websites and web applications easier. It's compatible with the latest versions of most browsers, including Firefox, Internet Explorer, Google Chrome, Opera, and Safari, though not on all platforms.

Bootstrap version 2.0 and up also supports *responsive web design*, which dynamically adjusts the layout of web pages according to the characteristics of whatever device is being used, whether that's a phone, tablet, or desktop machine. As of version 3.0, Bootstrap has a mobile-first design philosophy, empoying responsive design by default. It provides a grid system to allow developers (who may lack skills in responsive design) to write code that works equally well on all devices. The default 12-column grid system without responsive features enabled uses a 940-pixel wide container. With the responsive CSS file added, the grid becomes 724×1170 pixels wide, depending on your viewport. Below 767-pixel viewports, the columns become fluid and stack vertically.

For much more about Bootstrap, go to `http://getbootstrap.com`. Figure 14-2 shows a web page made with Bootstrap.

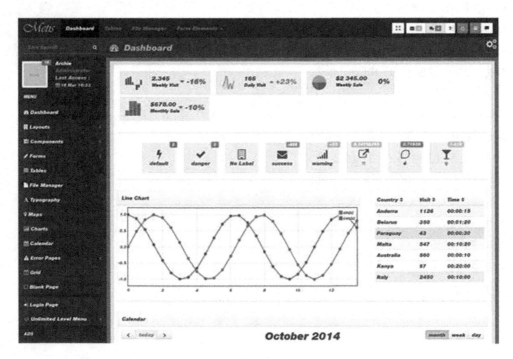

Figure 14-2. *Web page made with Bootstrap*

240

Installing ng-bootstrap

ng-bootstrap is an Angular version of the Bootstrap library that you can use to quickly build apps using Bootstrap widgets. The source code is available to `https://github.com/ng-bootstrap/ng-bootstrap`, and demos are available at `https://ng-bootstrap.github.io/#/components/accordion/examples`.

Here's how to install ng-bootstrap:

1. Build the app using the CLI in the usual manner.

2. Use npm to install both ng-bootstrap and Bootstrap modules:

   ```
   npm install --save @ng-bootstrap/ng-bootstrap bootstrap
   ```

3. Tell the CLI project to use the styles in the bootstrap CSS file. Edit .angular.json and add the following entry under styles:

   ```
   "../node_modules/bootstrap/dist/css/bootstrap.css",
   ```

4. Edit your module file (app.module.ts) and specify the `NgbModule` as an `import`. This will make the code in `NgbModule` available in this Angular module:

   ```
   imports: [
       NgbModule.forRoot(),
       BrowserModule
   ],
   ```

Bootstrap: Example widgets-ex100

This component allows the user to select a pizza using a group of buttons that act like a group of radio buttons, as shown in Figure 14-2.

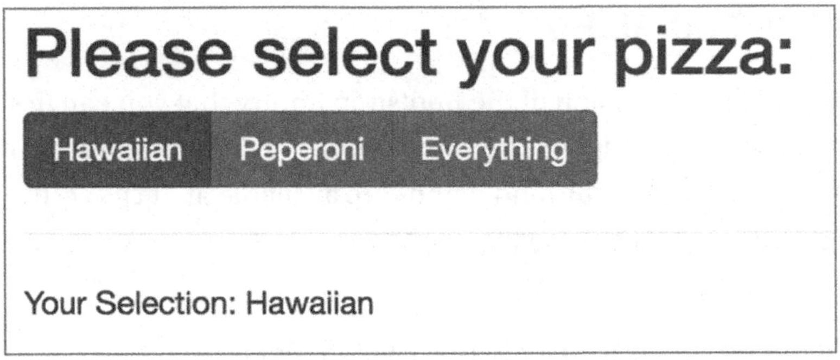

Please select your pizza:

Hawaiian   Peperoni   Everything

Your Selection: Hawaiian

Figure 14-3. *Selecting a pizza*

Let's go through the example:

1. *Build the app using the CLI*: Use the following command:

   ```
   ng new widgets-ex100 --inline-template --inline-style
   ```

2. *Install* ng-bootstrap *and* bootstrap: Use the following code:

   ```
   cd widgets-ex100
   npm install --save @ng-bootstrap/ng-bootstrap bootstrap
   ```

3. *Install Bootstrap styles into project*: Edit .angular-cli.json and add the following entry under styles:

   ```
   "../node_modules/bootstrap/dist/css/bootstrap.css",
   ```

   The style block should look like this:

   ```
   "styles": [
           "../node_modules/bootstrap/dist/css/bootstrap.css",
           "styles.css"
       ],
   ```

4. *Start* ng serve: Use this command:

   ```
   ng serve
   ```

5. *Open app*: Open a web browser and navigate to localhost:4200. You should see "welcome to app!"

6. *Edit module*: Edit app.module.ts and change it to the following:

```
import { BrowserModule } from '@angular/platform-browser';
import { NgModule } from '@angular/core';
import { FormsModule } from '@angular/forms';
import { NgbModule } from '@ng-bootstrap/ng-bootstrap';

import { AppComponent } from './app.component';

@NgModule({
  declarations: [
    AppComponent
  ],
  imports: [
    NgbModule.forRoot(),
    BrowserModule,
    FormsModule
  ],
  providers: [],
  bootstrap: [AppComponent]
})
export class AppModule { }
```

7. *Edit class*: Edit app.component.ts and change it to the following:

```
import { Component } from '@angular/core';
import { NgbModule } from '@ng-bootstrap/ng-bootstrap';

@Component({
  selector: 'app-root',
  template: `
    <div style="padding:10px">
    <h2>Please select your pizza:</h2>
    <div [(ngModel)]="model" ngbRadioGroup name="radioBasic">
      <label ngbButtonLabel class="btn btn-primary">
        <input ngbButton type="radio" value="Hawaiian"> Hawaiian
      </label>
      <label ngbButtonLabel class="btn btn-primary">
```

```
        <input ngbButton type="radio" value="Peperoni"> Peperoni
      </label>
      <label ngbButtonLabel class="btn btn-primary">
        <input ngbButton type="radio" value="Everything"> Everything
      </label>
    </div>
    <hr>
    Your Selection: {{model}}
    </div>
  `,
  styles: []
})

export class AppComponent {
  model = 'Hawaiian';
}
```

Your app should be working at localhost:4200.

Material Design

Material Design also uses grid-based layouts like Bootstrap. It enables responsive animations and transitions, padding, and depth effects light lighting and shadows. Material has a lok based on paper and ink.

Polymer is the implementation of Material Design for web application user interfaces. It contains the Polymer library, which provides a Web Components API for browsers and an elements catalog, including a paper elements collection featuring visual elements. Figure 14-4 show a Material Design web page. You can read much more about this product at www.material-ui.com.

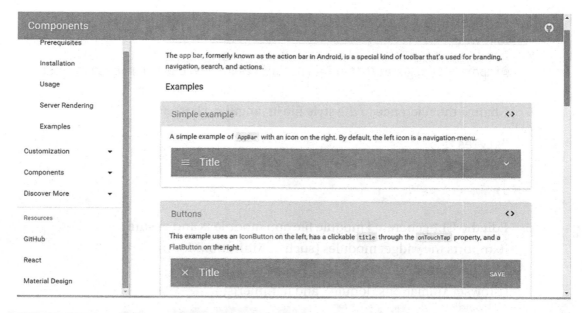

Figure 14-4. *Web page of Material Design*

Installing Angular Material

Angular Material is an Angular version of the Material library that you can to quickly build apps with Material components. The source code is available at `https://github.com/jelbourn/material2-app`, and the example is here: `https://material2-app.firebaseapp.com`.

Here's how to install Angular Material:

1. Build the app using the CLI in the usual manner.

2. Use npm to install Angular Material, Angular Animation, and CDK (Components Development Kit).

    ```
    npm install --save @angular/material
    npm install --save @angular/animations
    npm install --save @angular/cdk
    ```

3. Add the icons to your project by including them in the index.html file:

    ```
    <link href="https://fonts.googleapis.com/
    icon?family=Material+Icons" rel="stylesheet">
    ```

4. Rename the styles file styles.css to styles.scss and change it to the following:

```
@import '~@angular/material/prebuilt-themes/deeppurple-amber.css';
```

5. Change the reference to the style file in .angular-cli.json:

```
"styles": [
    "styles.scss"
],
```

6. Edit the CLI-generated module file app.module.ts and ensure it imports the widget modules (such as MdButtonModule, MdCheckboxModule), the animations module (BrowserAnimationsModule), and hammerjs:

```
import {MdButtonModule, MdCheckboxModule} from '@angular/material';
import {BrowserAnimationsModule} from '@angular/platform-browser/
animations';
import { hammerjs } from 'hammerjs';
@NgModule({
  ...
  imports: [MdButtonModule, MdCheckboxModule],
  [BrowserAnimationsModule]
  ...
}
```

Angular Material Design: Example widgets-ex200

This component allows the user to select the date with a Material-styled date picker popup, as shown in Figure 14-5.

Figure 14-5. *Date picker popup*

Let's do the example:

1. Build the app using the CLI:

    ```
    ng new widgets-ex200 --inline-template --inline-style
    ```

2. Install Angular Material, Animations and Component Development Kit.

    ```
    cd widgets-ex200
    npm install --save @angular/material
    npm install --save @angular/animations
    npm install --save @angular/cdk
    ```

3. Add the icons to your project by including them in the index.html file:

    ```
    <link href="https://fonts.googleapis.com/
    icon?family=Material+Icons" rel="stylesheet">
    ```

4. Rename the styles file styles.css to styles.scss and change it to the following:

```
@import '~@angular/material/prebuilt-themes/deeppurple-amber.css';
```

5. Change the reference to the style file in .angular-cli.json:

```
"styles": [
    "styles.scss"
],
```

6. Edit app.module.ts and change it to the following:

```
import { BrowserModule } from '@angular/platform-browser';
import { NgModule } from '@angular/core';
import { AppComponent } from './app.component';
import { BrowserAnimationsModule } from '@angular/platform-
browser/animations';
import {FormsModule, ReactiveFormsModule} from '@angular/forms';
import {
  MatNativeDateModule,
  MatFormFieldModule,
  MatInputModule,
  MatDatepickerModule
} from '@angular/material';
@NgModule({
  declarations: [
    AppComponent
  ],
  imports: [
    BrowserModule, BrowserAnimationsModule, MatNativeDateModule,
    MatFormFieldModule, MatInputModule, MatDatepickerModule
  ],
  providers: [],
  bootstrap: [AppComponent]
})
export class AppModule { }
```

7. Edit app.component.ts and change it to the following:

```
import { Component } from '@angular/core';

@Component({
selector: 'app-root',
template: `
  <mat-form-field>
  <input matInput [matDatepicker]="picker" placeholder="Choose a date">
  <mat-datepicker-toggle matSuffix [for]="picker"></mat-
  datepicker-toggle>
  <mat-datepicker #picker></mat-datepicker>
  </mat-form-field>
`,
styles: []
})

export class AppComponent {
  title = 'app';
}
```

8. Start ng serve:

```
ng serve
```

9. Open a web browser and navigate to localhost:4200. You should
   see the app running.

Your app should be working at localhost:4200.

Summary

If you're serious about building a polished Angular app, you should use a pre-built widget library module. Many applications use Bootstrap and Material. I'm currently working on an application that uses Bootstrap, and it has the advantage of offering a grid system, which takes away a lot of the pain of responsive design.

UI widget libraries definitely make it easier to write beautiful user interfaces with more maintainable, standard code. Dont waste your time re-inventing the wheel writing your own widget library! Remember that you can setup themes in widget libraries to customize them to your specifications.

CHAPTER 15

Routes and Navigation

In most web applications, users navigate from one page to the next as they perform application tasks. Users can navigate in these ways:

- Entering a URL in the address bar

- Following links, clicking buttons, and so on

- Going backward or forward in the browser history

In Angular applications, users can navigate in the same three ways but they're navigating through components (the building blocks of Angular apps). We can navigate because we have the Angular router. The router can interpret a browser URL as an instruction to navigate to a component and pass optional parameters (which contain information) to the component to give it contextual information and help it decide which specific content to present or what it needs to do.

We can bind the router to links on a page, and it will navigate to the appropriate component when the user clicks a link. We can navigate imperatively when the user clicks a button, selects from a drop-down, or responds to some other stimulus from any source.

The router logs activity in the browser's history, so the back and forward buttons work as well.

Router Routes on the Client Side

Any URL that contains a # character is a *fragment* URL. The portion of the URL to the left of the # identifies a resource that can be accessed (from the server), and the portion on the right, known as the *fragment identifier*, specifies a location within the resource (on the client). For example, in the URL www.cnn.com/index.html#section2, the fragment name is section2, and it specifies a location in the document index.html.

© Mark Clow 2018
M. Clow, *Angular 5 Projects*, https://doi.org/10.1007/978-1-4842-3279-8_15

The original purpose of fragments was to allow the user to jump to a link on a specified part of the current page, scrolling up or down. Now fragments are often used for client-side navigation, because by their nature they don't invoke a request to pull resources from the server.

HTML5 browsers can work with client-side and non-client-side routing for URLs, including those with hashes and those without. But some older browsers won't work with client-side routing for URLS that aren't hashed. *Hashed* means that the client-side part of the URL needs to be after the # sign (that is, it's a fragment).

If you're deploying a single page application to production,n you probably need to do the following:

1. Turn on hash routing on the router. This will make your single page application more compatible with older pre-HTML5 browsers. When you import the router module in your module, you should do the following:

```
@NgModule({
  imports: [
    RouterModule.forRoot(appRoutes, {useHash: true})
  ],
  ...
})
export class ...
```

2. Ensure that your 404 page on the server reroutes to the web page (for example, index.html) that contains the single page application. This will return pages to the single page app if for some reason the browser attempts to pull server resources in error.

Route Matching

If you specify a URL in your address bar of your web browser and the Angular application is loaded, the router will attempt to find the route that matches the URL. It goes through every permutation of possible route combination until it matches the complete URL. If you have multiple routes that can possibly match to the same url, the router will use the first route available, even if the second one looks more complete.

Router DSL

When you specify a route, you specify it using a text string, for example '/customers/123'. DSL stands for 'Domain Specific Language' and that term is used because your route text string can be interpreted and matched in many ways. Your route string can specify:

- An absolute route.

- A relative route from where you are at the moment.

- A route that references server resources.

- A route that references client-side resources (using fragment urls).

'DSL' is an intimidating term but don't worry, we will cover the different types of routes in this chapter and you will be up to speed quickly!

Router Module

Before you start using the component router, you should know that this module is included in the Node package dependencies but isn't included by default in the Angular CLI project. Routing isn't included in the application module.

However, you can change that by adding the `--routing` parameter to the end of the ng command. For example:

```
ng new router-ex300 --inline-template --inline-style --routing
```

Table 15-1 lists the objects in the router module. There are a lot of objects in the table, but don't worry—they'll become more understandable after some exercises.

Table 15-1. *Objects in the Router Module*

Object	Type	Description
RouterModule	Module	A separate Angular module that provides the necessary service providers and directives for navigating through application views.
Router		Displays the application component for the active URL. Manages navigation from one component to the next.
Routes		Defines an array of routes, each mapping a URL path to a component.
Route		Defines how the router should navigate to a component based on a URL pattern. Most routes consist of a path and a component type.
RouterOutlet	Directive	The directive (<router-outlet>) that marks where the router displays a view.
RouterLink	Directive	The directive for binding a clickable HTML element to a route. Clicking an element with a RouterLink directive that's bound to a string or a link parameters array triggers a navigation.
RouterLinkActive	Directive	The directive for adding/removing classes from an HTML element when an associated RouterLink contained on or inside the element becomes active/inactive.
ActivatedRoute		A service that's provided to each route component that contains route-specific information such as route parameters, static data, resolve data, global query params, and the global fragment.
RouterState		The current state of the router including a tree of the currently activated routes together with convenience methods for traversing the route tree.

Simple Routing: Example

This is a pizza-selection component that uses routing to allows the user to click links to display different types of pizzas, with each type of pizza in its own component. This example also shows the use of route parameters: you can route to the everything pizza with a size parameter of small or large. Figure 15-1 illustrates.

Figure 15-1. *Pizza selection*

This is example router-ex100:

1. *Build the app using the CLI*: Use the following code:

   ```
   ng new router-ex100 --routing --inline-template --inline-style
   ```

2. *Start* ng serve: Use the following code:

   ```
   cd router-ex100
   ng serve
   ```

3. *Open app*: Open a web browser and navigate to localhost:4200.
   You should see "welcome to app!"

255

4. *Edit routing class*: Edit app-routing.module.ts and change it to the following:

```
import { NgModule } from '@angular/core';
import { Routes, RouterModule } from '@angular/router';
import { PepperoniComponent, EverythingComponent} from './app.
component';

const routes: Routes = [
  { path: '',
    redirectTo: '/pepperoni',
    pathMatch: 'full'
  },
  {
    path: 'pepperoni',
    component: PepperoniComponent
  },
  {
    path: 'everything/:size',
    component: EverythingComponent
  }
];

@NgModule({
  imports: [RouterModule.forRoot(routes)],
  exports: [RouterModule]
})
export class AppRoutingModule { }
```

5. Step 5 – Edit Components Class

Edit 'app.component.ts' and change it to the following:

```
import { Component } from '@angular/core';
import { Router, ActivatedRoute, ActivatedRouteSnapshot} from
'@angular/router';

@Component({
  selector: 'pepperoni',
  template: `
```

```
    <h2>Pepperoni</h2>
    <img src="https://thumb1.shutterstock.com/display_pic_with_
    logo/55755/161642033/stock-photo-single-slice-of-pepperoni-meat-
    isolated-on-white-with-path-shot-from-above-161642033.jpg">
    `,
  styles: []
})
export class PepperoniComponent {
}

@Component({
  selector: 'everything',
  template: `
    <h2>Everything</h2>
    Size:{{size}}
    <img src="https://encrypted-tbn0.gstatic.com/images?q=tbn:ANd9
    GcROUXyx2jQrCBBBw2N4ofFVw2oWz7keZjDVUB4UDrASE9JHwQdi">
    `,
  styles: []
})
export class EverythingComponent {
  private size: String = '';
  constructor(private route: ActivatedRoute){
    route.params.subscribe(
      (params: Object) =>
      this.size = params['size']);
  }
}

@Component({
  selector: 'app-root',
  template: `
    <h1>
      Pizzas
    </h1>
```

```
      <a [routerLink]="['pepperoni']">Pepperoni</a>
      <a [routerLink]="['everything','small']">Everything Small</a>
      <a [routerLink]="['everything','large']">Everything Large</a>
      <router-outlet></router-outlet>
    `,
    styles: []
})
export class AppComponent {
  title = 'app';
}
```

6. *Edit module*: Edit app.module.ts and change it to the following:

```
import { BrowserModule } from '@angular/platform-browser';
import { NgModule } from '@angular/core';

import { AppRoutingModule } from './app-routing.module';
import { AppComponent, PepperoniComponent, EverythingComponent }
from './app.component';

@NgModule({
  declarations: [
    AppComponent,
    PepperoniComponent,
    EverythingComponent
  ],
  imports: [
    BrowserModule,
    AppRoutingModule
  ],
  providers: [],
  bootstrap: [AppComponent]
})
export class AppModule { }
```

Your app should be working at localhost:4200. Note the following:

- The file app-routing.module.ts was generated by the CLI. It defines a module AppRoutingModule just for the routing. This module contains a data structure that sets up URLs with accompanying components. Note how the first URL maps the default URL to another, and note how the path for the EverythingComponent specifies a `size` parameter.

```
{
  path: 'everything/:size',
  component: EverythingComponent
}
```

- The file app.component.ts contains all the components. It uses `RouterLink` directives to modify links to work with the Angular router. The EverythingComponent is used to display the `everything` pizza and can accept a `size` parameter. Note how it subscribes to the route parameters object to receive parameter updates. This is necessary in case the user switches from one size of `everything` to another, updating the `size` parameter.

```
constructor(private route: ActivatedRoute){
    route.params.subscribe(
      (params: Object) =>
      this.size = params['size']);
  }
```

- The file app.module.ts declares all the components so they can be accessed in the app module. It also imports the AppRoutingModule that we set up in app.routing.module.ts.

Nested Routing: Example

Nested routing means the ability to route and navigate to subcomponents that are inside other components that are navigated to. This is definitely possible in Angular, as you can see in this example.

Nested routing link URLs have more than one "level" because now there is a hierarchy of routes and their children, rather than just routes.

This will be example router-ex200, and Table 15-2 compares the URLs for this example with the ones for the previous example.

Table 15-2. *router-ex100 URLs vs. router-ex200 URLs*

Router-ex100	Router-ex200
/pepperoni	/pepperoni
/everything	/other/pasta
	/other/canzone

This is another pizza selection component that uses routing. However, this time it uses a nested route for the "other" menu and component. When you click the "other" link, you can select from a submenu of pasta or calzone, as shown in Figure 15-2. The display of these menu items is handled by nested routing.

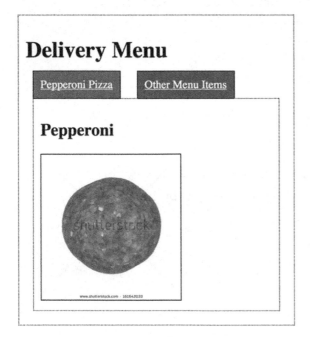

Figure 15-2. *Pasta or calzone?*

Let's do example router-ex200:

1. *Build the app using the CLI*: Use the following command:

   ```
   ng new router-ex200 --routing --inline-template --inline-style
   ```

2. *Start* ng serve: Use the following code:

   ```
   cd router-ex200
   ng serve
   ```

3. *Open app*: Open a web browser and navigate to localhost:4200. You should see "welcome to app!"

4. Edit routing class: Edit app-routing.module.ts and change it to the following:

   ```
   import { NgModule } from '@angular/core';
   import { Routes, RouterModule } from '@angular/router';
   import { PepperoniComponent } from './app.component';
   import { OtherComponent } from './app.other-component';
   import { NestedPastaComponent, NestedCalzoneComponent } from './
   app.other-component';

   const routes: Routes = [
     {
       path: '',
       redirectTo: '/pepperoni',
       pathMatch: 'full'
     },
     {
       path: 'pepperoni',
       component: PepperoniComponent
     },
     {
       path: 'other',
       component: OtherComponent,
       children: [
         {
   ```

```
        path: '',
        redirectTo: 'pasta',
        pathMatch: 'full'
      },
      {
        path: 'pasta',
        component: NestedPastaComponent
      },
      {
        path: 'calzone',
        component: NestedCalzoneComponent
      }
    ]
  }
];

@NgModule({
  imports: [RouterModule.forRoot(routes)],
  exports: [RouterModule]
})
export class AppRoutingModule {}
```

5. Edit components class: Edit app.component.ts and change it to
   the following:

```
import { Component } from '@angular/core';
import { Router, ActivatedRoute, ActivatedRouteSnapshot} from '@
angular/router';

@Component({
  selector: 'pepperoni',
  template: `
    <div>
      <h2>Pepperoni</h2>
```

```
      <img src="https://thumb1.shutterstock.com/display_pic_with_
      logo/55755/161642033/stock-photo-single-slice-of-pepperoni-meat-
      isolated-on-white-with-path-shot-from-above-161642033.jpg">
    </div>
  `,
  styles: []
})
export class PepperoniComponent {
}

@Component({
  selector: 'app-root',
  template: `
    <div>
      <h1>
        Delivery Menu
      </h1>
      <a [routerLink]="['pepperoni']" routerLinkActive="router-
      link-active">Pepperoni Pizza</a>
      <a [routerLink]="['other']" routerLinkActive="router-link-
      active">Other Menu Items</a>
      <router-outlet></router-outlet>
    </div>
  `,
  styles: []
})
export class AppComponent {
  title = 'app';
}
```

6. *Create other component*: Create app.other-component.ts and
    change it to the following:

```
import { Component } from '@angular/core';

@Component({
  selector: 'pasta',
  template: `
    <div>
      <h2>Pasta</h2>
      <img src="https://capetowncafe.files.wordpress.com/2015/04/
      spaghetti-recipe-wikipedia.jpg">
    </div>
  `,
  styles: []
})
export class NestedPastaComponent {
}

@Component({
  selector: 'calzone',
  template: `
    <div>
      <h2>Calzone</h2>
      <img src="https://upload.wikimedia.org/wikipedia/
      commons/5/54/Calzone_fritto.jpg">
    </div>
  `,
  styles: []
})

export class NestedCalzoneComponent {
}

@Component({
  selector: 'other',
  template: `
```

```
      <div>
        <h2>Other Menu Items</h2>
        <a [routerLink]="['pasta']" routerLinkActive="router-link-
        active">Pasta</a>
        <a [routerLink]="['calzone']" routerLinkActive="router-link-
        active">Calzone</a>
        <router-outlet></router-outlet>
        <br/>
        <br/>
      </div>
    `,
    styles: []
  })
  export class OtherComponent {
  }
```

7. *Edit module*: Edit app.module.ts and change it to the following:

```
import { BrowserModule } from '@angular/platform-browser';
import { NgModule } from '@angular/core';

import { AppRoutingModule } from './app-routing.module';
import { AppComponent, PepperoniComponent } from './app.component';
import { OtherComponent, NestedCalzoneComponent,
NestedPastaComponent } from './app.other-component';

@NgModule({
  declarations: [
    AppComponent,
    PepperoniComponent,
    OtherComponent,
    NestedCalzoneComponent,
    NestedPastaComponent
  ],
  imports: [
    BrowserModule,
    AppRoutingModule
  ],
```

```
    providers: [],
    bootstrap: [AppComponent]
})
export class AppModule { }
```

8. *Edit styles*: Edit styles.css and change it to the following:

```css
/* You can add global styles to this file, and also import other style
files */
img {
    width:200px;
    border: 1px solid #000000;
}
a {
    background-color: #0066CC;
    color: #ffffff;
    border: 1px solid #000000;
    padding: 10px;
    margin: 10px;
}
.router-link-active {
    background-color: #C14242;
}
div {
    border: 1px dotted #000000;
    margin: 10px;
    padding: 10px;
}
```

Your app should be working at localhost:4200. Note the following:

- The file app-routing.module.ts was generated by the CLI. It defines a module AppRoutingModule just for the routing. This module contains a data structure that sets up URLs with accompanying components. Note that this time the data structure contains child routing, using the `children` property:

```
{
    path: 'other',
    component: OtherComponent,
    children: [
        {
        path: '',
        redirectTo: 'pasta',
        pathMatch: 'full'
        },
        {
        path: 'pasta',
        component: NestedPastaComponent
        },
        {
        path: 'calzone',
        component: NestedCalzoneComponent
        }
    ]
}
```

- The file app.component.ts is used to define the app component and the pepperoni component (not nested). It also contains the non-nested router links and the router outlet, into which the non-nested components are injected.

- The file app.other-component.ts is used to define the other component (not nested) and the pasta and calzone nested components. The other component contains the nested router links and the router outlet, into which the nested components are injected.

267

- The file app.module.ts declares all the components so that they can be accessed in the app module. It also imports the AppRoutingModule that we set up in app.routing.module.ts.

- The file styles.css declares some styles (badly, I admit) that are used for the links and for a tabbed effect. Notice how the routerLinkActive style is set up on the router links to highlight the currently active links (this applies to nested and non-nested links).

Router links:

```
<a [routerLink]="['pepperoni']" routerLinkActive="router-link-active">
Pepperoni Pizza</a>
```

Styling for active router links:

```
.router-link-active {
    background-color: #C14242;
}
```

Route Configuration

Angular applications route by using a single instance of the router service. When navigation occurs, the router attempts to resolve a route for the new location. To resolve routes, routes must be configured for the router. The routes are configured as an array of route objects. Each route object needs a path (to resolve it) and, usually, a component that will be displayed in the router outlet for the resolved route. Route objects can also have more properties (more about that shortly).

You can configure route paths that redirect to other paths. For example, the following code redirects an empty route to the pepperoni route. In the case of an empty URL, we also need to add the pathMatch: 'full' property so Angular knows it should be matching exactly the empty string and not partially the empty string:

```
const routes: Routes = [
  {
    path: '',
    redirectTo: '/pepperoni',
```

```
        pathMatch: 'full'
    },
    ...
];
```

You can also add a CatchAll route by using the path **, and if the URL doesn't match any of the other routes it will match this route:

```
const routes:Routes = [
    ...
    {path: '**', component: CatchAllComponent}
];
```

When you configure your routes, you configure them using an array of route objects. Each route object can have a data property that contains other properties which can be extracted later by the target component for that route.

The following code sets up a route with data, including a message for the "not found" path:

```
{ path: '500', component: ErrorPageComponent, data: {message: 'Unexpected
Server Error'}}
```

The following code accesses that data so it can be used to show a message. Either this:

```
this.errorMessage = this.snapshot.data['message'];
```

Or this:

```
this.route.data.subscribe(
    (data: Data) => { this.errorMessage = data['message']; }
);
```

Note that this allows you to reuse the same component for different purposes with different data. For example, you could also set up a route for path 401 which would reuse the error page component but this time with the message "Unauthorized."

Route Path Parameters

You can pass data parameters to components in the routes as part of the URL path—for example, customer/123.

When you write the code for the component that receives the parameter, you have two different implementations to choose from:

- You can read the parameter from the route snapshot (which is a one-off snapshot of the route). This is useful when you're routing to a child component inside a parent component once only and this parameter never changes:

```
constructor(route: ActivatedRoute) {
  this.customerId = route.snapshot.paramMap.get('id');
}
```

- You can read the parameter by subscribing to an observable parameter map. This is useful when you're routing to a child component inside a parent component and the child component may *reroute* (being passed a new parameter) when something changes:

```
constructor(route: ActivatedRoute) {
  route.paramMap.subscribe(
    params => this.customerId = params.get('id')
  );
}
```

Route Query Parameters: Example

You can pass data parameters to components in the routes using query strings—for example, customer?id=123.

This works in a similar manner to path parameters. When you write the code for the component that receives the parameter, you have two different implementations to choose from:

- You can read the query parameter from the route snapshot, useful when routing to a child component inside a parent component once only and this parameter never changes:

```
constructor(route: ActivatedRoute) {
  this.customerId = route.snapshot.queryParams['id'];
}
```

- You can read the parameter by subscribing to an observable query parameter map—useful when routing to a child component inside a parent component and the child component may reroute when something changes:

```
constructor(route: ActivatedRoute) {
  route.queryParams.subscribe(
    params => this.customerId = params.get('id')
  );
}
```

This example is a component that shows a list of customers at the top, with details of the selected customer below, as shown in Figure 15-3. This will be example router-ex300.

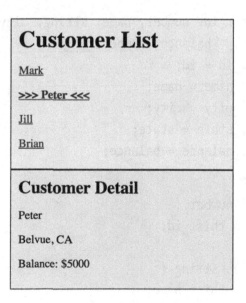

Figure 15-3. *List of customers and detail*

1. *Build the app using the CLI*: Use the following command:

    ```
    ng new router-ex300 --routing --inline-template --inline-style
    ```

2. *Start* ng serve: Use the following code:

    ```
    cd router-ex300
    ng serve
    ```

3. *Open app*: Open a web browser and navigate to localhost:4200.
    You should see "welcome to app!"

4. *Create customer class*: Create customer.ts:

    ```
    export class Customer {
        private _id: number;
        private _name: string;
        private _city: string;
        private _state: string;
        private _balance: number;

        constructor(id: number, name: string, city: string, state:
        string,      balance: number) {
            this._id = id;
            this._name = name;
            this._city = city;
            this._state = state;
            this._balance = balance;
        }

        get id(): number {
            return this._id;
        }
        get name(): string {
            return this._name;
        }
        get city(): string {
            return this._city;
        }
    ```

```
    get state(): string {
        return this._state;
    }
    get balance(): number {
        return this._balance;
    }
}
```

5. Create CustomerService class: Create customerService.ts:

```
import { Injectable } from '@angular/core';
import { Customer } from './customer';

@Injectable()
export class CustomerService {
  private _customers: Array<Customer> = [
      new Customer(1, 'Mark', 'Atlanta', 'GA', 12000),
      new Customer(2, 'Peter', 'Belvue', 'CA', 5000),
      new Customer(3,'Jill', 'Colombia', 'SC', 2000),
      new Customer(4, 'Brian', 'Augusta', 'GA', 2000)
  ];

  get customers() {
    return this._customers;
  }

  getCustomerById(id: number){
    for (let i=0,ii=this._customers.length;i<ii;i++){
      const customer = this._customers[i];
      if (customer.id == id){
        return customer;
      }
    }
    return null;
  }
}
```

6. *Edit app routing module*: Edit app-routing.module.ts and change
    it to the following:

```
import { NgModule } from '@angular/core';
import { Routes, RouterModule } from '@angular/router';
import { DetailComponent, PleaseSelectComponent } from './app.
component';

const routes: Routes = [
  {
    pathMatch: 'full',
    path: '',
    component: PleaseSelectComponent,
    children: []
  },
  {
    pathMatch: 'full',
    path: 'detail',
    component: DetailComponent,
    children: []
  }
];

@NgModule({
  imports: [RouterModule.forRoot(routes)],
  exports: [RouterModule]
})
export class AppRoutingModule { }
```

7. *Edit app component*: Edit app.component.ts and change it to the
    following:

```
import { Component } from '@angular/core';
import { ActivatedRoute } from '@angular/router';
import { CustomerService } from './customerService';
import { Customer } from './customer';
```

```
@Component({
  selector: 'pleaseSelect',
  template: `
    <div>
    <h2>Please make a selection.</h2>
    </div>
  `,
  styles: ['div { background-color: #FFFFFF; padding: 10px;
  border: 1px solid #000000 }']
})
export class PleaseSelectComponent {
}

@Component({
  selector: 'detail',
  template: `
    <div>
    <h2>Customer Detail {{id}}</h2>
    <p>{{customer.name}}<p>
    <p>{{customer.city}}, {{customer.state}}</p>
    <p>Balance: &#36;{{customer.balance}}</p>
    </div>
  `,
  styles: ['div { background-color: #FFE4E1 }']
})
export class DetailComponent {
  customer: Customer;
  constructor(
    private customerService: CustomerService,
    private route: ActivatedRoute) {
      route.queryParams.subscribe(
        (queryParams: Object) =>
        this.customer = customerService.getCustomerById(queryParams
        ['id']));
  }
}
```

```
@Component({
  selector: 'app-root',
  template: `
    <div>
    <h1>
      Customer List
    </h1>
    <p *ngFor="let customer of _customerService.customers">
      <a [routerLink]="['detail']" [queryParams]="{id: customer.
      id}" routerLinkActive="active">{{customer.name}}</a>
    </p>
    </div>
    <router-outlet></router-outlet>
  `,
  styles: ['div { background-color: #faebd7 }',]
})
export class AppComponent {
  constructor(private _customerService: CustomerService){
  }
}
```

8. *Edit app module*: Edit app.module.ts and change it to the following:

```
import { BrowserModule } from '@angular/platform-browser';
import { NgModule } from '@angular/core';

import { AppRoutingModule } from './app-routing.module';
import { AppComponent, DetailComponent, PleaseSelectComponent }
from './app.component';
import { CustomerService } from './customerService';
import { Customer } from './customer';

@NgModule({
  declarations: [
    AppComponent,
    DetailComponent,
    PleaseSelectComponent
  ],
```

```
  imports: [
    BrowserModule,
    AppRoutingModule
  ],
  providers: [CustomerService],
  bootstrap: [AppComponent]
})
export class AppModule { }
```

9. *Edit styles*: Edit styles.css and change it to the following:

```
div {
    padding: 10px; border: 1px solid #000000;
}
h1,h2 {
    margin: 0px;
}
.active {
    font-weight: bold;
}
.active::before {
    content: ">>> ";
}
.active::after {
    content: " <<<";
}
```

Your app should be working at localhost:4200. Note the following:

- The file customer.ts sets up the `customer` class.

- The file customerService.ts is a service injected into the app component and the Detail component. It contains a list of customers, along with methods to access the customer data.

- The file app-routing.module.ts sets up the route for the Please Select component and the Detail component.

- The file app.component.ts sets up the components. Note how it uses a different syntax for specifying query parameters to a router link:

```
<a [routerLink]="['detail']" [queryParams]="{id: customer.id}" rou
terLinkActive="active">{{customer.name}}</a>
```

- The file app.module.ts declares the components used, imports the app routing module, and sets up the `CustomerService` class as a provider for the customer dependency injection in the Detail and App components.

- The file 'styles.css' is used to setup common styles for the h1, h2 and div tags.

Router Imperative Navigation: Example

So far, we've written code that provides the user with the ability to click a link to navigate. *Imperative navigation* is different. This is not generating links; it's simply telling the router to go somewhere, performing navigation in your code. *Navigation* is an asynchronous event; it doesn't lock the code until completed. The imperative navigation methods discussed in this section return a `Promise` object when completed, which is a callback for success or failure. The two methods are `Router.navigate` and `Router.navigateByUrl`. To use imperative navigation, you first need to inject the router into your class using constructor injection.

- `Router.navigate`: This navigates to a component relatively (to the current route) or absolutely based on an array of commands or route elements. It returns a promise that resolves when navigation is complete. It uses the link DSL as specified earlier in router link DSL format. It's basically the same as clicking a router link.

- `Router.navigateByUrl`: This navigates to a complete absolute URL string. It returns a promise that resolves when navigation is complete. It's usually preferred to navigate with `navigate` instead of this method, because URLs are more brittle. If the given URL begins with a /, the router will navigate absolutely. If the given URL doesn't begin with /, the router will navigate relative to this component.

Both navigation methods return a *promise,* which enables the user to add two callback methods to handle the navigation result: the first one for a success handler, the second one for an error handler. There is example of this in the example below. Both navigation methods also have the ability to accept an additional parameter for a `NavigationExtras` object. This object allows you to pass additional information to the router to further specify the desired route.

This component allows the user to navigate between components and also go back, as shown in Figure 15-4. It also logs when navigation is completed. This is example router-ex400.

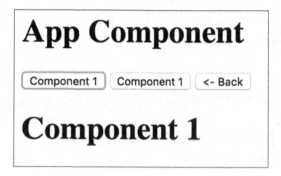

Figure 15-4. *Navigating between components*

Let's do the example:

1. *Build the app using the CLI*: Use the following command:

   ```
   ng new router-ex400 --routing --inline-template --inline-style
   ```

2. *Start* ng serve: Use the following code:

   ```
   cd router-ex400
   ng serve
   ```

3. *Open app*: Open a web browser and navigate to localhost:4200. You should see "welcome to app!"

4. *Edit routing module*: Edit app-routing.module.ts and change it to the following:

   ```
   import { NgModule } from '@angular/core';
   import { Routes, RouterModule } from '@angular/router';
   import { AppComponent, Component1, Component2 } from './app.
   component';
   ```

```
const routes: Routes = [
  {
    path: 'component1',
    component: Component1
  },
  {
    path: 'component2',
    component: Component2
  },
  {
    path: '**',
    component: Component1
  },
];

@NgModule({
  imports: [RouterModule.forRoot(routes)],
  exports: [RouterModule]
})
export class AppRoutingModule { }
```

5. *Edit* Component *class*: Edit app.component.ts and change it to the following:

```
import { Component } from '@angular/core';
import { Router } from '@angular/router';
import { Location } from '@angular/common';
@Component({
  selector: 'component1',
  template: `
    <h1>
      {{title}}
    </h1>
    <router-outlet></router-outlet>
  `,
  styles: []
})
```

```
export class Component1 {
  title = 'Component 1';
}

@Component({
  selector: 'component2',
  template: `
    <h1>
      {{title}}
    </h1>
    <router-outlet></router-outlet>
  `,
  styles: []
})
export class Component2 {
  title = 'Component 2';
}

@Component({
  selector: 'app-root',
  template: `
    <h1>
      {{title}}
    </h1>
    <button (click)="component1()">Component 1</button>
    <button (click)="component2()">Component 1</button>
    <button (click)="back()"><- Back</button>
    <router-outlet></router-outlet>
  `,
  styles: []
})
export class AppComponent {
  title = 'App Component';
  constructor(private router: Router, private location: Location)
{}
  component1(){
```

```
      this.router.navigate(['component1']).then(result => { console.
      log("navigation result: " + result)});
   }
   component2(){
      this.router.navigateByUrl("/component2");
   }
   back(){
      this.location.back();
   }
}
```

6. *Edit module*: Edit app.module.ts and change it to the following:

```
import { BrowserModule } from '@angular/platform-browser';
import { NgModule } from '@angular/core';

import { AppRoutingModule } from './app-routing.module';
import { AppComponent, Component1, Component2 } from './app.
component';

@NgModule({
  declarations: [
    AppComponent,
    Component1,
    Component2
  ],
  imports: [
    BrowserModule,
    AppRoutingModule
  ],
  providers: [],
  bootstrap: [AppComponent]
})
export class AppModule { }
```

Your app should be working at localhost:4200. Note the following:

- The app component injects the router and the location.

- It contains code to navigate imperatively when the user clicks a button.

- It contains a callback that's fired when navigation is completed.

- It also contains code in the location for the back button.

Router: Extracting Data

You can extract the information shown in Table 15-3 out of the Router object that's injected into your class.

Table 15-3. *Extracting Data from Router*

Property	Description
errorHandler	Error handler that's invoked when a navigation errors
navigated	Indicates if at least one navigation happened
urlHandlingStrategy	URL handling strategy
routeReuseStrategy	Route reuse strategy
routerState	Current router state
url	Current URL
events	An observable of router events, allows you to add callbacks to router events

You normally define the router routes using a configuration object, and this doesn't change. However you can reload a different configuration object into the router whenever you want using the resetConfig method. This would be very useful if you wanted to load the routes from the server or other data source.

Route Guards: Example

Routes enable the user to navigate through the application. Sometimes the user needs to do something before being allowed access to a certain part of the application—for example, log in. Route guards can be used to control access to certain routes.

There are two main types of route guards:

- CanActivate: Can the user navigate to a route? In this class, you can inject the router. This is useful to navigate the user away to another resource if the user isn't allowed to navigate to a route.

- CanDeactivate: Can the user move away from a route? Useful for prompting to save changes.

This example component displays menu links. Some of the links will only work once the user has logged in. This will be example router-ex500:

1. *Build the app using the CLI*: Use the following command:

   ```
   ng new router-ex500 --routing --inline-template --inline-style
   ```

2. *Start* ng serve: Use the following code:

   ```
   cd router-ex500
   ng serve
   ```

3. *Open app*: Open a web browser and navigate to localhost:4200. You should see "welcome to app!"

4. *Create activating service*: Create activate.service.ts and change it to the following:

   ```
   import { Injectable } from '@angular/core';
   import { UserService } from './user.service';
   import { CanActivate } from '@angular/router';

   @Injectable()
   export class ActivateService implements CanActivate{
       constructor(private _userService: UserService){}
   ```

```
    canActivate() {
        return this._userService.authenticated;
    }
}
```

5. *Edit routing module*: Edit app.routing.module.ts and change it to
   the following:

```
import { NgModule } from '@angular/core';
import { Routes, RouterModule } from '@angular/router';
import { AuthenticatedComponent, NonAuthenticatedComponent} from
'./app.component';
import { UserService } from './user.service';
import { ActivateService } from './activate.service';

const routes: Routes = [
  {
    path: 'authenticated',
    component: AuthenticatedComponent,
    canActivate: [
      ActivateService
    ]
  },
  {
    path: '**',
    component: NonAuthenticatedComponent
  }
];

@NgModule({
  imports: [RouterModule.forRoot(routes)],
  exports: [RouterModule],
  providers: [UserService, ActivateService]
})
export class AppRoutingModule { }
```

6. *Edit components*: Edit app.component.ts and change it to the
    following:

```
import { Component, ViewChild } from '@angular/core';
import { UserService } from './user.service';

@Component({
  selector: 'non-authenticated-component',
  template: `
    <div>
      <h2>Non-authenticated</h2>
      <p>This component can be accessed without authentication.</p>
    </div>
    `,
  styles: []
})
export class NonAuthenticatedComponent {
}

@Component({
  selector: 'authenticated-component',
  template: `
    <div>
      <h2>Authenticated</h2>
      <p>This component cannot be accessed without authentication.</p>
    </div>
    `,
  styles: []
})
export class AuthenticatedComponent {
}

@Component({
  selector: 'app-root',
  template: `
    <span *ngIf="!_userService.authenticated">
    User:<input type="input" #name />
```

```
    Password:<input type="input" #password />
    <input type="button" (click)="login()" value="Login" />"
    </span>
    <hr/>
    Authenticated:{{_userService.authenticated}}
    <hr/>
    <a [routerLink]="['non-authenticated']">Non-Authenticated</a>
    <a [routerLink]="['authenticated']">Authenticated</a>
    <router-outlet></router-outlet>
    `,
    styles: []
})
export class AppComponent {
    loggedIn: boolean = false;
    @ViewChild('name') name;
    @ViewChild('password') password;
    constructor(private _userService: UserService){}
    login(){
        this._userService.authenticate(
            this.name.nativeElement.value,
            this.password.nativeElement.value);
    }
}
```

7. *Edit app module*: Edit app.module.ts and change it to the following:

```
import { BrowserModule } from '@angular/platform-browser';
import { NgModule } from '@angular/core';

import { AppRoutingModule } from './app-routing.module';
import { AppComponent, AuthenticatedComponent,
NonAuthenticatedComponent } from './app.component';
import { UserService } from './user.service';

@NgModule({
  declarations: [
    AppComponent,
```

```
    AuthenticatedComponent,
    NonAuthenticatedComponent
  ],
  imports: [
    BrowserModule,
    AppRoutingModule
  ],
  providers: [UserService],
  bootstrap: [AppComponent]
})
export class AppModule { }
```

8. *Create user service*: Create user.service.ts and change it to the following:

```
import { Injectable } from '@angular/core';

@Injectable()
export class UserService {
    private _authenticated: boolean = false;
    public get authenticated(): boolean{
        return this._authenticated;
    }
    public set authenticated(value: boolean){
        this._authenticated = value;
    }
    public authenticate(name, password){
        if ((name === 'user') && (password === 'password')){
            this._authenticated = true;
        }
    }
}
```

Your app should be working at localhost:4200. Note the following:

- The service activate.service.ts is a route guard that allows or disallows a route from being activated. The `canActivate` method is invoked: `true` allows the activation, and `false` doesn't allow the activation. This service is injected into the routing module so it can be used in the route configuration.

- The service user.service.ts is a service that tracks the state of the user—whether they're authenticated or not. This service is injected into the service activate.service.ts and the app component.

Summary

Hopefully this chaper will be very useful to you and you'll use it to write the routing in your Angular application. Remember that your routing will probably get quite complicated, possibly with multiple router modules and router outlets. You can try to put all your routing together in one routing module or you can try to spread it into multiple. One routing module may be simpler but this may cause more merge conflicts when developers are constantly changing this one file. Remember you can use route guards to enforce security, allowing or preventing access to various components.

The next chapter talks about reactive programming and how Angular applications can use new technology to handle streams of data flowing in applications.

CHAPTER 16

Observers, Reactive Programming, and RxJS

Reactive Extensions for JavaScript (RxJS) is a Reactive streams library that allows you to work with asynchronous data streams, and it's included in Angular. The project is actively developed by Microsoft in collaboration with a community of open source developers.

The purpose of this chapter is to introduce RxJS basic concepts and cover some of the library's functionality. I'll cover using RxJS and Angular together in another chapter.

Reactive programming is a programming paradigm focused on data flows and change. It allows you to express static or dynamic data flows with ease, and the execution model will automatically propagate changes through the data flow. Reactive Extensions code is available on almost every computing platform, not just JavaScript, and its purpose is to bring the capability for Reactive programming to the computing platform.

Asynchronous Data Streams

RxJS libraries compose asynchronous and event-based Reactive programs using observable collections in JavaScript. What are asynchronous data streams? Let's break it down:

- *Asynchronous*: In JavaScript, this means we can call a function and register a *callback* to be notified when results are available, so we can continue with execution and avoid the web page being unresponsive. This is used for AJAX calls, DOM events, promises, web workers, and WebSockets.

- *Data*: Raw information in the form of JavaScript data types, such as number, string, objects (arrays, sets, maps).

© Mark Clow 2018
M. Clow, *Angular 5 Projects*, https://doi.org/10.1007/978-1-4842-3279-8_16

- *Streams*: Sequences of data made available over time. For example, in contrast to to arrays, you don't need all the information to be present in order to start using them.

Examples of asynchronous data streams include things that you're watching:

- Stock quotes

- Tweets

- Computer events, for example mouse clicks

- Web service requests

Observable Sequences (Observables)

In RxJS, you represent asynchronous data streams using *observable sequences*, also called just *observables*. You could watch stock quotes or mouse clicks using observables. Observables are flexible and can be used with push or pull patterns:

- *Push*: When using the push pattern, we subscribe to the source stream and react to new data as soon as it's made available (emitted). You can listen to a stream and react accordingly.

- *Pull*: When using the pull pattern, we're using the same operations but synchronously. This happens when using arrays, generators, or iterables.

Because observables are data streams, you can query them using operators implemented by the observable type. Here are just a few of the many things you can do with observable operators:

- Filter out stock changes for stocks you don't own

- Aggregate—get all the typing in the first five seconds

- Perform time-based operations on multiple events

Observers: Example

If observables are things that can be watched, observers are the things that watch them, as illustrated in Figure 16-1.

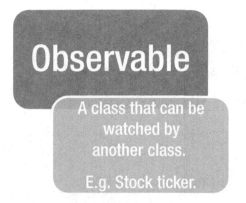

Figure 16-1. *Observables and observers*

Observers are classes that can respond to events, or things happening. To respond, they must implement the following methods:

- onNext: An observable calls this method when the observable emits an item. onNext takes the item emitted by the observable as a parameter.

- onError: An observable calls this method when it fails to create the expected data or hits some other error, stopping the observable. The observable won't make any more calls to onNext or onCompleted. The onError method takes an indication of what caused the error as its parameter.

- onCompleted: An observable calls this method after it calls onNext for the last time, if there haven't been any errors.

In this example, we'll create an observable with two events and then observe it. Figure 16-2 shows the console you'll see. This will be example rxjs-ex100.

```
Next: event1,event2
Completed
```

Figure 16-2. *Console showing events*

Let's do the example:

1. *Build the app using the CLI*: Use the following command:

   ```
   ng new rxjs-ex100 --inline-template --inline-style
   ```

2. *Start* ng serve: Use the following code:

   ```
   cd rxjs-ex100
   ng serve
   ```

3. *Open app*: Open a web browser and navigate to localhost:4200. You should see "welcome to app!"

4. *Edit class*: Edit app.component.ts and change it to the following:

   ```
   import { Component } from '@angular/core';
   import * as Rx from 'rxjs';
   @Component({
     selector: 'app-root',
     template: `
     `,
     styles: []
   })
   export class AppComponent {
     constructor(){
       const array: Array<string> = ['event1', 'event2'];
       const observable: Rx.Observable<string[]> = Rx.Observable.
       of(array);
       const subscription: Rx.Subscription = observable.subscribe(
         // Observer
         function (x) {
             console.log('Next: ' + x);
         },
         function (err) {
             console.log('Error: ' + err);
         },
         function () {
             console.log('Completed');
         }
   ```

```
    );
  }
}
```

Your app should be working at localhost:4200. Open developer tools in your browser, reload the page and look at the console output. Note that the app component does the following:

- An array is created.

- An observable is created from the array.

- A subscription is created from a subscription to the observable. This subscription implements observer code to handle events.

Subscriptions

A *subscription* is like a connection between an Observable and an Observer. Figure 16-3 illustrates this relationship.

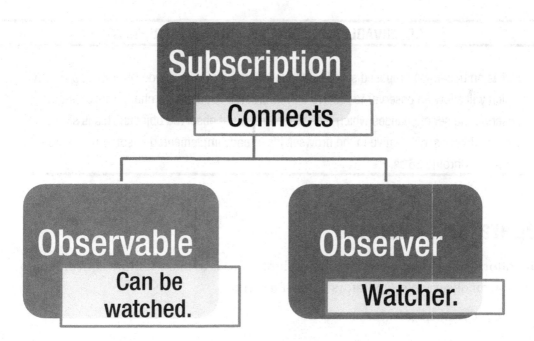

Figure 16-3. A subscription connects observable and observer

You use a subscription to link an observable and an observer together:

```
const subscription: Rx.Subscription = observable.subscribe(
    // Observer
    function (x) {
        console.log('Next: ' + x);
    },
    function (err) {
        console.log('Error: ' + err);
    },
    function () {
        console.log('Completed');
    }
  );
```

To unlink an observable and observer, call the method dispose in the subscription:

```
subscription.dispose();
```

OBSERVABLES, OBSERVERS, AND JAVASCRIPT ES7

ES7 is an upcoming proposed standard for JavaScript that will include Object.observe, which will allow an observer to receive a time-ordered sequence of change records that describe the set of changes which took place to a set of observed objects. This is similar to what RxJS does, only native in the browser. It's already implemented in some browsers—for example, Chrome 36.ss.

Operators: Example

Operators perform a variety of tasks. Their purpose is to make it more convenient to observe an observable. Operators do the following:

- Create observables
- Combine observables
- Filter observables

- Handle errors

- Perform utilities

Most operators operate on an observable and return an observable. This allows you to apply operators one after the other, in a chain. Each operator in the chain modifies the observable that results from the operation of the previous operator.

In this example we'll create an observable with two events and then we'll observe it. If you look at the console, you'll see event logs. This will be example rxjs-ex200.

Let's do the example:

1. *Build the app using the CLI*: Use the following command:

   ```
   ng new rxjs-ex200 --inline-template --inline-style
   ```

2. *Start* ng serve: Use the following code:

   ```
   cd rxjs-ex200
   ng serve
   ```

3. *Open app*: Open a web browser and navigate to localhost:4200. You should see "welcome to app!"

4. *Edit class*: Edit app.component.ts and change it to the following:

   ```
   import { Component } from '@angular/core';
   import * as Rx from 'rxjs';
   @Component({
     selector: 'app-root',
     template: `
     `,
     styles: []
   })
   export class AppComponent {
     constructor(){
       const observable: Rx.Observable<number> = Rx.Observable.
       range(0,100);
       const subscription: Rx.Subscription = observable.subscribe(
         // Observer
         val => { console.log(`Next: ${val}`) },
   ```

```
      err => { console.log(`Error: ${err}`) },
      () => { console.log(`Completed`) }
    );
  }
}
```

Your app should be working at localhost:4200. Open developer tools in your browser, reload the page and look at the console output. Note the following:

- The range operator creates a range of events.

- The observer uses arrow functions to handle the events.

Operators That Create Observables

There are many operators that are used just to create observables. This section talks about several of these.

from

This operator creates an observable from other objects that emits multiple values. The following creates an observable from an array that emits two values:

```
const array: Array<string> = ['event1', 'event2'];
const observable: Rx.Observable<string> = Rx.Observable.from(array);
```

interval

interval creates an observable that emits a value after each period—for example, 0,1,2,3,4. Figure 16-4 shows an observable emitting a value every 1/2 second (500 ms).

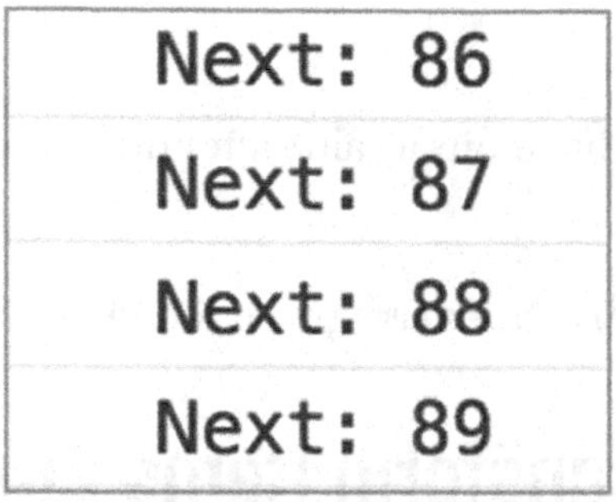

| Next: 86 |
| Next: 87 |
| Next: 88 |
| Next: 89 |

Figure 16-4. *Observable emitting a value every half second*

Here's the code:

```
const observable: Rx.Observable<number> = Rx.Observable.interval(500);
var observable: Rx.Observable<number> = new Rx.Observable.interval(500);
```

of (Was just)

of converts an item into an observable that emits just that item. The following code creates an observable that emits 500 only once:

```
const observable: Rx.Observable<number> = Rx.Observable.of(500);
```

range

range creates an observable that emits a range of integers. The following code creates an observable that emits 1 to 100:

```
const observable: Rx.Observable<number> = Rx.Observable.range(0,100);
```

repeat

repeat creates an observable that emits the repetition of a given element a specific number of times. The following code creates an observable that emits 1 2 3 1 2 3 1 2 3 1 2 3:

```
const observable: Rx.Observable<number> = Rx.Observable.range(1,3).repeat(4);
```

timer

`timer` creates an observable that emits a value after due time has elapsed and then after each period:

```
const observable: Rx.Observable<number> = Rx.Observable.timer(2000,500);
```

Operators That Transform Items Emitted by Observables

You've seen how to create observables that emit values. Now let's look at how to modify these values.

buffer

`buffer` is an operator to periodically gather items from an observable into bundles and emit these bundles rather than emitting the items one at a time. The following code creates an observable that emits a value every 100 milliseconds. It then bundles emissions up every 5000 milliseconds:

```
const observable: Rx.Observable<any> = Rx.Observable
    .timer(0,100)
    .buffer( Rx.Observable.timer(0, 5000) );
```

Figure 16-5 shows the results.

```
Next:                                              app.component.ts:18

Next:                                              app.component.ts:18
0,1,2,3,4,5,6,7,8,9,10,11,12,13,14,15,16,17,18,19,20,21,22,23,24,
25,26,27,28,29,30,31,32,33,34,35,36,37,38,39,40,41,42,43,44,45,46
,47,48,49

Next:                                              app.component.ts:18
50,51,52,53,54,55,56,57,58,59,60,61,62,63,64,65,66,67,68,69,70,71
,72,73,74,75,76,77,78,79,80,81,82,83,84,85,86,87,88,89,90,91,92,9
3,94,95,96,97,98

Next:                                              app.component.ts:18
99,100,101,102,103,104,105,106,107,108,109,110,111,112,113,114,11
5,116,117,118,119,120,121,122,123,124,125,126,127,128,129,130,131
,132,133,134,135,136,137,138,139,140,141,142,143,144,145,146,147
```

Figure 16-5. *Gathering observables into bundles*

map

map is an operator commonly used to transform the items emitted by an observable by applying a function to each item. The following code simply puts a pipe around the emitted value, and the results are shown in Figure 16-6.

```
const observable: Rx.Observable<string> = Rx.Observable.range(0,100)
    .map((val) =>  '|' + val + '|' );
```

```
Next:  |0|
Next:  |1|
Next:  |2|
```

Figure 16-6. *Putting pipes around emitted values*

scan

scan is an operator used to sequentially apply a function to each item emitted by an observable and emit each successive value. It's like map except the result from the first function call is fed into the second, and so on. The results of the following code are shown in Figure 16-7:

```
const observable: Rx.Observable<number> = Rx.Observable.range(1,5)
    .scan((val) =>  { val++; return val * val } );
```

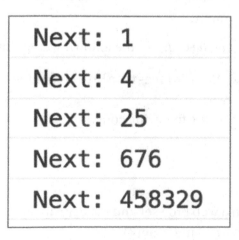

```
Next: 1
Next: 4
Next: 25
Next: 676
Next: 458329
```

Figure 16-7. *Emitting values of functions applied*

Operators That Filter Items Emitted by Observables

You don't always need to watch everything. Sometimes you need to only watch certain things.

debounce: Example

debounce is an operator used to ensure that an observer only emits one item during a certain period of time. It's useful in observing UI elements—for example, if you have a filter box and you don't want it to respond too fast and get ahead of itself with multiple requests. debounce will stop the networks and computers from getting overloaded with too many search requests.

This will be example rxjs-ex300, and its results are shown in Figure 16-8.

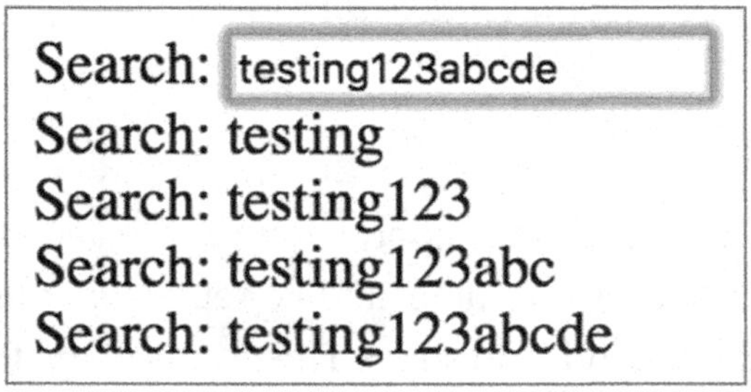

```
Search: testing123abcde
Search: testing
Search: testing123
Search: testing123abc
Search: testing123abcde
```

Figure 16-8.   *Emitting only one item*

This example has a searchbox that uses the debounce and distinctUntilChanged methods to filter the user's input:

1. *Build the app using the CLI*: Use the following command:

   ```
   ng new rxjs-ex300 --inline-template --inline-style
   ```

2. *Start* ng serve: Use the following code:

   ```
   cd rxjs-ex300
   ng serve
   ```

3. *Open app*: Open a web browser and navigate to localhost:4200.
   You should see "welcome to app!"

4. *Edit class*: Edit app.component.ts and change it to the following:

```
import { Component } from '@angular/core';
import * as Rx from 'rxjs';

@Component({
  selector: 'app-root',
  template: `
    Search: <input type="text" (keyup)="onChange($event.target.value)"/>
    <div *ngFor="let log of _logs">Search: {{log}}</div>
  `,
  styles: []
})
export class AppComponent {
  _searchText: string;
  _searchSubject: Rx.Subject<string>;
  _logs: Array<string> = [];

  constructor() {

    // Create new Subject.
    this._searchSubject = new Rx.Subject<string>();

    // Set the Subject up to subscribe to events and filter them by
    // debounce events and ensure they are distinct.
    this._searchSubject
          .debounceTime(300)
          .distinctUntilChanged()
          .subscribe(
            // Handle event. Log it.
            searchText => this._logs.push(searchText)
          );
  }
  public onChange(searchText: string) {

    // Emit an event to the Subject.
    this._searchSubject.next(searchText);
  }
}
```

Your app should be working at localhost:4200. Note the following:

- The constructor sets up the Rxjs subject _searchSubject to subscribe to events and filter them. After filtering, each event is added to a log, which is displayed in the component. A *subject* is an object than can act both as an observer and as an observable. Because it's an observer, it can subscribe to one or more observables, and because it's an observable, it can pass through the items it observes by re-emitting them, and it can also emit new items.

- The onChange method is fired when the user types a key on the search box. The code in this method events a string event to the _searchSubject Rxjs subject.

distinct

distinct is an operator used to suppress the emission of duplicate items. The following example generates a new value every 1/2 second. We then use map to transform it into the string "unchanging value". Then we add distinct to suppress duplicate values. Thus, we only ever get one value emitted:

```
const observable: Rx.Observable<string> = Rx.Observable.interval(500)
    .map((val) => 'unchanging value').distinct();
```

filter

filter is an operator used to emit only the first item, or the first item that meets a condition, from an observable. The following code generates a new value every 1/2 second and then filters out any value not divisible by 7:

```
const observable: Rx.Observable<number> = Rx.Observable.range(0,100)
    .filter((val) => val % 7 === 0);
```

The results are shown in Figure 16-9.

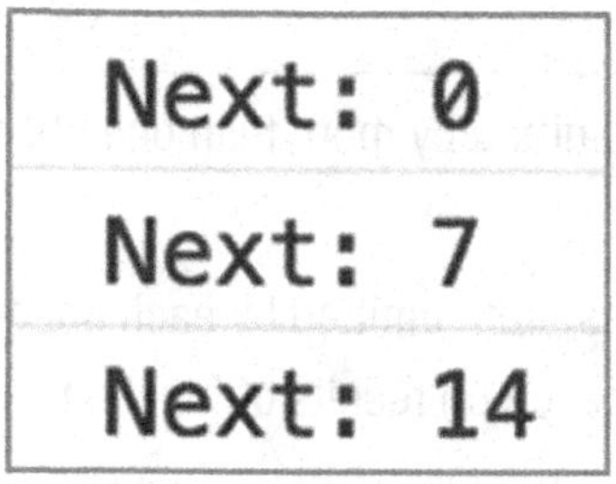

Figure 16-9. *Generating a new value and filtering*

take

take is an operator used to emit only the first *n* items emitted by an observable. The following code emits new values from 0 to 100 but only takes the first three:

```
const observable: Rx.Observable<number> = Rx.Observable.range(0,100)
    .take(3);
```

Operators that Combine Other Observables

Table 16-1 lists operators that combine other operators.

Table 16-1. *Operators That Combine Other Operators*

Operator	Description
And/Then/When	Combine items emitted by more than one observable using pattern and plan intermediaries
CombineLatest	Combine the latest item emitted by each observable using a specified function and emit items based on results of function
Join	Combine items emitted by two observables when one observable's item is emitted in a time frame defined by an item emitted by the other observable
Merge	Combine several observables into one by merging what they emit
StartWith	Emit a particular sequence of items before emitting items from the source observable
Switch	Convert an observable that emits observables into a single observable that emits the items emitted by the most-recently-emitted of those observables.
Zip	Combine the emissions of a number of observables via a function and emit single items for each combination based on the results of the function.

share

The share operator allows you to share an instance of a subscription to one or more observers. share creates a subscription when the number of observers goes from zero to one and then shares that subscription with all subsequent observers until the number of observers returns to zero, at which point the subscription is disposed. It's useful if you want to watch the same thing from multiple places. Figure 16-10 shows an example, and Figure 16-11 shows the console logs produced in the second screen.

```
var obs = Rx.Observable.interval(500).take(5)
          .do(i => console.log("obs value "+ i) )
          .share();


obs.subscribe(value => console.log("observer 1 received " + value));


obs.subscribe(value => console.log("observer 2 received " + value));
```

Figure 16-10. *The share operator in action*

```
obs value 0
observer 1 received 0
observer 2 received 0

obs value 1
observer 1 received 1
observer 2 received 1
```

Figure 16-11. Console logs produced by the share operator

Summary

This important chapter introduced asynchronous data streams and RxJs. I hope you followed the exercises because soon we'll be using *events*, which are a form of asynchronous data stream that you'll observe in your application. We'll use subjects, observables, and observers when working with Angular events, and we'll be using the operators introduced in this chapter.

The next chapter goes into more detail about using RxJs with Angular.

CHAPTER 17

RxJS with Angular

In the previous chapter, we went through the core concepts of Reactive extensions and learned about observables, observers, subscriptions, and operators in RxJS. Now we're going to see how we can use Reactive Extensions with Angular.

Reactive Extensions weren't around at the time of writing AngularJS, but promises were. AngularJS used a lot of promise objects, including by the $http, $interval, and $timeout modules. Promise objects could be used to represent asynchronous results: success (return value) or failure (return error). Promise objects were used in HTTP communication with the server and many other objects. Figure 17-1 shows an example.

In Angular, promises are going away in favor of observables. They haven't completely gone away, though.

```
function asyncGreet(name) {
  // perform some asynchronous operation, resolve or reject the promise when appropriate.
  return $q(function(resolve, reject) {
    setTimeout(function() {
      if (okToGreet(name)) {
        resolve('Hello, ' + name + '!');
      } else {
        reject('Greeting ' + name + ' is not allowed.');
      }
    }, 1000);
  });
}

var promise = asyncGreet('Robin Hood');
promise.then(function(greeting) {
  alert('Success: ' + greeting);
}, function(reason) {
  alert('Failed: ' + reason);
});
```

Figure 17-1. *Promise objects in AngularJS*

© Mark Clow 2018
M. Clow, *Angular 5 Projects*, https://doi.org/10.1007/978-1-4842-3279-8_17

Observables have a few advantages over promises:

- Promises only emitted one value/error. Observables can emit multiple values over time. For example, with an observable you can listen for events on a web socket for a period of time. You can only listen once with a promise.

- You can use operators with observers to map, filter, and more.

- You can cancel observables.

Observables and Angular

Angular uses observables for asynchronous data streams in DOM events and HTTP services. In listening for DOM (Document Object Model) events, you can observe a steady stream of data of what the user is doing in the user interface, such as keystrokes, mouse events, and so on. For Http services, you can listen for server responses, having a connection open and responding to incoming data.

Observables and DOM Events: Example

The DOM is a way of representing and interacting with objects in HTML documents. Document nodes are organized in a structure called the DOM tree, and objects in the tree are addressed and manipulated using methods on the objects.

Angular DOM events can be observable. To use DOM events, we'll use the module Rx.DOM (HTML DOM bindings for RxJS) through rx.angular.

You can filter events and combine watching multiple different events and observing in one place.

This example detects when the user hasn't done anything for a period of 5 seconds. When that happens, we add a line saying "idle" to the component's display, as shown in Figure 17-2. This will be example rxjs-and-angular-ex100.

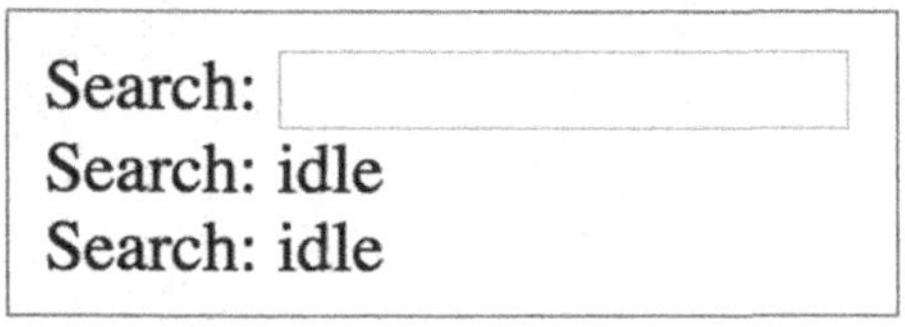

Search: [   ]
Search: idle
Search: idle

Figure 17-2. *Displaying idle users*

Let's do the example:

1. *Build the app using the CLI*: Use the following command:

   ```
   ng new rxjs-and-angular-ex100 --inline-template --inline-style
   ```

2. *Start* ng serve: Use the following code:

   ```
   cd rxjs-and-angular-ex100
   ng serve
   ```

3. *Open app*: Open a web browser and navigate to localhost:4200.
   You should see "welcome to app!"

4. *Edit class*: Edit app.component.ts and change it to the following:

   ```
   import { Component } from '@angular/core';
   import * as Rx from 'rxjs';

   @Component({
     selector: 'app-root',
     template: `
       Search: <input type="text">
       <div *ngFor="let log of _logs">Search: {{log}}</div>
       `,
     styles: []
   })
   export class AppComponent {
     _logs: Array<string> = [];
     constructor(){
       const observable: Rx.Observable<any> = Rx.Observable.merge(
         Rx.Observable.fromEvent(document,'keydown'),
         Rx.Observable.fromEvent(document,'click'),
         Rx.Observable.fromEvent(document,'mousemove'),
         Rx.Observable.fromEvent(document,'scroll'),
         Rx.Observable.fromEvent(document,'touchstart')
       );
   ```

```
        const idleEventObservable = observable.bufferTime(5000)
          .filter(function(arr) {
            return arr.length == 0;
          })
        .subscribe(idleEvent => this._logs.push('idle'));
      }
    }
```

Your app should be working at localhost:4200. Note that in the constructor, we merge the emissions from the document events keydown, click, mousemove, scroll, and touchstart into one observable. We buffer it to every 5 seconds and filter out occurrences when events occur within that time. We then subscribe to the result, and when it occurs we add an "idle" log, which is displayed in the component.

Observables and HTTP Services

$http and Http Module

AngularJS had its own Http module. The $http service was a core AngularJS service that facilitated communication with the remote HTTP servers via the browser's XMLHttpRequest object or via JSONP.

The Angular 2 & 4 Http module (@angular/http) was similar to the Http module in the first version of Angular, except that it used uses Reactive Extensions—in other words, observables. Reactive Extensions bring a lot to the table, offering all the operators mentioned in prior chapters.

When Angular 5 was released, it included a new HttpClient module (@angular/common/http) to replace the previous Http module. You can still use the old Http module (@angular/http) but it has been deprecated and will be removed in a future version.

The next chapter covers the new Angular HttpClient module.

Summary

This chapter was very short, but you should now understand the following:

- Angular uses observables for handling DOM events and the results of HTTP service calls (calling an HTTP service on a server and receiving the result).

- Observables enable the user to handle streams of data using RxJS. For example, you could make an HTTP call to get some data and use the RxJS map operator to transform the result.

I've used RxJs to process DOM events a few times, but I frequently use RxJs operators with HTTP services very frequently. I'll introduce HTTP services and how to use them with RxJs in the next chapter.

CHAPTER 18

HTTP and the HttpClient Module

Ninety-nine percent of Angular projects involve communication between a client (a browser) and some remote server. Normally this is done with HTTP. So, it's very important to know how HTTP communication works and how you can write code for it. That's what this chapter is about.

The HyperText Transfer Protocol (HTTP) is designed to enable communications between clients and servers. HTTP works as a request-response protocol between a client and server. We will cover this in more detail in this chapter.

HTTP methods have been around for a long time (since way before AJAX and different types of web applications). HTTP methods can be used in traditional server-side web applications and in client-side AJAX web applications also.

Whenever a client talks to a web server using HTTP, it includes information about the request method. The method describes what the client wants the server to do—the intent of the request. The most commonly used methods are GET and POST. The GET method is used to request data from the server. The POST method is used to send data to the server in order to save it or update it.

The most commonly used HTTP methods are as follows:

- POST
- GET
- PUT
- PATCH
- DELETE

© Mark Clow 2018
M. Clow, *Angular 5 Projects*, https://doi.org/10.1007/978-1-4842-3279-8_18

HTTP headers allow client and server to pass additional information with requests or responses. A *request header* consists of its name, which is case-insensitive, followed by a colon (:), followed by its value (with no line breaks).

If you use the developer tools in your browser, you can see the network communications, including the HTTP calls. If you examine the HTTP requests using the Developer Tools of your web browser, you'll see the requests made to the server and those returned back.

Figures 18-1 and 18-2 show HTTP request and response headers.

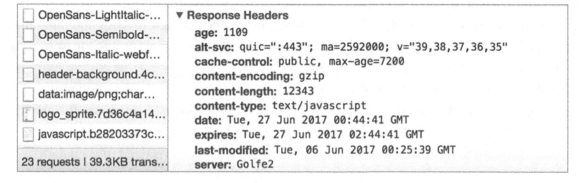

Figure 18-1. *HTTP request headers*

OpenSans-LightItalic-...	▼ Response Headers
OpenSans-Semibold-...	age: 1109
OpenSans-Italic-webf...	alt-svc: quic=":443"; ma=2592000; v="39,38,37,36,35"
	cache-control: public, max-age=7200
header-background.4c...	content-encoding: gzip
data:image/png;char...	content-length: 12343
	content-type: text/javascript
logo_sprite.7d36c4a14...	date: Tue, 27 Jun 2017 00:44:41 GMT
javascript.b28203373c...	expires: Tue, 27 Jun 2017 02:44:41 GMT
	last-modified: Tue, 06 Jun 2017 00:25:39 GMT
23 requests I 39.3KB trans...	server: Golfe2

Figure 18-2. *HTTP response headers*

Http Body

The http body allows the client and the server to pass additional information with the request or the response after the header. Http bodies are not always required because a body of information is not always needed. For example, Http 'get' requests don't need to include information in the body – all the information is already contained in the header.

Here is an example of the http body of a response from a server:

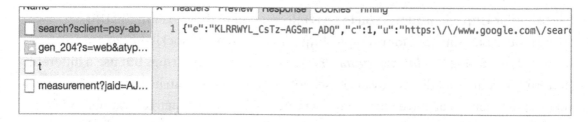

Passing Information with HTTP

There are various ways to pass information from the browser to the server. The server normally returns the information in the body, although it can pass information by returning data in the HTTP headers.

Query Parameters

The Angular Http client allows you to pass information to the server in the URL using query parameters. For example, http://localhost:4200/sockjs-node/info?t=1498649243238.

Some characters are not allowed to be part of a URL (for example, spaces), and other characters may have a special meaning in a URL. To get around this, the URL syntax allows for encoding on parameters to ensure a valid URL. For example, the space character between *Atlantic* and *City* in the following URL is encoded as *%20*: https:// trailapi-trailapi.p.mashape.com/?q[city_cont]=Atlantic%20City.

This encoding can be performed when building the URL with string concatenation, using the JavaScript method encodeURIComponent. If you use an Angular object (such as URLSearchParams) to build the query parameter string, it will automatically do this for you.

When navigating in your browser, query parameters are visible to the user on the address bar. When performing an AJAX request using the Angular Http client, though, they won't be visible.

Query parameters can't be used to pass as much information as the request body can.

Matrix Parameters

The Angular Http client allows you to pass information to the server in the URL using matrix parameters—for example, http://localhost:4200/sockjs-node/info;t=1498649243238. *Matrix parameters* are similar to query strings but use a different pattern. They also act differently because, not having a ?, they can be cached. Also, matrix parameters can have more than one value. You can use matrix parameters in Angular by specifying a URL that includes them. However, Angular currently does not have any built-in objects to create URLs with matrix parameters.

Matrix parameters can't be used to pass as much information as the request body can.

Path Parameters

The Angular Http client allows you to pass information to the server in the URL using path parameters—for example, http://localhost:4200/api/badges/9243238.

Passing Data in the Request Body

In the old days, HTML *forms* (with form tags and input fields) were the best way to send data to the server. The user would fill in a form and hit Submit, and the data would be posted (using the HTTP POST method) to the server in the request body.

Now the Angular Http client allows you to do the same thing programmatically: pass information to the server in the request body using the Http client's POST method.

You can pass more data in the request body than by passing it in the URL using query or matrix parameters.

REST

A *RESTful* application is a server application that exposes its state and functionality as a set of resources that the clients (browsers) can manipulate, and conforms to a certain set of principles. Examples of resources might be a list of clients or their orders.

All resources are uniquely addressable, usually through URIs, although other addressing can be used. For example, you could use orders/23 to access order number 23, or orders/24 to access order number 24.

All resources can be manipulated through a constrained set of well-known actions, usually CRUD (create, read, update, delete), represented most often through the HTTP methods POST, GET, PUT, and DELETE. Sometimes just some of these HTML methods are used, not all of them. For example, you could use an HTTP DELETE to orders/23 to delete that order.

The data for all resources is transferred through any of a constrained number of well-known representations, usually HTML, XML, or JSON. JSON is most common.

JSON

JSON stands for *JavaScript Object Notation*. It's a data format used to pass data between the client and the server, in both directions. JSON is the same data format used by the JavaScript language. It uses a comma to separate items and a colon to separate the name of a property with the data for that property. It uses different types of brackets to denote objects and arrays.

Here's JSON for passing an object containing data. Note how the { and } brackets are used to denote the start and end of an object:

```
{ "name":"John", "age":31, "city":"New York" }
```

Here's JSON for passing an array. Note how the [and] brackets are used to denote the start and end of an array:

```
[ "Ford", "BMW", "Fiat"]
```

Here's JSON for passing an array of objects. Note how the brackets are combined to create a cars object that has two properties: Nissan and Ford. Each property has an array of models:

```
{
    "cars": {
        "Nissan": [
            {"model":"Sentra", "doors":4},
            {"model":"Maxima", "doors":4}
        ],
```

```
        "Ford": [
            {"model":"Taurus", "doors":4},
            {"model":"Escort", "doors":4}
        ]
    }
}
```

The Angular Http Client

The Angular Http client is a service that you can inject into your classes to perform HTTP communication with a server. This service is available through the new Angular 5 Http Client module @angular/common/http, which replaces the old Angular 4 Http module @angular/common/http. You'll need to modify your module class (the one for your project) to import this module:

```
@NgModule({
  imports: [
        ...
        HttpClientModule,
        ...
  ],
  declarations: [ AppComponent ],
  bootstrap: [ AppComponent ]
})
```

You can inject the Angular Http service directly into your components in this manner:

```
@Injectable()
class CustomerComponent {
  ...
  constructor(private http: HttpClient) {
  ...
  }
}
```

That's fine for prototyping but not advisable for code maintainability in the long term. You shouldn't really use HttpClient directly for data access outside a service class. Instead you should write service classes that use the Http Client then inject those classes into your code where you need data access. If you look at the official Angular documentation at angular.io, you'll see the following: *This is a golden rule: always delegate data access to a supporting service class.*

Below is an example of a service class using the HttpClient:

```
@Injectable()
class CustomerCommunicationService {
  ...
  constructor(private http: HttpClient) {
  ...
  }
}

class CustomerComponent {
  ...
  constructor(private http: CustomerCommunicationService) {
  ...

  // perform data access
  }
}
```

Generics

With Angular 5, the new HttpClientModule allows us to use generics when we invoke HTTP requests. Generics enable us to tell Angular the type of response that we expect to receive back from the HTTP request. The type of response could be a 'any' (to allow any type of response), a variable type (for example a String), a class or an interface. For example, the code below performs an http 'get', specifying the expected response to be an array of Language objects:

```
this._http.get<Array<Language>>('https://languagetool.org/api/v2/languages');
```

This enables Angular to parse the response for us so that we don't have to. No more having to call JSON.parse to convert the response string to an object.

Asynchronous Operations

In JavaScript, making HTTP requests is an *asynchronous* operation. It sends the HTTP request to the API and *doesn't* wait for a response before continuing with the next line of code. When the API responds milliseconds or seconds or minutes later, then we get notified and we can start processing the response.

In Angular, there are two ways of handling these asynchronous operations: we can use promises or observables (covered a couple of chapters ago).

Normally we make calls to our supporting service classes, and they return the asynchronous result, which we handle in the component.

Request Options

Soon I'll cover each type of HTTP call you can make, but first let's talk about request options. When you invoke HTTP communication with a server, you have many ways of configuring the communication. What headers should you use? What media should you accept from the server? What credentials should you pass to the server? You set these options in an Angular object called RequestOptionsArgs and pass this as an argument to the Angular Http client method call.

Here's an example of the use of the RequestOptionsArg when making a GET call. Note how this object is used to specify the URL, the HTTP method, parameters, authentication token, and body:

```
var basicOptions:RequestOptionsArgs = {
  url: 'bankInfo',
  method: RequestMethods.Get,
  params: {
    accountNumber: accountNumber
  },
  headers: new HttpHeaders().set('Authentication': authenticationStr),
  body: null
};
```

HTTP GET Method: Example

The GET method is very commonly used to "get" data from a server. It typically doesn't use the request body. For example, for the URL /customers/getinfo.php?id=123, there is no request body. Here some aspects of GET:

- It's idempotent—calling the same PUT multiple times has the same effect as calling it once.

- It can remain in the browser history.

- It can be bookmarked.

- It has length restrictions.

- Request uses HTTP header.

- Response returned as HTTP body.

The GET method should be implemented in an indempotent manner on the server. In other words, making multiple, identical requests has the same effect as making a single request. Note that although idempotent operations produce the same result on the server (no side effects), the response itself may not be the same (for example, a resource's state may change between requests).

Figure 18-3 shows a component that gets the list of languages and language codes from Snapchat.

Countries

- Asturian (ast)
- Belarusian (be)
- Breton (br)
- Catalan (ca)
- Catalan (Valencian) (ca)
- Chinese (zh)

Figure 18-3. *Getting a list of languages and language codes from Snapchat*

This will be example http-ex100:

1. *Build the app using the CLI*: Use the following command:

```
ng new http-ex100 --inline-template --inline-style
```

2. *Start* ng serve: Use the following code:

```
cd http-ex100
ng serve
```

3. *Open app*: Open a web browser and navigate to localhost:4200.
   You should see "welcome to app!"

4. *Edit module*: Edit app.module.ts and change it to the following:

```
import { BrowserModule } from '@angular/platform-browser';
import { NgModule } from '@angular/core';
import { AppComponent } from './app.component';
import { SwaggerService } from './swagger.service';
import { HttpClientModule } from '@angular/common/http';

@NgModule({
  declarations: [
    AppComponent
  ],
  imports: [
    BrowserModule, HttpClientModule
  ],
  providers: [SwaggerService],
  bootstrap: [AppComponent]
})
export class AppModule { }
```

5. Create *service*: Create swagger.service.ts::

```
import { Injectable } from '@angular/core';
import { HttpClient } from '@angular/common/http';
import { Language } from './language';
```

```
@Injectable()
export class SwaggerService {
    constructor(private _http: HttpClient){}

    getLanguages() {
        return this._http.get<Array<Language>>('https://
        languagetool.org/api/v2/languages');
    }
}
```

6. *Create data object class*: Create language.ts.

```
export class Language {
    private _code: string;
    private _name: string;
    public get code() {
        return this._code;
    }
    public get name() {
        return this._name;
    }
    public set code(newValue: string){
        this._code = newValue;
    }
    public set name(newValue: string){
        this._name = newValue;
    }
}
```

7. *Edit component*: Edit app.component.ts and change it to the
    following:

```
import { Component, OnInit } from '@angular/core';
import { SwaggerService } from './swagger.service';
import { Language } from './language';

@Component({
  selector: 'app-root',
```

```
    template: `
    <h1>Countries</h1>
    <ul>
    <li *ngFor="let language of _languages">
    {{language.name}} ({{language.code}})
    </li>
    </ul>
    `
    ,
    styles: []
})
export class AppComponent implements OnInit{
  _languages = new Array<Language>();

  constructor(private _swaggerService: SwaggerService) {}

  ngOnInit(){
    this._swaggerService.getLanguages().subscribe(
      res => {
       this._languages = res;
      },
      error => { console.log('an error occurred'); }
    )
  }
}
```

Your app should be working at localhost:4200, and you should see a list of languages. Note the following:

- The file swagger.service.ts creates a service that has the injectable annotation to enable it to be injected into the app component. This service has a constructor into which the Angular Http module is injected. It also contains the method getLanguages, which makes an HTTP call to a server, which returns an observable. Note that the get method specifies the response type as 'Language' using a generic (see the <Array<Language>>).

- The file 'language.ts' defines the language data object which we will use to pass data from the service to the component.

- The file app.component.ts creates a component. Note that the swagger service is injected into this component using the constructor. When the component initializes, it calls the swagger service and subscribes to the observable result with two methods: the first one for success and the second one for failure.

- The first method (the "success" one) accepts the HTTP result as a parameter and sets the instance variable `_langages` to the returned array of JavaScript objects, which is then visible in the component.

HTTP GET Method Using Parameters: Example

We've covered GET, but "get" what? A GET uses parameters to get a specific thing (or things)—very useful if you want to get the information for a specific customer off the server. You can do that by simply modifying the URI of the GET to include query parameters, or you can do it using the Angular search or parameter objects embedded into the `RequestOptionsArgs` object.

Figure 18-4 shows an example of performing an HTTP GET in three different ways using query parameters, triggered by three different buttons.

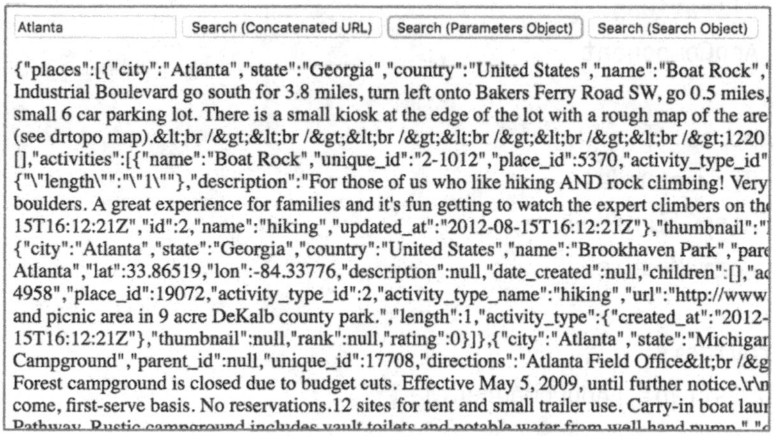

Atlanta | Search (Concatenated URL) | Search (Parameters Object) | Search (Search Object)

{"places":[{"city":"Atlanta","state":"Georgia","country":"United States","name":"Boat Rock",'
Industrial Boulevard go south for 3.8 miles, turn left onto Bakers Ferry Road SW, go 0.5 miles,
small 6 car parking lot. There is a small kiosk at the edge of the lot with a rough map of the are
(see drtopo map).

1220
[],"activities":[{"name":"Boat Rock","unique_id":"2-1012","place_id":5370,"activity_type_id"
{"\"length\"":"\"1\""},"description":"For those of us who like hiking AND rock climbing! Very
boulders. A great experience for families and it's fun getting to watch the expert climbers on th
15T16:12:21Z","id":2,"name":"hiking","updated_at":"2012-08-15T16:12:21Z"},"thumbnail":"
{"city":"Atlanta","state":"Georgia","country":"United States","name":"Brookhaven Park","par
Atlanta","lat":33.86519,"lon":-84.33776,"description":null,"date_created":null,"children":[],"ac
4958","place_id":19072,"activity_type_id":2,"activity_type_name":"hiking","url":"http://www
and picnic area in 9 acre DeKalb county park.","length":1,"activity_type":{"created_at":"2012-
15T16:12:21Z"},"thumbnail":null,"rank":null,"rating":0}]},{"city":"Atlanta","state":"Michigar
Campground","parent_id":null,"unique_id":17708,"directions":"Atlanta Field Office<br /&g
Forest campground is closed due to budget cuts. Effective May 5, 2009, until further notice.\r\n
come, first-serve basis. No reservations.12 sites for tent and small trailer use. Carry-in boat laur
Pathway. Rustic campground includes vault toilets and potable water from well hand pump." "c

Figure 18-4. GET in three different ways

This will be example http-ex200:

1. *Build the app using the CLI*: Use the following command:

   ```
   ng new http-ex200 --inline-template --inline-style
   ```

2. *Start* ng serve: Use the following code:

   ```
   cd http-ex200
   ng serve
   ```

3. *Open app*: Open a web browser and navigate to localhost:4200. You should see "welcome to app!"

4. *Edit module*: Edit app.module.ts and change it to the following:

   ```
   import { BrowserModule } from '@angular/platform-browser';
   import { NgModule } from '@angular/core';
   import { FormsModule } from '@angular/forms';
   import { AppComponent } from './app.component';
   import { HttpClientModule } from '@angular/common/http';

   @NgModule({
     declarations: [
       AppComponent
     ],
     imports: [
       BrowserModule,
       HttpClientModule,
       FormsModule
     ],
     providers: [],
     bootstrap: [AppComponent]
   })
   export class AppModule { }
   ```

5. *Edit component*: Edit app.component.ts and change it to the following:

```
import { Component } from '@angular/core';
import { HttpClient, HttpHeaders, HttpParams } from '@angular/
common/http';

@Component({
  selector: 'app-root',
  template: `
    <input [(ngModel)]="_search" placeholder="city">
    <button (click)="doSearchConcatenatedUrl()">Search
    (Concatenated URL)
    </button>
    <button (click)="doSeachHttpParams1()">Search
    (Http Params1)</button>
    <button (click)="doSeachHttpParams2()">Search (Http Params2)
    </button>
    <p>JSON {{_result | json}}</p>
  `,
  styles: []
})
export class AppComponent {
  _search = 'Atlanta';
  _result = {};

  constructor(private _http: HttpClient){
  }

  doSearchConcatenatedUrl(){
    const concatenatedUrl: string =
      "https://trailapi-trailapi.p.mashape.com?q[city_cont]=" +
      encodeURIComponent(this._search);
    const mashapeKey =
'OxWYjpdztcmsheZU9AWLNQcE9g9wp1qdRkFjsneaEp2Yf68nYH';
    const httpHeaders: HttpHeaders = new HttpHeaders(
      {'Content-Type': 'application/json',
      'X-Mashape-Key': mashapeKey});
```

```
      this._http.get(concatenatedUrl, { headers: httpHeaders }).subscribe(
        res => { this._result = res; });
    }

  doSeachHttpParams1(){
    const url: string =
      'https://trailapi-trailapi.p.mashape.com';
    const mashapeKey = 'OxWYjpdztcmsheZU9AWLNQcE9g9wp1qdRkFjsnea
    Ep2Yf68nYH';
    const httpHeaders = new HttpHeaders(
      {'Content-Type': 'application/json',
       'X-Mashape-Key': mashapeKey});
    const params = new HttpParams({
      fromString: 'q[city_cont]=' + this._search;
    });
    this._http.get(url, {headers: httpHeaders, params: params}).
    subscribe(
        res => { this._result = res; });
    }
  doSeachHttpParams2(){
    const url: string =
      'https://trailapi-trailapi.p.mashape.com';
    const mashapeKey = 'OxWYjpdztcmsheZU9AWLNQcE9g9wp1qdRkFjsnea
    Ep2Yf68nYH';

    const httpHeaders = new HttpHeaders(
      {'Content-Type': 'application/json',
       'X-Mashape-Key': mashapeKey});
    const params = new HttpParams().set('q[city_cont]', this._search);
    this._http.get(url, {headers: httpHeaders, params: params}).
    subscribe(
        res => { this._result = res; });
    }
  }
```

Your app should be working at localhost:4200. Note the following:

- The method doSearchConcatenatedUrl manually builds the URL string by appending the URL with the encoded 'q[city_cont]' parameter set to the encoded input string. The GET method is called on the Http client.

- The method doSeachHttpParams1 builds an HttpParams object from a query string similar to in the method 'doSearchConcatenatedUrl' above. The GET method is called on the Http client, passing the HttpParams object within the second argument. Note the HttpParams object does the encoding for us.

- The method doSeachHttpParams2 creates an HttpParams object and sets the 'q[city_cont]' parameter to the input string. The GET method is called on the Http client, passing the HttpParams object within the second.

Http GET Method Using Path Parameters: Example

This is an example of performing an HTTP GET using path parameters. The user is shown a list of articles, and each one has a Show button, as shown in Figure 18-5. The user can click the Show button, and an HTTP GET will be called, with path parameters, to get the details of the article, which is then displayed on a popup modal.

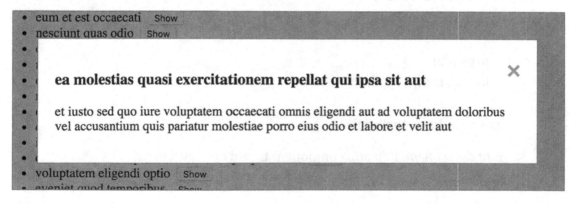

Figure 18-5. *Showing an article from a list*

This will be example http-ex300:

1. *Build the app using the CLI*: Use the following command:

```
ng new http-ex300 --inline-template --inline-style
```

2. *Start* ng serve: Use the following code:

```
cd http-ex300
ng serve
```

3. *Open app*: Open a web browser and navigate to localhost:4200. You should see "welcome to app!"

4. *Edit module*: Edit app.module.ts and change it to the following:

```
import { BrowserModule } from '@angular/platform-browser';
import { NgModule } from '@angular/core';

import { AppComponent } from './app.component';

import { HttpClientModule } from '@angular/common/http';

@NgModule({
  declarations: [
    AppComponent
  ],
  imports: [
    BrowserModule,
    HttpClientModule
  ],
  providers: [],
  bootstrap: [AppComponent]
})
export class AppModule { }
```

5. *Edit component*: Edit app.component.ts and change it to the following:

```
import { Component, OnInit, AfterViewInit, ViewChild } from
'@angular/core';
import { HttpClient } from '@angular/common/http';
```

```
@Component({
  selector: 'app-root',
  template: `
<ul>
<li *ngFor="let post of _posts">
  {{post.title}}  <button (click)="showPost(post.
  id)">Show</button>
</li>
</ul>
<div #modal id="myModal" class="modal">
  <div class="modal-content">
    <span class="close" (click)="closeModal()">&times;</span>
    <h3>{{this._post.title}}</h3>
    <p>{{this._post.body}}</p>
  </div>
</div>
  `,
  styles: []
})
export class AppComponent implements OnInit {
  _posts = [];
  _post = {};
  @ViewChild('modal') _myModal: any;

  constructor(private _http: HttpClient) {
  }

  ngOnInit() {
    return this._http.get<any>("http://jsonplaceholder.typicode.
    com/posts").subscribe(
      res => {
        this._posts = res;
      }
    );
  }
```

```
showPost(postId: number) {

  this._http.get<any>(`http://jsonplaceholder.typicode.com/
  posts/${postId}`).subscribe(
    res => {
      this._post = res;
      this._myModal.nativeElement.style.display = 'block';
    }
  )
}

closeModal() {
  this._myModal.nativeElement.style.display = 'none';
}

}
```

6. *Edit styles*: Edit styles.css and change it to the following:

```
.modal {
    display: none;
    position: fixed;
    z-index: 1;
    left: 0;
    top: 0;
    width: 100%;
    height: 100%;
    overflow: auto;
    background-color: rgb(0,0,0);
    background-color: rgba(0,0,0,0.2);
}

.modal-content {
    background-color: #fefefe;
    margin: 15% auto;
    padding: 20px;
    border: 1px solid #888;
    width: 60%;
}
```

```
.close {
    color: #aaa;
    float: right;
    font-size: 28px;
    font-weight: bold;
}
.close:hover,
.close:focus {
    color: black;
    text-decoration: none;
    cursor: pointer;
}
```

Note that In the app component method showPost, we use template literals to inject the post ID into the URL string.

HTTP POST Method: Example

POST is very commonly used to post data to a server. It typically sends the data in the request body. For example, for the URL /customers/new, the request body is name=Mark&city=Atlanta&state=GA.

Here are some important aspects of HTTP POST:

- It's not idempotent—calling the same put multiple times will result in a different effect from calling it once.

- It can't be cached.

- It can't remain in the browser history.

- It can't be bookmarked.

- It doesn't have length restrictions.

- The request uses HTTP body.

- The response is returned as HTTP body.

By its very nature, HTTP POST isn't idempotent. It has side effects—for example, adding a customer twice by posting the data twice (double posting).

Figure 18-6 shows an example of performing an HTTP POST. The user can input a title and a body and click Add to post them to the server. The server returns information to the browser, which is added to the list "You added" at the bottom.

Figure 18-6. *HTTP POST*

This will be example http-ex400:

1. *Build the app using the CLI*: Use the following command:

   ```
   ng new http-ex400 --inline-template --inline-style
   ```

2. *Start* ng serve: Use the following code:

   ```
   cd http-ex400
   ng serve
   ```

3. *Open app*: Open a web browser and navigate to localhost:4200. You should see "welcome to app!"

4. *Edit module*: Edit app.module.ts and change it to the following:

   ```
   import { BrowserModule } from '@angular/platform-browser';
   import { NgModule } from '@angular/core';
   import { HttpClientModule } from '@angular/common/http';
   ```

```
import { FormsModule } from '@angular/forms';
import { AppComponent } from './app.component';
@NgModule({
  declarations: [
    AppComponent
  ],
  imports: [
    BrowserModule,
    HttpClientModule,
    FormsModule
  ],
  providers: [],
  bootstrap: [AppComponent]
})
export class AppModule { }
```

5. *Edit component*: Edit app.component.ts and change it to the following:

```
import { Component, OnInit, AfterViewInit, ViewChild } from
'@angular/core';
import { HttpClient } from '@angular/common/http';

@Component({
  selector: 'app-root',
  template: `
    <div>
    Title:
    <br/>
    <input type="text" [(ngModel)]="_title" size="50" />
    <br/>
    <br/>
    Body:
    <br/>
    <textarea [(ngModel)]='_body' rows="2" cols="50">
    </textarea>
    <br/>
```

```
          <button (click)="onAdd()">Add</button>
          </div>
          <p><b>You Added:</b></p>
          <p *ngIf="_added.length == 0">None</p>
          <p *ngFor="let added of _added">
            {{added.title}}
          </p>
        `,
      styles: ['div { padding: 20px; background-color: #C0C0C0 }']
    })
    export class AppComponent {
      _title: string;
      _body: string;
      _added: Array<any> = new Array<any>();

      constructor(private _http: HttpClient) {
      }

      onAdd(){
        const requestBody = {
          title: this._title || '[Unspecified]',
          body: this._body || '[Unspecified]',
        };
        this._http.post("http://jsonplaceholder.typicode.com/posts",
        requestBody).subscribe(
          res => {
            this._added.push(res);
          }
        )
      }
    }
```

Note the following:

- In the app component method onAdd we create the object that's
  going to be posted to the server in the request body.

- In the app component method onAdd we use the or operator to ensure that we pass something valid to the server—either this._title (if that exists) or the text "[Unspecified]":

  title: this._title || '[Unspecified]'

- In the app component method onAdd we subscribe to the HTTP POST and use an arrow function to process the returned result. We add the returned result to the array of _added so it appears at the bottom.

HTTP PUT Method Using Path Parameters

The PUT method is similar to the POST method except that with a REST service it's typically used to update a resource rather than create it.

Some important aspects of HTTP PUT include the following:

- It's idempotent—calling the same PUT multiple times has the same effect as calling it once.

- It doesn't have length restrictions

- It's not cacheable.

- The request uses HTTP body.

- The response is returned as HTTP header.

HTTP PATCH Method Using Path Parameters

The PATCH method is like PUT except that it's not idempotent. For example, it would be useful to increase the value on a resource by a certain amount.

Some important aspects of PATCH include the following:

- It's not idempotent—calling the same PUT multiple times has a different effect as calling it once.

- It doesn't have length restrictions.

- It's not cacheable.

- The request uses HTTP body.

- The response is returned as HTTP header.

HTTP DELETE Method Using Path Parameters

The DELETE method is used to remove a resource from the server. Note the following:

- It's not idempotent—calling the DELETE multiple times has the same effect as calling it once.

- It's not cacheable.

- The request uses HTTP body.

- The response is returned as HTTP header.

Modifying the Server Response: Example

Remember that the Http client service calls return observable objects. That means the server returns an asynchronous data stream to the client (the browser) and that you can use the RxJS module to process that data using the operators discussed in Chapter 16. This includes the map operator we can use to transform the data.

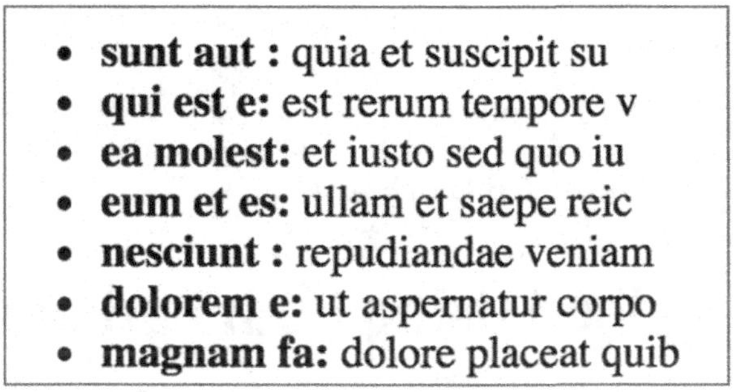

- **sunt aut :** quia et suscipit su
- **qui est e:** est rerum tempore v
- **ea molest:** et iusto sed quo iu
- **eum et es:** ullam et saepe reic
- **nesciunt :** repudiandae veniam
- **dolorem e:** ut aspernatur corpo
- **magnam fa:** dolore placeat quib

Figure 18-7. *Using map to modify a response*

Figure 18-7 shows an example of using the RxJS map operator (with a function) to modify the response returned from the server. In this case, we use it to transform data into *typed* data (data structured in a class).

This will be example http-ex500:

1. *Build the app using the CLI*: Use the following command:

```
ng new http-ex500 --inline-template --inline-style
```

2. *Start* ng serve: Use the following code:

```
cd http-ex500
ng serve
```

3. *Open app*: Open a web browser and navigate to localhost:4200.
    You should see "welcome to app!"

4. *Create class*: Create the following typescript class post.ts in the app:

```
export class Post {
    _title: string = "";
    _body: string = "";

    constructor(title: string, body: string){
        const titleNaN = title || '';
        const bodyNaN = body || '';
        this._title = titleNaN.length > 10 ? titleNaN.
        substring(0,9): titleNaN;
        this._body = bodyNaN.length > 20 ? bodyNaN.
        substring(0,19): bodyNaN;
    }

    get title(): string{
        return this._title;
    }

    get body(): string{
        return this._body;
    }

}
```

5. *Edit module*: Edit app.module.ts and change it to the following:

```
import { BrowserModule } from '@angular/platform-browser';
import { NgModule } from '@angular/core';
import { AppComponent } from './app.component';
import { HttpClientModule } from '@angular/common/http';
```

```
@NgModule({
  declarations: [
    AppComponent
  ],
  imports: [
    BrowserModule,
    HttpClientModule
  ],
  providers: [],
  bootstrap: [AppComponent]
})
export class AppModule { }
```

6. *Edit component*: Edit app.component.ts and change it to the following:

```
import { Component } from '@angular/core';
import { HttpClient } from '@angular/common/http';
import { Post } from './Post';
import 'rxjs/Rx';

@Component({
  selector: 'app-root',
  template: `
    <ul>
      <li *ngFor="let post of _posts">
        <b>{{post.title}}:</b> {{post.body}}
      </li>
    </ul>
    `,
  styles: []
})
export class AppComponent {
  _posts: Array<Post>;
  constructor(private _http: HttpClient) {}
  ngOnInit() {
```

```
      return this._http.get<Array<Post>>("http://jsonplaceholder.
      typicode.com/posts")
        .map(
          response => {
            const postsArray: Array<Post> = new Array<Post>();
            for (const responseItem of response){
              const post =
                new Post(responseItem['title'], responseItem['body']);
              postsArray.push(post);
            }
            return postsArray;
          }
        )
        .subscribe(
          response => {
            this._posts = response;
          }
        );
    }
  }
```

We create the typescript class Post to store each post. Note that this class has a constructor that trims the title and body of each post. And we use the or trick to convert "non-truthy" values to an empty string:

```
const titleNaN = title || '';
```

We use the following code to get data from the server. We use the map to convert the response (an array of objects) into a typed array of Post classes. We then subscribe to the result:

```
  return this._http.get("http://jsonplaceholder.typicode.com/posts")
    .map(
      response => {
        const postsArray: Array<Post> = new Array<Post>();
        for (const responseItem of response){
          const post =
```

```
        new Post(responseItem['title'], responseItem['body']);
      postsArray.push(post);
    }
    return postsArray;
  }
)
.subscribe(
  response => {
    this._posts = response;
  }
);
```

Handling a Server Error Response: Example

When you subscribe to an HTTP method call, you supply a handler method that processes the results. However, you can supply other handler methods too—one to handle errors and another to handle completion:

```
.subscribe(
    function(response) { console.log("Success " + response)},
    function(error) { console.log("Error " + error)},
    function() { console.log("Completion")}
);
```

This is an example of handling a server error and displaying an appropriate error message (shown in Figure 18-8.

Figure 18-8. *Displaying an error message*

This will be example http-ex600:

1. *Build the app using the CLI*: Use the following command:

    ```
    ng new http-ex600 --inline-template --inline-style
    ```

2. *Start* ng serve: Use the following code:

```
cd http-ex600
ng serve
```

3. *Open app*: Open a web browser and navigate to localhost:4200. You should see "welcome to app!"

4. Create service class: Create the following typescript class service.ts in the app:

```
import { Injectable } from '@angular/core';
import { HttpClient } from '@angular/common/http';
import { Observable } from 'rxjs/Observable';
import 'rxjs/Rx';

@Injectable()
export class Service {

  constructor(private _http: HttpClient) {
  }

  getPosts() : Observable<any> {
    return this._http.get("http://jsonplaceholder.typicode.com/postss");
  };

}
```

5. *Edit module*: Edit app.module.ts and change it to the following:

```
import { BrowserModule } from '@angular/platform-browser';
import { NgModule } from '@angular/core';
import { AppComponent } from './app.component';
import { HttpClientModule } from '@angular/common/http';
import { Service } from './Service';

@NgModule({
  declarations: [
    AppComponent
  ],
  imports: [
```

345

```
    BrowserModule,
    HttpClientModule
  ],
  providers: [HttpClientModule, Service],
  bootstrap: [AppComponent]
})
export class AppModule { }
```

6. *Edit component*: Edit app.component.ts and change it to the following:

```
import { Component } from '@angular/core';
import { Service } from './Service';
import 'rxjs/Rx';

@Component({
  selector: 'app-root',
  template: `
    <ul>
      <li *ngFor="let post of _posts">
        <b>{{post.title}}:</b> {{post.body}}
      </li>
    </ul>
    <div *ngIf="_error">
      Error: {{_error.status}}: {{_error.statusText}}
    </div>
  `,
  styles: ['div {font-size:20px; padding: 5px; background-color:
  red;color: white}']
})
export class AppComponent {
  _posts = [];
  _error;

  constructor(private _service: Service) {}

  ngOnInit() {
    this._service.getPosts()
      .subscribe(
```

```
      response => {
        this._posts = response;
      },
      error => {
        this._error = error;
      }
    );
  }
}
```

Note the following:

- The service class `service.ts` uses an incorrect URL that will throw a 404 error.

- The component app.component.ts calls the method `getPosts` and subscribes to its result, using two methods, each one implemented with an arrow function. The first processes a successful result, and the second processes an error. In this example, we process the error, setting the instance variable _error to its result.

- The _error instance variable is referred to in the template. If set, it shows a message in red.

Asynchronous Pipes: Example

The async pipe subscribes to an observable or promise and returns the latest value it has emitted. When a new value is emitted, the async pipe marks the component to be checked for changes. When the component gets destroyed, the async pipe unsubscribes automatically to avoid potential memory leaks.

Figure 18-9 shows an example of using a map to transform the output from a server and then using a pipe to output it.

> # Post Title Names
>
> sunt aut facere repellat provident occaecati excepturi optio reprehenderitqui
> est esseea molestias quasi exercitationem repellat qui ipsa sit auteum et est
> occaecatinesciunt quas odiodolorem eum magni eos aperiam quiamagnam
> facilis autemdolorem dolore est ipsamnesciunt iure omnis dolorem tempora
> et accusantiumoptio molestias id quia eumet ea vero quia laudantium
> autemin quibusdam tempore odit est doloremdolorum ut in voluptas mollitia
> et saepe quo animivoluptatem eligendi optioeveniet quod temporibussint

Figure 18-9. *Using a pipe to output*

This will be example http-ex700:

1. *Build the app using the CLI*: Use the following command:

   ```
   ng new http-ex700 --inline-template --inline-style
   ```

2. *Start* ng serve: Use the following code:

   ```
   cd http-ex700
   ng serve
   ```

3. *Open app*: Open a web browser and navigate to localhost:4200.
   You should see "welcome to app!"

4. *Edit module*: Edit app.module.ts and change it to the following:

   ```
   import { BrowserModule } from '@angular/platform-browser';
   import { NgModule } from '@angular/core';
   import { AppComponent } from './app.component';
   import { HttpClientModule } from '@angular/common/http';

   @NgModule({
     declarations: [
       AppComponent
     ],
     imports: [
       BrowserModule,
       HttpClientModule
     ],
   ```

```
    providers: [HttpClientModule],
    bootstrap: [AppComponent]
})
export class AppModule { }
```

5. *Edit component*: Edit app.component.ts and change it to the
    following:

```
import { Component } from '@angular/core';
import { Injectable } from '@angular/core';
import { HttpClient } from '@angular/common/http';
import 'rxjs/Rx';
import { Observable } from 'rxjs/Observable';

@Component({
  selector: 'app-root',
  template: `
    <h1>Post Title Names</h1>
    <p>{{_result|async}}</p>
  `,
  styles: []
})
export class AppComponent {
  _result: any;

  constructor(private _http: HttpClient) {}

  ngOnInit() {
    this._result =
      this._http.get<Array<any>>("http://jsonplaceholder.typicode.
      com/posts")
      .map(
        response => {
          let titles = '';
          for (const responseItem of response){
            titles += responseItem['title'];
          }
          return titles;
```

```
          }
        );
     }
  }
```

Note the following:

- The component app.component.ts calls the HTTP GET method to return a list of posts. It uses the map operator (and a function) to convert it into a string of all the titles of the posts. It then assigns the result to the _result instance variable.

- The component app.component.ts uses a template to display the value of the _result instance variable.

Summary

This important chapter covered the basics of HTTP communication and how to use the Http services to get and send data to the server. I recommend that you complete all the exercises because the Http service will be very important to you in future work writing single page applications. Remember that the Http Services that you will be working with may have their own custom headers and content types. For example your server developers may introduce a custom header to return error information from the server to the client in the event of an error. You may also need to add security tokens to each Http Service call. You will need to know how these Http Services work and how you can extend their functionality to work how you want.

The next chapter is also important: it covers forms, another feature of Angular you will use all the time.

CHAPTER 19

Forms

You can't enter data in an application without forms. AngularJS allowed the user to create forms quickly, using the `NgModel` directive to bind the input element to the data in the $scope. You can also do the same in Angular, but Angular 4 has a new Forms module that makes it easier to do the following:

- Create forms dynamically

- Validate input with common validators (required)

- Validate input with custom validators

- Test forms

Two Ways of Writing Forms

You can continue writing forms in a similar way to how you used to in AngularJS, but I recommend using the new Forms module because it does more work for you. The Forms module offers two main way of working with forms: template-driven forms and reactive forms. Both ways work with the same Forms module.

Template-Driven Forms

This is similar to how things were done in Angular.JS. We build the HTML template and add a few directives to specify addition information (such as validation rules), and Angular takes charge of building the model objects for us behind the scenes: the underlying forms, form groups, and controls.

- *Advantages*: Simple, quick to get started, perfect for simple forms, don't need to know how form model objects work

- *Disadvantages*: HTML and business rules are coupled, no unit testing

© Mark Clow 2018
M. Clow, *Angular 5 Projects*, https://doi.org/10.1007/978-1-4842-3279-8_19

Reactive Forms

Reactive forms are different. We build the model objects ourselves (including validation form rules), and the form binds (and syncs) to the template. I typically use Reactive Forms more than Template-Driven forms.

- *Advantages*: More control, perfect for more advanced forms, enable unit testing, HTML and business rules are decoupled

- *Disadvantages*: Need to know how form model objects work, take more time to develop

As of the time of writing this book, the Angular CLI generates projects with the Node dependency to the Forms module already set up. All you have to do is adjust your module to import the forms module. Here's an example of the app.module.ts file:

```
import { BrowserModule } from '@angular/platform-browser';
import { NgModule } from '@angular/core';
import { FormsModule } from '@angular/forms';

import { AppComponent } from './app.component';

@NgModule({
  declarations: [
    AppComponent
  ],
  imports: [
    BrowserModule,
    FormsModule
  ],
  providers: [],
  bootstrap: [AppComponent]
})
export class AppModule { }
```

Form Model Objects

This section applies to both ways of writing forms: template and Reactive. Both use the same model objects. Let's take a quick look at them.

NgForm

Stores state information for the form, including the following:

- Values for all the controls inside the form

- Groups of fields in the form

- Fields in the form

- Validators

FormGroup

Stores the value and validity state of a group of FormControl instances:

- Values for all the controls inside the form group

FormControl

Stores the value and validity state of an individual control—for instance a listbox:

- Value

- Validation state

- Status (for example, disabled)

You can add a subscriber to respond to form control value changes:

```
this.form.controls['make'].valueChanges.subscribe(
        (value) => { console.log(value); }
);
```

You can add a subscriber to respond to form control status changes:

```
this.form.controls['make'].statusChanges.subscribe(
        (value) => { console.log(value); }
);
```

Example output:

```
INVALID
VALID
```

FormArray

This is used to track the value and state of multiple FormControls, FormGroups, or FormArrays. It's useful for dealing with multiple form objects and tracking overall validity and state.

Forms and CSS

This section applies to both methods of writing forms: template and Reactive. When you have form validation, you need to highlight invalid data when it occurs. The Forms module has been designed to work with CSS to make it very easy to highlight invalid user input. The styles listed in Table 19-1 are automatically added to the form elements—all you need to do is add the CSS code to produce the required visual effect.

Table 19-1. *Styles Added to Form Elements*

Style	Description
ng-touched	Style applied if control has lost focus
ng-untouched	Style applied if control hasn't lost focus yet
ng-valid	Style applied if control passes validation
ng-invalid	Style applied if control doesn't pass validation
ng-dirty	Style applied if user has already interacted with the control
ng-pristine	Style applied if user hasn't interacted with the control yet

Template Forms: Example

As mentioned earlier, template forms use directives to create the form model objects. You build the input form and inputs in the template and add a few directives, and the form is ready and working. Template forms are perfect for quickly building simple forms that have simple validation.

Template forms work asynchronously. So, the model objects aren't available until the view has been initialized and the directives have been processed. Not all the model objects are even available in the AfterViewInit lifecycle method.

To use Angular template forms, your application module needs to import the Forms module from the @angular/forms node module:

```
import { BrowserModule } from '@angular/platform-browser';
import { NgModule } from '@angular/core';
import { FormsModule } from '@angular/forms';

import { AppComponent } from './app.component';

@NgModule({
  declarations: [
    AppComponent
  ],
  imports: [
    BrowserModule,
    FormsModule
  ],
  providers: [],
  bootstrap: [AppComponent]
})
export class AppModule { }
```

Let's go through creating a template form and see what's needed to make it work. This will be example forms-ex100.

1. *Build the app using the CLI*: Use the following command:

   ```
   ng new forms-ex100 --inline-template --inline-style
   ```

2. *Start* ng serve: Use the following code:

   ```
   cd forms-ex100
   ng serve
   ```

3. *Open app*: Open a web browser and navigate to localhost:4200. You should see "app works!"

4. *Edit module*: Edit app.module.ts and change it to the following:

```
import { BrowserModule } from '@angular/platform-browser';
import { NgModule } from '@angular/core';
import { FormsModule } from '@angular/forms';

import { AppComponent } from './app.component';

@NgModule({
  declarations: [
    AppComponent
  ],
  imports: [
    BrowserModule,
    FormsModule
  ],
  providers: [],
  bootstrap: [AppComponent]
})
export class AppModule { }
```

5. *Edit component*: Edit app.component.ts and change it to the following:

```
import { Component, ViewChild } from '@angular/core';
import { NgForm, RequiredValidator } from '@angular/forms';

@Component({
  selector: 'app-root',
  template: `
  <form #f novalidate>
    <p>First Name <input name="fname"/></p>
    <p>Last Name <input name="lname"/></p>
    Valid: {{ f.valid }}
    Data: {{ f.value | json }}
  </form>
  `,
  styles: []
```

```
})
export class AppComponent {
  @ViewChild('f') f: NgForm;
}
```

6. *View app*: Notice that this component just displays the input forms, as shown in Figure 19-1. It doesn't display any further information.

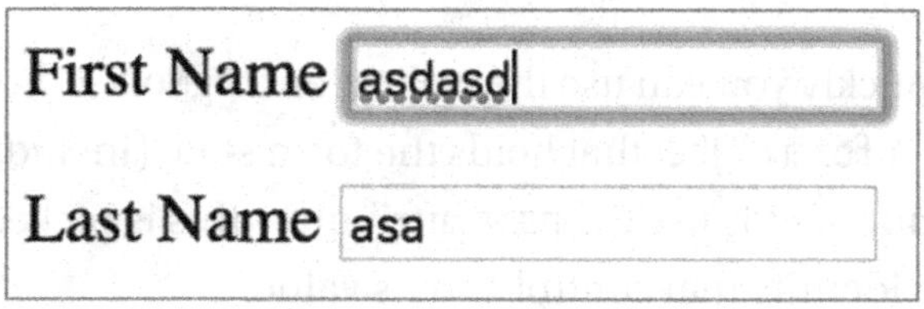

First Name asdasd

Last Name asa

Figure 19-1. *Displaying input forms*

7. *Edit component*: Now we'll add some directives to the form and input tags to get the form working as a template form. The changes are highlighted in bold in the following code:

```
import { Component, ViewChild } from '@angular/core';
import { NgForm, RequiredValidator } from '@angular/forms';

@Component({
  selector: 'app-root',
  template: `
  <form #f="ngForm" novalidate>
    <p>First Name <input name="fname" ngModel required /></p>
    <p>Last Name <input name="lname" ngModel required /></p>
    Valid: {{ f.valid }}
    Data: {{ f.value | json }}
  </form>  `,
  styles: []
})
export class AppComponent {
    @ViewChild('f') f: NgForm;
}
```

8. *View app*: Note that this component displays the input forms and the state of the form in Figure 19-2—its validity and its data.

First Name	peter
Last Name	smith|
Valid: true Data: { "fname": "peter", "lname": "smith" }	

Figure 19-2. *State of the form*

This shows how quickly you can use the ngForm and ngModel directives to make a template form, with a form object that holds the form state (including data). Note also how the HTML input fields use the name attribute—this is picked up by the form directives and used to identify that control and its value.

Template Variables and Data Binding: Example

Sometimes you need access to each control to access its state, its value, and so on. You can use the following syntax to set a template variable to the ngModel of the control (that is, its FormControl object). You can also use the ViewChild to access the FormControl as a variable:

```
import { Component, ViewChild } from '@angular/core';
import { NgForm, FormControl, RequiredValidator } from '@angular/forms';

@Component({
  selector: 'app-root',
  template: `
<form #f="ngForm" novalidate>
  <p>First Name <input name="fname" ngModel #fname="ngModel" required />
  </p>
  <h2>Form Template Variable</h2>
  Valid {{ fname.valid}}
  Data: {{ fname.value | json }}
  <h2>From Instance Variable</h2>
  Valid {{ fname2.valid}}
  Data: {{ fname2.value | json }}
```

```
    </form>   `,
    styles: []
})
export class AppComponent {
    @ViewChild('f') f: NgForm;
    @ViewChild('fname') fname2: FormControl;
}
```

You can also use template variables to query form control states, as listed in Table 19-2. This makes it very easy to add logic in the template to hide and show error messages.

Table 19-2. *Template Variables*

Variable	Description
.touched	Has the user performed any input in this field? Returns true or false.
.valid	Does the field input pass validation? Returns true or false.
.value	The current form value.
.hasError('required')	Has the specified error occurred? Returns true or false.

Sometimes you need to two-way bind each control's value to the model so that you can get and set each control's value as required. This is useful if you want to set the form control. Change the ngModel directive to use two-way binding and link it to the instance variable—in the following case, _name:

```
<input type="text" class="form-control" name="name" placeholder="Name
(last, first)" [(ngModel)]="_name" required>
```

Let's go through creating a template form and binding the form controls to instance variables. And let's build this form with bootstrap styling so it looks good. The submit form has a button that enables or disables according to the user's input, as shown in Figure 19-3.

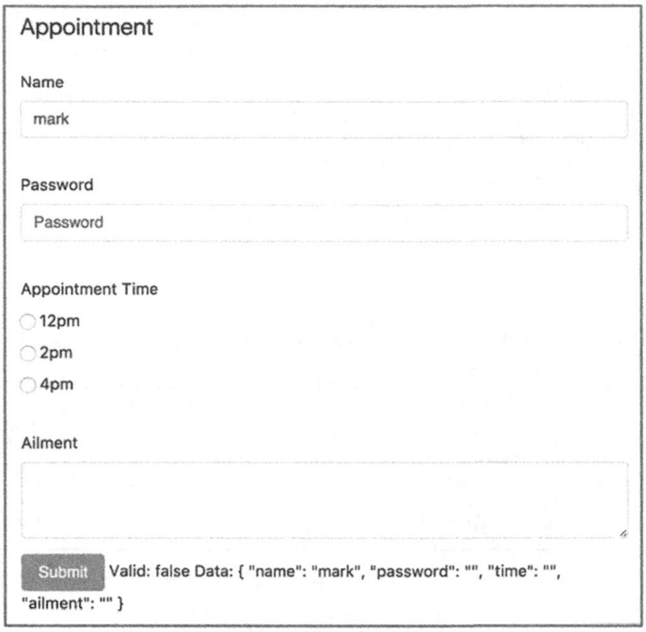

Figure 19-3. *Creating a template form binding form controls to instance variables*

This will be example forms-ex200:

1. *Build the app using the CLI*: Use the following command:

   ```
   ng new forms-ex200 --inline-template --inline-style
   ```

2. *Start* ng serve: Use the following code:

   ```
   cd forms-ex200
   ng serve
   ```

3. *Open app*: Open a web browser and navigate to localhost:4200. You should see "app works!"

4. *Edit web page*: Edit the file index.html and change it to the following:

   ```
   <!doctype html>
   <html lang="en">
   <head>
     <meta charset="utf-8">
     <title>FormsEx200</title>
     <base href="/">
   ```

```
<link rel="stylesheet" href="https://maxcdn.bootstrapcdn.
com/bootstrap/4.0.0-alpha.6/css/bootstrap.min.css"
integrity="sha384-rwoIResjU2yc3z8GV/NPeZWAv56rSmLldC3R/
AZzGRnGxQQKnKkoFVhFQhNUwEyJ" crossorigin="anonymous">
<script src="https://code.jquery.com/jquery-3.1.1.slim.min.
js" integrity="sha384-A7FZj7v+d/sdmMqp/nOQwliLvUsJfDHW+k9Omg/a/
EheAdgtzNs3hpfag6Ed950n" crossorigin="anonymous"></script>
<script src="https://cdnjs.cloudflare.com/ajax/libs/
tether/1.4.0/js/tether.min.js" integrity="sha384-DztdAPBW
PRXSA/3eYEEUWrWCy7G5KFbe8fFjk5JAIxUYHKkDx6Qin1DkWx51bBrb"
crossorigin="anonymous"></script>
<script src="https://maxcdn.bootstrapcdn.com/bootstrap/4.0.0-
alpha.6/js/bootstrap.min.js" integrity="sha384-vBWWzlZJ8
ea9aCX4pEW3rVHjgjt7zpkNpZk+02D9phzyeVkE+joOieGizqPLForn"
crossorigin="anonymous"></script>

<meta name="viewport" content="width=device-width, initial-scale=1">
<link rel="icon" type="image/x-icon" href="favicon.ico">
</head>
<body>
  <app-root></app-root>
</body>
</html>
```

5. *Edit module*: Edit the file app.module.ts and change it to the
   following:

```
import { BrowserModule } from '@angular/platform-browser';
import { NgModule } from '@angular/core';
import { FormsModule } from '@angular/forms';

import { AppComponent } from './app.component';

@NgModule({
  declarations: [
    AppComponent
  ],
```

```
    imports: [
      BrowserModule,
      FormsModule
    ],
    providers: [],
    bootstrap: [AppComponent]
})
export class AppModule { }
```

6. *Edit component*: Edit the file app.component.ts and change it to
   the following:

```
import { Component, ViewChild } from '@angular/core';
import { NgForm, RequiredValidator } from '@angular/forms';

@Component({
  selector: 'app-root',
  template: `
<form #appointmentForm="ngForm" novalidate (ngSubmit) =
"onSubmitForm(appointmentForm)">
  <legend>Appointment</legend>
  <div class="form-group">
    <label for="name">Name</label>
    <input type="text" class="form-control" name="name"
    placeholder="Name (last, first)" [(ngModel)]="_name" required>
  </div>
  <div class="form-group">
    <label for="password">Password</label>
    <input type="password" class="form-control" name="password"
    placeholder="Password" [(ngModel)]="_password" required>
  </div>
  <div class="form-group">
    <div class="form-check">
      <div>
        <label>Appointment Time</label>
      </div>
```

```
        <label class="form-check-label">
          <input type="radio" class="form-check-input" name="time"
          value="12pm" [(ngModel)]="_time" required>
          12pm
        </label>
      </div>
      <div class="form-check">
        <label class="form-check-label">
          <input type="radio" class="form-check-input" name="time"
          value="2pm" [(ngModel)]="_time" required>
          2pm
        </label>
      </div>
      <div class="form-check">
        <label class="form-check-label">
          <input type="radio" class="form-check-input" name="time"
          value="4pm" [(ngModel)]="_time" required>
          4pm
        </label>
      </div>
    </div>
    <div class="form-group">
      <label for="exampleTextarea">Ailment</label><textarea
      class="form-control" name="ailment" rows="3" [(ngModel)]=
      "_ailment" required ></textarea>
    </div>
    <button type="submit" class="btn btn-primary" [disabled]=
    "!_appointmentForm.valid">Submit</button>
    Valid: {{ _appointmentForm.valid }}
    Data: {{ _appointmentForm.value | json }}
  </form>
  `,
  styles: ['form { padding: 20px }', '.form-group { padding-top: 20px }']
})
```

```
export class AppComponent {
  @ViewChild('appointmentForm') _appointmentForm: NgForm;
  _name: string = 'mark';
  _password: string = '';
  _time: string = '';
  _ailment: string = '';

  onSubmitForm() {
    alert("Submitting data:" + JSON.stringify
    (this._appointmentForm.value));
  }
}
```

Your app should be working at localhost:4200. Note that the file index.html is modified to link to the bootstrap CSS and JavaScript files.

The file app.component does the following:

- Sets up a form that is a template variable appointmentForm. The form fires the method onSubmitForm when it's submitted.

- Sets up input fields and uses two-way binding with the ngModel directive to link the value of each field to an instance variable.

- Contains the following markup in the template to enable or disable the Submit button:

  ```
  <button type="submit" class="btn btn-primary" [disabled]="!_
  appointmentForm.valid">Submit</button>
  ```

- Displays form validity and values underneath.

Template Forms and CSS: Example

Let's go through creating an input form with color coding to form validation state. Green indicates valid input, red indicates invalid input. There's also code for error messages, as shown in Figure 19-4.

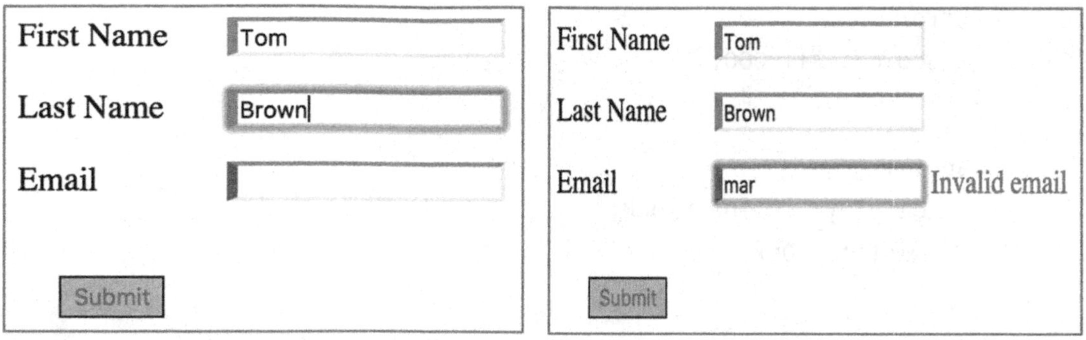

Figure 19-4. *Input form with color coding*

This will be example forms-ex300:

1. *Build the app using the CLI*: Use the following command:

   ```
   ng new forms-ex300 --inline-template --inline-style
   ```

2. *Start* ng serve: Use the following code:

   ```
   cd forms-ex300
   ng serve
   ```

3. *Open app*: Open a web browser and navigate to localhost:4200. You should see "app works!"

4. *Edit styles*: Edit the file styles.css and change it to the following:

   ```
   input.ng-valid {
     border-left: 5px solid #42A948; /* green */
   }

   input.ng-invalid {
     border-left: 5px solid #a94442; /* red */
   }
   ```

```
.error {
    color: #ff0000;
}

label {
    display: inline-block;
    width: 100px;
}

button {
    border: 1px solid black;
    margin: 20px;
}
```

5. *Edit module*: Edit file app.module.ts and change it to the
    following:

```
import { BrowserModule } from '@angular/platform-browser';
import { NgModule } from '@angular/core';
import { FormsModule } from '@angular/forms';

import { AppComponent } from './app.component';

@NgModule({
  declarations: [
    AppComponent
  ],
  imports: [
    BrowserModule,
    FormsModule
  ],
  providers: [],
  bootstrap: [AppComponent]
})
export class AppModule { }
```

6. *Edit component*: Edit the file app.component.ts and change it to
    the following:

```
import { Component, ViewChild } from '@angular/core';
import { NgForm, FormControl, RequiredValidator } from '@angular/forms';

@Component({
  selector: 'app-root',
  template: `
  <form #f="ngForm" novalidate>
    <p><label>First Name</label><input name="fname" ngModel
    #fname="ngModel" required />
    <span class="error" *ngIf="fname.touched && fname.
    hasError('required')">Required</span>
    </p>
    <p><label>Last Name</label><input name="lname" ngModel
    #lname="ngModel" required />
    <span class="error" *ngIf="lname.touched && lname.
    hasError('required')">Required</span>
    </p>
    <p><label>Email</label><input name="email" ngModel
    #email="ngModel" required email />
    <span class="error" *ngIf="email.touched && email.
    hasError('required')">Required</span>
    <span class="error" *ngIf="email.value && email.touched &&
    email.hasError('email')">Invalid email</span>
    </p>
    <button (click)="onSubmit()" [disabled]="!f.valid">
    Submit</button>
  </form>`,
  styles: []
})
export class AppComponent {
    onSubmit(){
      alert('Submitted');
    }
}
```

Your app should be working at localhost:4200. Note the following:

- The file styles.css applies the required styles to the appropriate states—for example, setting the `ng-valid` style to show a green indicator when the form control has valid data.

- The file app.component.ts contains logic to display error messages based on the form control states.

Reactive Forms: Example

You build the model objects for the form—they're the same ones as the template forms—and then bind them to the input controls in the template. So, you're building the form controls in your class and amending your template to link to those controls. This gives you complete control over the form, its values, and its validations. You can directly manipulate the model objects (for example, change values), and the binding immediately takes affect synchronously. In fact, value and validity updates are always synchronous and under your control.

To use Angular template forms, your application module needs to import the Reactive Forms module from the @angular/forms node module:

```
import { BrowserModule } from '@angular/platform-browser';
import { NgModule } from '@angular/core';
import { ReactiveFormsModule } from '@angular/forms';

import { AppComponent } from './app.component';

@NgModule({
  declarations: [
    AppComponent
  ],
  imports: [
    BrowserModule,
    ReactiveFormsModule
  ],
  providers: [],
  bootstrap: [AppComponent]
})
export class AppModule { }
```

To bind a template to a model, you create the HTML form, and HTML inputs in the component's template. Then you create a form model in your component's class. Now you bind the two together using the following directives:

- `<form [formGroup]="registerForm">`: Connects the form model with the form HTML in the template.

- `<fieldset formGroupName="address">`: Connects the form group with the fieldset HTML in the template.

- `<input formControlName="name">`: Connects the form control in the model with the form input HTML in the template.

Let's go through creating a reactive form and see what's needed to make it work. This will be example forms-ex400:

1. *Build the app using the CLI*: Use the following command:

   ```
   ng new forms-ex400 --inline-template --inline-style
   ```

2. *Start* ng serve: Use the following code:

   ```
   cd forms-ex400
   ng serve
   ```

3. *Open app*: Open a web browser and navigate to localhost:4200. You should see "app works!"

4. *Edit styles*: Edit the file styles.css and change it to the following:

   ```css
   input.ng-valid {
     border-left: 5px solid #42A948; /* green */
   }

   input.ng-invalid {
     border-left: 5px solid #a94442; /* red */
   }

   .error {
       color: #ff0000;
   }
   ```

```
label {
    display: inline-block;
    width: 100px;
}

button {
    border: 1px solid black;
    margin: 20px;
}
```

5. *Edit module*: Edit the file app.module.ts and change it to the
   following:

```
import { BrowserModule } from '@angular/platform-browser';
import { NgModule } from '@angular/core';
import { ReactiveFormsModule } from '@angular/forms';

import { AppComponent } from './app.component';

@NgModule({
  declarations: [
    AppComponent
  ],
  imports: [
    BrowserModule,
    ReactiveFormsModule
  ],
  providers: [],
  bootstrap: [AppComponent]
})
export class AppModule { }
```

6. *Edit component*: Edit the file app.component.ts and change it to
   the following:

```
import { Component, OnInit } from '@angular/core';
import { FormGroup, FormControl, FormControlName, Validators }
from '@angular/forms';
```

```
@Component({
  selector: 'app-root',
  template: `
    <form #form [formGroup]="formGroup" (ngSubmit)="onSubmit(form)"
    novalidate>
      <label>Name:
        <input formControlName="name">
      </label>
      <br/>
      <label>Location:
        <input formControlName="location">
      </label>
      <br/>
      <input type="submit" value="Submit" [disabled]="!formGroup.valid">
    </form>
  `,
  styles: []
})
export class AppComponent implements OnInit{

  formGroup: FormGroup;

  ngOnInit(){
    this.formGroup = new FormGroup({
      name: new FormControl('', Validators.required),
      location: new FormControl('', Validators.required)
    });
  }
  onSubmit(form: FormGroup){
    alert('sumit');
  }
}
```

Your app should be working at localhost:4200. Note the following:

- The file styles.css sets up the CSS styles.

- The file app.component.ts contains the HTML in the template for the form.

- The file app.component.ts initializes the model, a form group with form controls in the ngInit method, when the component initializes.

  - The file app.component.ts links the HTML in the template to the model. It links HTML form to formGroup using the following:

    ```
    <form #form [formGroup]="formGroup" (ngSubmit)="onSubmit(form)" novalidate>
    ```

  - It links HTML input to formControl using the following:

    ```
    <input formControlName="name">
    ```

Reactive Forms: FormBuilder

The FormBuilder class is designed to help you build the form model with less code. Inject the FormBuilder into your component's class and use its methods as listed in Table 19-3.

Table 19-3. *FormBuilder Methods*

Method	Purpose	Arguments	Returns
group	Create a form group	Configuration object, extra parameters (validators, async validators)	FormGroup
control	Create a form control	Current form state (value/disabled status), array of validators, array of async validators	FormControl
array	Create a form array	Configuration object (array), validator, async validator	FormArray

We'll start using FormBuilder in the upcoming examples.

Reactive Forms: Form Group Nesting Example

Sometimes our forms consist of multiple different elements. For example, if you were entering a customer order, the information could be structured in the following manner:

- Name

- Address

- Order

  - Order items

- Credit card info

Each of those elements can contain one or more form controls, so we need to be able to manage each. This is where form groups come in. In this case, you could have the hierarchy of form groups shown in Figure 19-5.

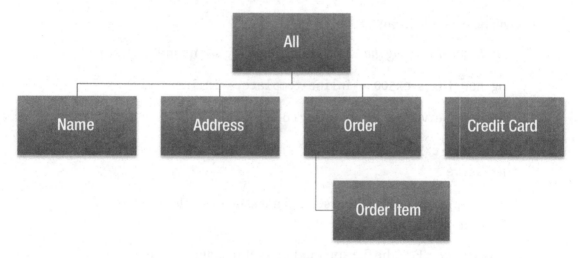

***Figure 19-5.** Hierarchy of form groups*

This example enables the user to enter and submit an order including the customer name, customer address, and a list of items, as shown in Figure 19-6.

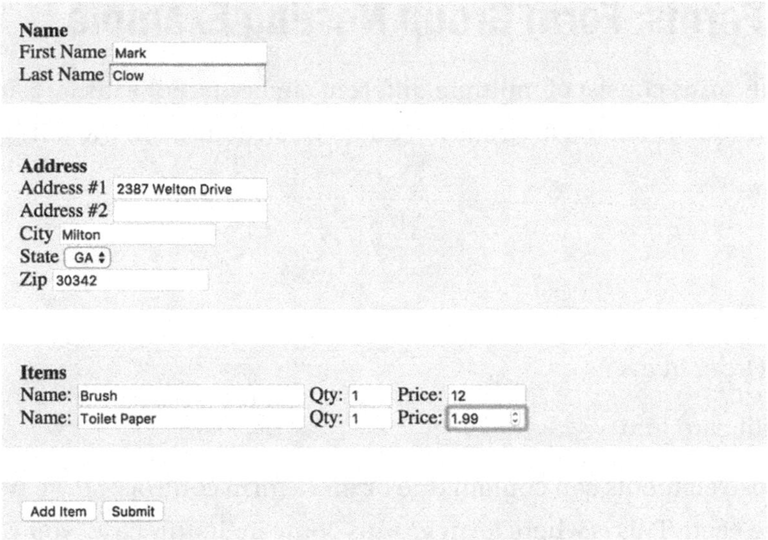

Name
First Name Mark
Last Name Clow

Address
Address #1 2387 Welton Drive
Address #2
City Milton
State [GA ▼]
Zip 30342

Items
Name: Brush   Qty: 1   Price: 12
Name: Toilet Paper   Qty: 1   Price: [1.99   ▼]

[Add Item] [Submit]

Figure 19-6. *Entering and submitting an order*

This will be example forms-ex500:

1. *Build the app using the CLI*: Use the following command:

   ```
   ng new forms-ex500 --inline-template --inline-style
   ```

2. *Start* ng serve: Use the following code:

   ```
   cd forms-ex500
   ng serve
   ```

3. *Open app*: Open a web browser and navigate to localhost:4200.
   You should see "app works!"

4. *Edit module*: Edit the file app.module.ts and change it to the
   following:

   ```
   import { BrowserModule } from '@angular/platform-browser';
   import { NgModule } from '@angular/core';
   import { ReactiveFormsModule } from '@angular/forms';

   import { AppComponent } from './app.component';

   @NgModule({
   ```

```
  declarations: [
    AppComponent
  ],
  imports: [
    BrowserModule,
    ReactiveFormsModule
  ],
  providers: [],
  bootstrap: [AppComponent]
})
export class AppModule { }
```

5. *Edit component class*: Edit the file app.component.ts and change it to the following:

```
import { Component, OnInit } from '@angular/core';
import { FormGroup, FormArray, FormBuilder, Validators } from '@angular/forms';

@Component({
  selector: 'app-root',
  templateUrl: 'app.component.html',
  styles: ['div { background-color: #f2f2f2; padding: 15px;
  margin: 5px }',
    'p { margin: 0px }'
  ]
})

export class AppComponent implements OnInit {

  public _parentForm: FormGroup;
  public _name: FormGroup;
  public _addr: FormGroup;
  public _items: FormArray;

  constructor(private _fb: FormBuilder){}

  ngOnInit() {
    this._name = this._fb.group({
```

```
            fname: ['', [Validators.required]],
            lname: ['', [Validators.required]]
        });
    this._addr = this._fb.group({
            addr1: ['', [Validators.required]],
            addr2: [''],
            city: ['', [Validators.required]],
            state: ['', [Validators.required]],
            zip: ['', [Validators.required, Validators.minLength(5),
            Validators.maxLength(5)]],
        });
    this._items = this._fb.array(
        [this.createItemFormGroup()]
    );
    this._parentForm = this._fb.group({
        name: this._name,
        addr: this._addr,
        items: this._items
    });
}

createItemFormGroup(){
    return this._fb.group({
            name: ['', Validators.required],
            qty: ['1', Validators.required],
            price: ['', Validators.required]
        });
}

addItem(){
    this._items.push(this.createItemFormGroup());
}

deleteItem(index){
    delete this._items[index];
}
```

```
  onSubmit(form: FormGroup){
    alert('Submitted');
  }
}
```

6. *Edit component template*: Edit the file app.component.html and change it to the following:

```
<form [formGroup]="_parentForm" novalidate (ngSubmit)="onSubmit
(parentForm)">
  <div formGroupName="name">
    <b>Name</b>
    <br/>
    <label>First Name
      <input type="text" formControlName="fname">
      <small *ngIf="_name.controls.fname.touched && !_name.
      controls.fname.valid">Required.</small>
    </label>
    <br/>
    <label>Last Name
      <input type="text" formControlName="lname">
      <small *ngIf="_name.controls.lname.touched && !_name.
      controls.lname.valid">Required.</small>
    </label>
  </div>
  <br/>
  <div formGroupName="addr">
    <b>Address</b>
    <br/>
    <label class="left">Address #1
      <input type="text" formControlName="addr1">
      <small *ngIf="_addr.controls.addr1.touched && !_addr.
      controls.addr1.valid">Required.</small>
    </label>
    <br/>
    <label>Address #2
```

```
        <input type="text" formControlName="addr2">
      </label>
      <br/>
      <label>City
        <input type="text" formControlName="city">
        <small *ngIf="_addr.controls.city.touched && !_addr.
        controls.city.valid">Required.</small>
      </label>
      <br/>
      <label>State
        <select formControlName="state">
          <option>AL</option>
          <option>GA</option>
          <option>FL</option>
        </select>
        <small *ngIf="_addr.controls.state.touched && !_addr.
        controls.state.valid">Required.</small>
      </label>
      <br/>
      <label>Zip
        <input type="number" formControlName="zip">
        <small *ngIf="_addr.controls.zip.touched && !_addr.controls.
        zip.valid">Required.</small>
      </label>
    </div>
    <br/>
    <div formArrayName="items">
      <b>Items</b>
      <br/>
      <p [formGroupName]="i" *ngFor="let item of _items.controls;let
      i=index">
        <label>Name: <input type="text" formControlName="name"
        size="30">
          <small *ngIf="item.controls.name.touched && !item.
          controls.name.valid">Required.</small>
        </label>
```

```
<label>Qty: <input type="number" formControlName="qty"
min="1" max="10">
  <small *ngIf="item.controls.qty.touched && !item.controls.
  qty.valid">Required.</small>
</label>
<label>Price: <input type="number"
formControlName="price" min="0.01" max="1000" step=".01">
  <small *ngIf="item.controls.price.touched && !item.
  controls.price.valid">Required.</small>
</label>
  </p>
</div>
<br/>
<div>
  <input type="button" value="Add Item" (click)="addItem()"/>
  <input type="submit" value="Submit" [disabled]="!_parentForm.valid"/>
</div>
</form>
```

Your app should be working at localhost:4200. Note the following:

- We have at least four fixed FormGroup objects: one for the name, one for the address, one for the first item, and another for the parent form.

- The FormArray contains one FormGroup object, but it can contain other FormGroup objects if the user clicks the Add Item button.

- The overall form validity still controls the enablement and disablement of the Submit button.

Validators

Angular provides some validators for our forms. You can add multiple validators to the same FormControl (an item in the FormGroup):

- Required validation:

```
this.form = fb.group({
        'name': ['', Validators.required],
    });
```

- Minimum length validation:

```
this.form = fb.group({
        'name': ['', Validators.required, Validators.minLength(4)]
    });
```

- Maximum length validation:

```
this.form = fb.group({
        'name': ['', Validators.required, Validators.maxLength(4)]
    });
}
```

Combining Multiple Validators

The Validators class provides the compose method to allow the user to specify multiple validators to a control:

```
constructor(private fb: FormBuilder){
    this.form = fb.group({
        'name': ['', Validators.compose( [Validators.required,
        Validators.maxLength(6)] ) ],
    });
}
```

Custom Validation Example

The Angular Forms module allows you to create a custom class to validate your input. The validation method is static and returns a validation result only when there's an error. If everything is okay, this method returns a null. This custom class can be used when specifying the field in the FormBuilder and can also be used in the component template to provide a visual cue.

This component won't allow the user to enter *mercedes*, as shown in Figure 19-7.

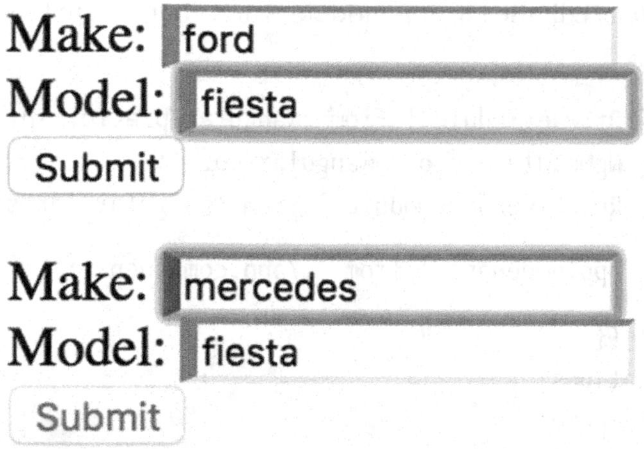

Figure 19-7. *Custom validation*

This will be example forms-ex600:

1. *Build the app using the CLI*: Use the following command:

   ```
   ng new forms-ex600 --inline-template --inline-style
   ```

2. *Start* ng serve: Use the following code:

   ```
   cd forms-ex600
   ng serve
   ```

3. *Open app*: Open a web browser and navigate to localhost:4200. You should see "app works!"

4. *Edit styles*: Edit the file styles.css and change it to the following:

   ```
   input.ng-valid {
     border-left: 5px solid #42A948; /* green */
   }

   input.ng-invalid {
     border-left: 5px solid #a94442; /* red */
   }
   ```

5. *Edit module*: Edit the file app.module.ts and change it to the following:

```
import { BrowserModule } from '@angular/platform-browser';
import { NgModule } from '@angular/core';
import { ReactiveFormsModule } from '@angular/forms';

import { AppComponent } from './app.component';

@NgModule({
  declarations: [
    AppComponent
  ],
  imports: [
    BrowserModule,
    ReactiveFormsModule
  ],
  providers: [],
  bootstrap: [AppComponent]
})
export class AppModule { }
```

6. *Edit component*: Edit the file app.component.ts and change it to the following:

```
import { Component, OnInit } from '@angular/core';
import { AbstractControl, FormGroup, FormControl, FormControlName,
Validators } from '@angular/forms';

export function validateNotMercedes(control: AbstractControl) {
    return (control.value.toLowerCase() != 'mercedes') ?
      null :
      { validateNotMercedes: {
        valid: false
      }
    }
}
```

```
@Component({
  selector: 'app-root',
  template: `
    <form #form [formGroup]="formGroup" (ngSubmit)="onSubmit(form)"
    novalidate>
      <label>Make:
        <input formControlName="make">
      </label>
      <br/>
      <label>Model:
        <input formControlName="model">
      </label>
      <br/>
      <input type="submit" value="Submit" [disabled]="!formGroup.valid">
    </form>
  `,
  styles: []
})
export class AppComponent implements OnInit{

  formGroup: FormGroup;

  ngOnInit(){
    this.formGroup = new FormGroup({
      make: new FormControl('', [Validators.required,
      validateNotMercedes]),
      model: new FormControl('', Validators.required)
    });
  }

  onSubmit(form: FormGroup){
    alert('sumit');
  }
}
```

Your app should be working at localhost:4200. Note the following:

- The code in file app.component.ts exports the `validateNotMercedes` function to validate the make. Note that it returns a null to indicate validity—otherwise, it returns an object with the property `valid` set to false.

- The code in file app.component.ts sets up the form group using the `FormControl` objects. Notice how here the `make` `FormControl` specifies the `validateNotMercedes` function as a validator.

Summary

You don't have to use the Angular form modules, but they do a lot of work for you and save you a lot of time. Angular offers you two options: the quick-and-easy template forms and the more advanced Reactive forms. You need to know both because they're both very useful and well implemented. They may take some time to learn, but the payoff is woth it.

The next chapter covers pipes. Pipes aren't essential but can be useful.

CHAPTER 20

Pipes

Pipes have been around since AngularJS. They're useful at transforming data, especially when the same transformation is used throughout the application. Pipes make it easy to add these transformations into your component template.

Angular Pipes

Angular includes several pipes to add to your template. You don't need to import them or add them as directives or anything—just start using them.

lowercase

Lowercase: {{ "The Quick Brown Fox Jumped Over The Lazy Dogs" | lowercase }}

Produces:

Lowercase: the quick brown fox jumped over the lazy dogs

uppercase

Uppercase: {{ "The Quick Brown Fox Jumped Over The Lazy Dogs" | uppercase }}

Produces:

Uppercase: THE QUICK BROWN FOX JUMPED OVER THE LAZY DOGS

© Mark Clow 2018
M. Clow, *Angular 5 Projects*, https://doi.org/10.1007/978-1-4842-3279-8_20

currency

Currency: {{ 2012.55 | currency }}

> Produces:

Currency: USD2,012.55

UK (gbp) pound currency

UK Pound Currency: {{ 2012.55 | currency: 'gbp':true }}

> Produces:

UK Pound Currency: £2,012.55

percent

Percentage: {{ 0.5 | percent }}

> Produces:

Percentage: 50%

date

Date: {{ dt | date }}

> Produces:

Date: Jul 12, 2017

shortdate

Short Date: {{ dt | date:shortdate }}

Produces:

Short Date: Jul 12, 2017

Special Date Format

Special Date Format: {{ dt | date:'yMMMMEEEEd' }}

Produces:

Special Date Format: Wednesday, July 12, 2017

Table 20-1 lists the predefined date formats.

Table 20-1. *Predefined Date Formats*

Name	Format	Example (English/US)
medium	yMMMdjms	Sep 3, 2010, 12:05:08 PM
short	yMdjm	9/3/2010, 12:05 PM
fullDate	yMMMMEEEEd	Friday, September 3, 2010
longDate	yMMMMd	September 3, 2010
mediumDate	yMMMd	Sep 3, 2010
shortDate	yMd	9/3/2010
mediumTime	jms	12:05:08 PM
shortTime	jm	12:05 PM

Table 20-2 shows how date format elements can be combined.

Table 20-2. *Combining Date Formats*

Name	Format	Text Form Full	Text Form Short	Numeric Form	Numeric Form 2 Digit
era	G	GGGG	G		
year	y			y	yy
month	M	MMMM	MMM	M	MM
day	D			d	dd
weekday	E	EEEE	EEE		
hour	J			j	jj
12 hour	H			h	hh
24 hour	H			H	HH
minute	M			m	MM
second	S			s	ss
timezone	z / Z	z	Z		

json

```
{{ {customerName: 'Mark', 'address': '2312 welton av 30333'} | json }}
```

Produces:

```
{ "customerName": "Mark", "address": "2312 welton av 30333" }
```

The preceding example does the following:

- Generates a JavaScript object containing two properties: a customer name and address

- Passes this JavaScript object to the json pipe

- The json pipe outputs a JSON representation of the supplied object

Angular Pipes: Example

The component shown in Figure 20-1 displays information using the variety of Angular pipes.

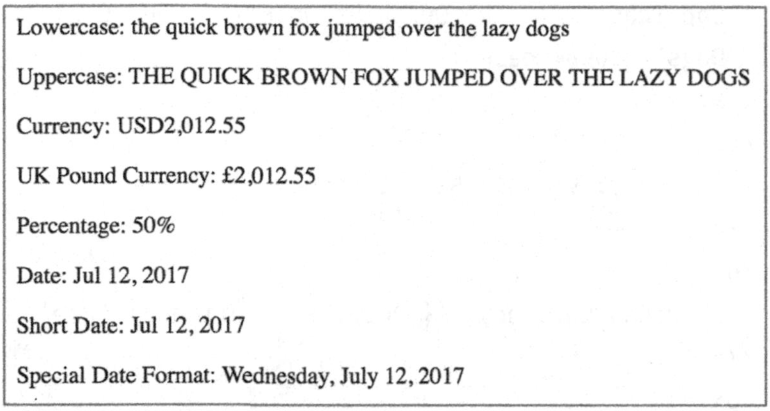

> Lowercase: the quick brown fox jumped over the lazy dogs
>
> Uppercase: THE QUICK BROWN FOX JUMPED OVER THE LAZY DOGS
>
> Currency: USD2,012.55
>
> UK Pound Currency: £2,012.55
>
> Percentage: 50%
>
> Date: Jul 12, 2017
>
> Short Date: Jul 12, 2017
>
> Special Date Format: Wednesday, July 12, 2017

Figure 20-1. *Showing various Angular pipes*

This will be example pipes-ex100:

1. *Build the app using the CLI:* Use the following command:

   ```
   ng new pipes-ex100 --inline-template --inline-style
   ```

2. *Start* ng serve: Use the following code:

   ```
   cd pipes-ex100
   ng serve
   ```

3. *Open app*: Open web browser and navigate to localhost:4200. You should see "app works!"

4. *Edit component*: Edit the file app.component.ts and change it to the following:

   ```
   import { Component } from '@angular/core';

   @Component({
     selector: 'app-root',
     template: `
       <p>
         Lowercase: {{ "The Quick Brown Fox Jumped Over The Lazy
         Dogs" | lowercase }}
       </p>
       <p>
   ```

```
        Uppercase: {{ "The Quick Brown Fox Jumped Over The Lazy
        Dogs" | uppercase }}
      </p>
      <p>
        Currency: {{ 2012.55 | currency }}
      </p>
      <p>
        UK Pound Currency: {{ 2012.55 | currency: 'gbp':true }}
      </p>
      <p>
        Percentage: {{ 0.5 | percent }}
      </p>
      <p>
        Date: {{ dt | date }}
      </p>
      <p>
        Short Date: {{ dt | date:shortdate }}
      </p>
      <p>
        Special Date Format: {{ dt | date:'yMMMMEEEEd' }}
      </p>
    `,
    styles: []
})
export class AppComponent {
  dt = new Date();
}
```

The app should be working and displaying the formatted data.

Custom Pipes: Example

Writing custom pipes is straightforward. However, some new syntax is introduced so there are a few things to remember:

- The component that uses a custom pipe needs to declare the `Pipe` class both as an import and specify it in the `@Component` annotation.

- The pipe class is prefixed by the `@Pipe` annotation. It also needs to import the `Pipe` and `PipeTransform`, as well as implement the `PipeTransform` interface.

You can get the Angular CLI command `ng generate pipe <pipe name>` to generate a custom pipe in a CLI-generated project. Ignore the *<pipe name>*.pipe.spec.ts file (it's for testing), but edit the *<pipe name>*.pipe.ts file:

```
ng generate pipe reverse

installing pipe
  create src/app/reverse.pipe.spec.ts
  create src/app/reverse.pipe.ts
  update src/app/app.module.ts
```

Your custom pipe should be a TypeScript class that implements the `PipeTransform` interface:

```
interface PipeTransform {
  transform(value: any, ...args: any[]): any
}
```

The component shown in Figure 20-2 allows the user to reverse some text. It also has an optional argument—the number of spaces to be put between each character of the reversed text.

> My name is eniaC leahciM
>
> My name is e n i a C l e a h c i M

Figure 20-2. *Reversing text with a pipe*

This will be example pipes-ex200:

1. *Build the app using the CLI*: Use the following command:

```
ng new pipes-ex200
```

2. *Start* ng serve: Use the following code:

```
cd pipes-ex200
ng serve
```

3. *Open app*: Open a web browser and navigate to localhost:4200. You should see "app works!"

4. *Generate pipe*: Generate the custom pipe using the CLI:

```
ng generate pipe reverse
```

5. *Edit pipe*: Edit the file reverse.pipe.ts and change it to the following:

```
import { Pipe, PipeTransform } from '@angular/core';

@Pipe({
  name: 'reverse'
})
export class ReversePipe implements PipeTransform {

  transform(value: any, args?: any): any {
    let spaces = 0;
    if (args){
      spaces = parseInt(args);
    }
    let reversed = '';
    for (let i=value.length-1;i>=0;i--){
      reversed += value.substring(i, i+1);
      reversed += Array(spaces + 1).join(' ');
    }
    return reversed;
  }
}
```

6. *Edit component*: Edit the file app.component.ts and change it to the following:

```
import { Component } from '@angular/core';
import { ReversePipe } from './reverse.pipe';
@Component({
  selector: 'app-root',
  template: `
    <p>My name is {{name | reverse}}
    <p>My name is {{name | reverse:5}}
  `,
  styles: []
})
export class AppComponent {
  name: string = 'Michael Caine';
}
```

The app should be working and displaying the formatted data. Note the following:

1. The class `ReversePipe` implements the `PipeTransform` interface as any pipe would.

2. The class `ReversePipe` adds extra spaces by using the `Array` object constructor. If you supply a single value to the constructor, it sets the array length to that value. The `join` method then specifies a string to separate each element of the array.

Summary

This short chapter showed how pipes can be useful. I use them in the following circumstances:

- When I require data to be formatted in a standard manner throughout the application—for example, currency.

- When I want to debug some instance variables, I sometimes add them to the template with a `json` pipe. This makes their current state visible at all times so I can see how they change.

We're going to step it up in the next chapter and cover more advanced subjects: zones and change detection.

CHAPTER 21

Zones and Change Detection

Angular uses a JavaScript module called Zone.js, the purpose of which is to produce an execution context that persists across asynchronous tasks. Currently, the browser DOM and JavaScript have a limited number of asynchronous activities, such as DOM events, promises, and server calls. Zone.js can intercept these activities and give your code the opportunity to take action before and after the asynchronous activity completes. This is useful when you need to see all the information pertinent to that task, especially when an error occurs.

Changes occur as a result of something, such as the following:

- *A DOM event*: Example: someone clicks on something.

- *Communication*: Example: the browser gets data back from the server.

- *A timer event happens*: Example: refresh every 10 seconds.

When dealing with Model View Controller (MVC) remember that the Model is the data, and the View displays the Data in the Model.

The purpose of change detection in Angular is to look for changes in the Model and to ensure that the View (that is, the DOM) is kept up-to-date with it. Change detection can get complicated because it needs to figure out when the View needs to be redrawn when code is running.

The following is an example of some code that changes the Model. An HTTP call is made to the server, and data is returned. A customer list is updated in the Model. So now this change needs to be detected by Angular, and the UI needs to be refreshed:

```
@Component()
class App implements OnInit{
```

© Mark Clow 2018
M. Clow, *Angular 5 Projects*, https://doi.org/10.1007/978-1-4842-3279-8_21

```
customers:Customer[] = [];
constructor(private http: Http) {}
ngOnInit() {
  this.http.get('/customers)
    .map(res => res.json())
    .subscribe(customers => this.customers = customers);
}
}
```

How does Angular know that something may have changed and that it should look for changes? Because NgZone tells it!

NgZone Is Zone.js for Angular

The NgZone class is a wrapper around the zone.js framework. The dependency injector can also pass in the zone through constructor injection.

Event Loop and Messages

JavaScript has a concurrency model based on an *event loop*. JavaScript runtime contains a message queue, which is a list of messages to be processed. Messages are taken out of the queue and processed by the browser UI thread. So, the browser basically works in a loop, picking up and processing messages to do things, as illustrated in Figure 21-1.

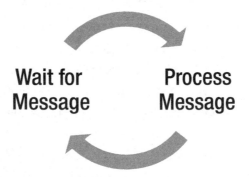

Wait for Message   **Process Message**

Figure 21-1. *Event loop*

Browser UI Thread

The browser UI thread is a single thread that updates the user interface by running the event loop code, processing messages. Each message is processed completely before the next message is processed. Only one thread is used to update the user interface (the document that the user views). If the browser UI thread is overloaded, the browser displays the message shown in Figure 21-2 (or one similar) to the user.

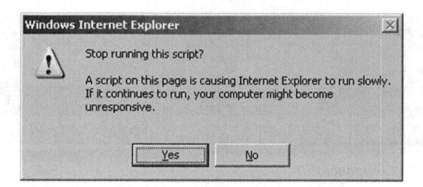

Figure 21-2. *Browser UI thread is overloaded*

Monkey Patching

With NgZone/Zones.js, system JavaScript code is "monkey patched" (when it has to be) so that it hooks into the event loop code to see what's happening with the messages being processed. This enables it to provide additional information about events occurring or code being called in the zone—for example, an asynchronous server call completing.

Note   A *monkey patch* is a way for a program to extend or modify supporting system software locally. In terms of Angular and Zone.js, Zone will monkey patch JavaScript core code when it has to in order to provide execution information.

NgZone emits onTurnStart and onTurnEnd events to inform observers of when something is about to occur and when something has occurred.

NgZone is used by Angular to look for events that require change detection. In core Angular code, Angular listens for the NgZone onTurnDone event. When this event fires, Angular performs change detection on the model and updates the UI.

Angular and Change Detection

Angular applications are built as multiple LEGO-like components, as I've put it before, with a tree-like hierarchy. You have the main Application component, and then you have subcomponents, and so forth.

Figure 21-3 illustrates the component UI, and Figure 21-4 illustrates the component tree.

Figure 21-3. *Component UI*

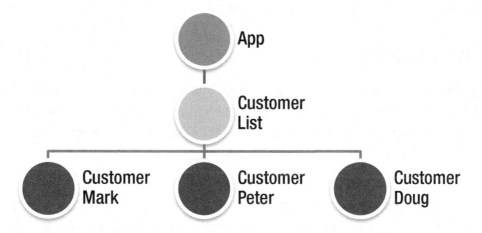

Figure 21-4. *Component tree*

Each Angular component has its own change detector for its variables. You don't see it happen, but Angular creates the change detector classes when it runs. So, if you have a tree of components, then you have a tree of change detectors. Core Angular code scans the tree for changes (calling each change detector) from the bottom up to see what's changed.

Note   *Mutable* objects can change. *Immutable* objects can't. Obviously, the change detection is quicker when it runs against objects that don't change. If you want your Angular code to run faster, start looking into using immutable objects for things that don't change.

We know that NgZone is used for Change Detection in Angular. NgZone is a class that's useful to us (as well as to the system Angular code) because it allows us to run asynchronous processes inside or outside the Angular zone.

When you run methods inside the Angular zone:

- They update the Angular UI.

- They run slower.

We run asynchronous processes inside the Angular zone when we need the change detection to occur and need to have the UI constantly updated. To run asynchronous processes inside the Angular zone, this we call the run method in the injected NGZone object, passing in the process function.

When you run methods outside the Angular zone:

- They don't update the Angular UI.

- They run faster.

We run asynchronous processes outside the Angular zone when we don't need the change detection to occur and we don't want the UI constantly updated. This may seem unnecessary, but when ultimate performance is required, this should be considered. To run asynchronous processes outside the Angular Zone, we call the runOutsideAngular method in the injected NgZone object, passing in the process method.

Running Asynchronous Code within the Angular Zone: Example

This example is based on the default Angular TypeScript Plunker application. The file app.ts is shown in Figure 21-5.

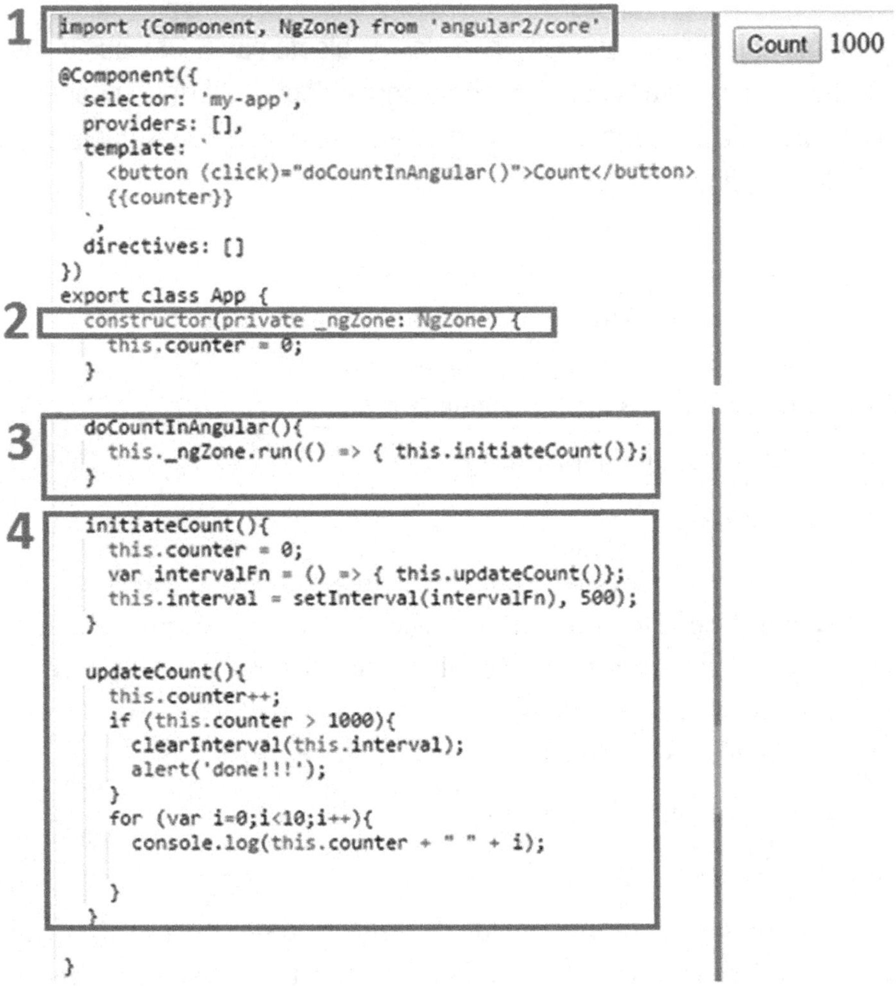

```
import {Component, NgZone} from 'angular2/core'

@Component({
  selector: 'my-app',
  providers: [],
  template: `
    <button (click)="doCountInAngular()">Count</button>
    {{counter}}
    `,
  directives: []
})
export class App {
  constructor(private _ngZone: NgZone) {
    this.counter = 0;
  }

  doCountInAngular(){
    this._ngZone.run(() => { this.initiateCount()};
  }

  initiateCount(){
    this.counter = 0;
    var intervalFn = () => { this.updateCount()};
    this.interval = setInterval(intervalFn), 500);
  }

  updateCount(){
    this.counter++;
    if (this.counter > 1000){
      clearInterval(this.interval);
      alert('done!!!');
    }
    for (var i=0;i<10;i++){
      console.log(this.counter + " " + i);
    }

  }
}

}
```

Count   1000

Figure 21-5. *Running asynchronous code within the Angular zone*

Let's go through the example:

1. Import NgZone.

2. Use constructor injection to inject an instance of NgZone.

3. This method is fired by a Count button that runs the
   initiateCount method using the injected NgZone. Notice that
   it calls the method run to run the method inside the injected
   Angular zone.

4. The methods initiateCount and updateCount produce console logs as an asynchronous task, using the interval timer. They update the counter and finish counting when the counter is over 1000.

When you run this app and click the Count button, you see the counter updating 1, 2, 3, 4 ... all the way up to 1000, and then the alert appears. The user interface shows the count. That's because the count is being performed in a function inside the Angular zone, with NgZone watching the events and causing change detection. The change detection detects that the count variable has changed and updates the UI, as shown in Figure 21-6.

Figure 21-6. count variable updates the UI

Running Asynchronous Code Outside the Angular Zone: Example

This example is also based on the default Angular TypeScript Plunker application. The file app.ts is shown in Figure 21-7.

1. Import NgZone.

2. Use constructor injection to inject an instance of NgZone.

3. This method is fired by Count button. It runs the initiateCount method using the injected NgZone. Notice that it calls the method runOutsideAngular to run the method outside the injected Angular zone.

4. The methods initiateCount and updateCount produce console logs as an asynchronous task, using the interval timer. They update the counter and finish counting when the counter is over 1000.

```
import {Component, NgZone} from 'angular2/core'

@Component({
  selector: 'my-app',
  providers: [],
  template: `
    <button (click)="doCountOutsideAngular()">Count</button>
    {{counter}}
    `,
  directives: []
})
export class App {
  constructor(private _ngZone: NgZone) {
    this.counter = 0;
  }

  doCountOutsideAngular(){
 //   this._ngZone.run(() => { this.initiateCount()};
    this._ngZone.runOutsideAngular(() => { this.initiateCount()};
  }

  initiateCount(){
    this.counter = 0;
    var intervalFn = () => { this.updateCount()};
    this.interval = setInterval(intervalFn), 500);
  }

  updateCount(){
    this.counter++;
    if (this.counter > 1000){
      clearInterval(this.interval);
      alert('done!!!');
    }
    for (var i=0;i<10;i++){
      console.log(this.counter + " " + i);
    }
  }
}
```

Count | 0

Figure 21-7. *Running asynchronous code outside the Angular zone*

When you run this application and click Count, you don't see the counter change. The user interface shows the count as 0 until the alert appears, as shown in Figure 21-8. That's because the count is being performed in a function outside the Angular zone, without NgZone watching the events and causing change detection. Notice how it's a bit faster?

Figure 21-8. count *variable not updated until alert*

Summary

This chapter attempted to introduce some of the internal workings of Angular. It's not intended to cover every detail of this subject—that would require many chapters.

This chapter (briefly) introduced the concept of immutability, something you need to know about, especially if you are going to do Functional Programming in the future. *Immutability* is the concept of objects that can't be modified once created. As a developer, you need to consider using immutable objects whenever possible because they have many benefits:

- They simplify coding (because there are fewer moving parts), and you know that objects don't change values.

- They work much better with the Angular change detection algorithm.

- When you restrict as much as possible the number of ways objects can be changed in your application, you make your code simpler and keep more control over what things are being changed.

- They minimize the side effects that sometimes occur when objects are mutated.

- They work much better with multi-threading.

The next chapter will introduce testing your Angular code.

CHAPTER 22

Testing

This book is mainly about how to get started being productive with Angular, but it would be incomplete without at least introducing ways to test the code that you write. The testing framework is quite complicated, so don't expect to know everything about it after reading this chapter.

I'll introduce some of the concepts and then go into the details of writing code to automate the testing of a project that was generated with the Angular CLI.

Unit testing is the testing of the smallest possible units of the application, either in a manual or automated form. The point of unit testing is to ensure that the code is performing as expected and that new code doesn't break old code. The process of test-driven development is the development of code in the following order:

1. Writing the test code (the test harness)

2. Writing application code to pass the tests

3. Cleaning up and refactoring application code to pass coding standards

4. Check that it still passes the tests

This process should be applied to smaller units of code, and this process should be repeated frequently. Unit tests are essential in the modern process of software development.

Software development uses the process of developers checking out the latest code from a central repository and working on it. After work is completed (and the code is tested), the developers check in the completed code. *Continual integration* is the process of integrating (or merging) all developer code into a shared codebase several times a day. Integrating code as often as possible highlights merging issues quickly and avoids larger code incompatibilities. The aim is to check out code for as short as time as possible and check in and integrate the changes as soon as possible before someone changes things too much in the meantime.

© Mark Clow 2018

M. Clow, *Angular 5 Projects*, https://doi.org/10.1007/978-1-4842-3279-8_22

Figure 22-1 shows a (very general) diagram of the development process working. It doesn't take into account code branches, merging issues, and other factors.

Figure 22-1. *The development process*

Automating the unit tests takes some up-front work but in the long run saves people time. Automated tests can find problems very quickly and they should be used at least in the following two situations:

- When a user is about to check in code changes, they should invoke the automated unit tests on their local machine to ensure that the code is working as expected.

- The build server should invoke the automated unit tests whenever a developer checks in code changes. The build server should also track the results of these tests and let people know whether they passed or failed.

Integration testing occurs after unit testing has occurred. It tests the combined code, simulating a user running the complete application. This is a higher level of testing—testing areas of the system without knowing anything about its structure or implementation. Integration testing ensures that the application works as expected for the user and that the component parts of the application work together.

Your Angular application is made up of components that have dependencies. You need to develop your unit tests so that they test units of code in isolation. For example, if you want to test a component that uses a service to get data from a server, you probably need to test the component and service separately. You'll probably need to do the following:

- Write code to test the component, injecting it with a mock (dummy) version of the service that acts in a predetermined manner. The *mock* service simulates an output from the service. That way you can test that the component processes the output from the service as expected.

- Write code to test the service, injecting it with a mock version of the communication layer (the back end) that talks to the server (for example, the Http service). The mock communication layer simulates connections, and these mock connections have the ability to simulate a response from the server. That way, you don't need a real server, and you can test that the component processes the output from the server as expected.

One thing that complicates testing is that a lot of the code we're testing is *asynchronous*, meaning it doesn't block and wait until the code completes. The testing library (and your testing code) has code to deal with asynchronous operations, and this complicates things even further. Sometimes the code has to be run in a special asynchronous zone to simulate these operations.

Karma

Karma is an automated test runner that was developed by the Angular team during the development of AngularJS. Karma can run unit tests fast and on real browsers.

You use Karma to start a server on which a group of Jasmine tests are run. Karma opens a web browser and automates it to perform tests, and you can see it running the tests in that browser. Sometimes it even leaves the browser open after the tests.

When you build your CLI project, it creates the file karma.conf.js to allow you to configure Karma for the project. Configuration options include the base path, which test files to include/exclude, autowatch files, which browsers to test on, colors, timeouts, testing framework (for example, Jasmine, covered in the next section), server hostname, and port (for example, localhost:8080), logging, plugins, preprocessors, reporters, single run, and so on.

Tip   The single run configuration is useful if you want to leave your browser open after tests finish. This is sometimes useful if there's a failure and you need to see what went on by looking at the browser's developer tools.

Jasmine

Jasmine is an open source, automated, unit testing JavaScript framework that's very commonly used with Angular and other JavaScript libraries.

When you write Jasmine tests, you have to follow the Jasime way of doing things. You write sets of described tests in .spec.ts files (one or more per file), and each described set of tests contains multiple tests. Each test does something with the code it tests, gets a result, and then checks the result for validity. Figure 22-2 illustrates the Jasmine structure.

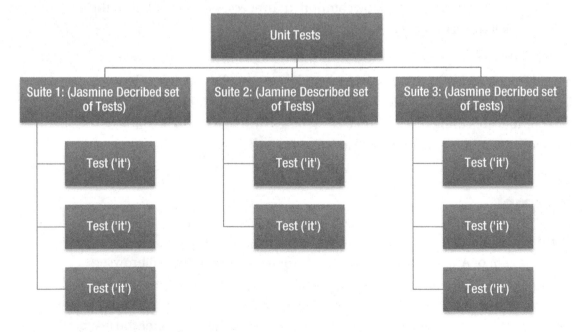

Figure 22-2. *Jasmine structure*

Jasmine unit tests have a two-level structure:

- A *"described" suite of tests*: Developers use the `describe` function to set up a suite of tests that are executed together. For example, connectivity tests. Notice that the `describe` method is also used to provide the dependencies for the object to be tested. Variables declared in a `describe` are available to any `it` block of code inside the suite.

- `it` *blocks of code that perform tests inside the "described" suite of tests*: Developers use the `it` function to set up a test where code is performed and a comparison occurs between the expected and actual results. Developers use the `expect` method inside a test to set result expectations. If they're met, the code passes the test—if not, it fails. Jasmine uses "matchers" to compare expected and actual results—for example, `expect(a).toEqual(12)`:

```
describe("[The class you are about to test]", () => {
    beforeEachProviders(() => {
      return [Array of dependencies];
    });
    it("test1", injectAsync([TestComponentBuilder],
    (tcb: TestComponentBuilder) => {
      return tcb.createAsync([The class you are about to test]).
      then((fixture) => {

            // test code ...
        // expect a result
      });
    }));

    it("test2", injectAsync([TestComponentBuilder], (tcb:
    TestComponentBuilder) => {
      return tcb.createAsync([The class you are about to test]).
      then((fixture) => {
```

```
                    // test code ...
               // expect a result
          });
       }));

     });
```

Jasmine Concepts

Table 22-1. *Jasmine Concepts*

Name	Description	Code Keyword
Suite	Described set of tests that corresponds to an area of code that needs testing. There is usually one suite of tests per unit test file, such as app.component.suite.ts. However, you can have more than one described set of tests in a unit test file.	describe
Spec	A test that performs code and checks the result against expectations. There can be multiple specs in a suite.	it
Expectations	Used within a test to check the result.	expect
Matchers	Used by an expectation to specify the expectation as a rule.	toBe, toEqual, toBeNull, toContain, toThrow, toThrowError, and so on

Table 22 are the Jasmine concepts you need to learn and the code keyword associated with each concept. Take a look at the code for a basic Jasmine test (underneath the table) and see how it corresponds to the concepts in the table.

```
describe("CalcUtils", function() {                        // suite
//Spec for sum operation
    it("2 plus 2 equals 4", function() {                  // spec
      var calc = new CalcUtils();
      expect(calc.sum(2,2))                               // expect
            .toEqual(4);                                   // matcher
    });
```

```
    //Spec for sum operation with decimal
    it("2.5 plus 2 equals 4.5", function() {                    // spec
        var calc = new CalcUtils();
        expect(calc.sum(2.5,2))                                 // expect
                .toEqual(4.5);                                  // matcher
    });
});
```

Jasmine Setup and Teardown

You have a suite of tests (described) which contains one or more tests (specs). Quite often the specs will be quite similar and will be testing the same object again and again. This can cause repetitive code because in every spec you would be instantiating the object to test, testing it, and then destroying it. You can see this in the code that follows Table 22-1.

Jasmine offers a solution to this: the setup and teardown methods. These functions are invoked immediately before and immediately after each test (spec) is run. This enables you to set up all your tests and clean up all of your tests with as little code as possible.

Take a look at how the setup cleans up the code we just looked at:

```
describe("CalcUtils", function() {                              // suite
    var calc;

    //This will be called before running each spec
    beforeEach(function() {                                     // setup
        var calc = new CalcUtils();
    });

    describe("calculation tests", function(){                   // suite

        //Spec for sum operation
        it("2 plus 2 equals 4", function() {                    // spec
            expect(calc.sum(2,2))                               // expect
                    .toEqual(4);                                // matcher
        });
```

```
        //Spec for sum operation with decimal
        it("2 plus 2 equals 4", function() {           // spec
            expect(calc.sum(2.5,2))                     // expect
                    .toEqual(4.5);                      // matcher
        });

    });
});
```

CLI

When we use the Angular CLI to generate our Angular project, it automatically (by default) generates unit test code for you that works with Karma and Jasmine. For example, when you generate the Angular project it generates an application component called app.component.ts and a unit test file called app.component.spec.ts. This unit test file already has methods stubbed out to unit test your component.

Running Unit Tests

When you issue the following command, Angular performs a compile of the project (the one in the current working directory) then invokes Karma to run all the unit tests:

```
ng test
```

This command includes a file watcher. If you change one of the project files, it will automatically rebuild the project and rerun the tests.

Unit Test Files

When you use the Angular CLI to generate an Angular project, the project generates unit test files that use Karma and Jasmine. These unit tests files

- Typically end with .spec.ts.

- Follow the Jasmine format, having a describe block that contains a block of it tests.

- Can be modified, allowing you to add more tests.

- Can be written from scratch, and Karma will pick up and run them for you.

- Use many of the Angular testing objects in the Angular @angular/core/testing module.

Dependency Injection

Each described suite of tests is kind of like a "mini module" because it runs code that has dependencies and therefore needs to set them up like a module does (an Angular @NgModule).

Angular Testing Objects

Angular provides a module @angular/core/testing that contains helper objects to make it easier to write unit tests:

```
import { TestBed, async } from '@angular/core/testing';
```

Table 22-2 lists the objects you're most likely to use in the testing module.

Table 22-2. *Angular Testing Objects*

Name	Type	Description
TestBed	Class	Enables the developer to create an enclosure in which the code to be tested can run and provides the following: • Instantiation of component within enclosure • Methods to control dependency injection for component • Methods to query the component's DOM elements • Methods to invoke Angular change detection • Method to compile the components being tested
async	Function	It takes a parameter-less function and *returns a function* that becomes the true argument to the beforeEach. It lest you perform the initialization code in the beforeEach (the spec setup) asynchronously.

ComponentFixture

The TestBed method createComponent enables you to create the component inside a testing enclosure and returns you an instance of a ComponentFixture object. One of the reasons that the component fixture is very useful is that it provides access to the component being debugged.

The debugElement property of ComponentFixture represents the Angular component and its corresponding DOM elements. It contains the following properties shown in Table 22-3.

Table 22-3. *debugElement Properties*

Property	Description
componentInstance	A reference to your component class, useful if you want to access instance variables and methods within your component
nativeElement	A reference to your component class's corresponding html element in the DOM, useful if you want to access the DOM to see how your component is being rendered by the template

ComponentInstance

Within the debugElement property of the fixture, the user can access the Angular component via the componentInstance property. Once you access the debugElement you can call your methods in your component to test it.

NativeElement

Also within the debugElement, the user can access the DOM element via the nativeElement property. nativeElement gives us the root element of the HTML generated by the Angular component. This root element is represented by an HTMLElement object, which is a fully fledged object with many properties and methods.

The HTMLElement object is not Angular-specific, but it's a very commonly used object in web development. Refer to https://developer.mozilla.org/en-US/docs/Web/API/HTMLElement for more information.

When you get the nativeElement for the debugElement, this returns the HTMLElement object for your component, not the entire DOM!

Sometimes developers make the mistake of expecting this element to contain HTML elements that are outside the scope of your component. They won't be available!

Some of the more useful methods and properties of the HTMLElement are listed in Table 22-4.

Table 22-4. *HTMLElement Methods and Properties*

Name	Description
innerText (property)	Useful for returning the text inside the element. Remember that this element may include unexpected whitespace.
innerHTML (property)	Returns the HTML syntax of the markup inside the element belonging to the component.
outerHTML (property)	Returns the HTML syntax of the markup inside the element, including its descendants.
querySelector (method)	Returns the first element that's a descendent of the element on which it's invoked that matches the specified group of selectors. Useful for finding an element inside the element belonging to the component. For example, the following code expects that the button with CSS class button-primary button is defined: `expect(element.querySelector("button.button-primary")). toBeDefined();`
querySelectorAll (method)	Returns a NodeList of all elements descended from the element on which it's invoked that match the specified group of CSS selectors. Useful for finding sub-elements inside the element belonging to the component. For example, this code gets a list of text-area elements in the element: `let textAreas = element.querySelectorAll("text-area");`
getAttribute ([name]) (method)	Returns an attribute (identified by name) for the element—for example, disabled. The following code expects that the approveButton is disabled: `expect(approveButton.getAttribute("disabled")) .toBeDefined();`

CLI Unit Test: Examples

This first example won't be exciting but it will show the generation of an example CLI project and examine the generated test code. This will be example testing-ex100:

1. *Build the app using the CLI*: Use the following command:

   ```
   ng new testing-ex100 --inline-template --inline-style
   ```

2. *Navigate to folder*: Use the following command:

   ```
   cd testing-ex100
   ```

3. *Open file*: Open app.component.spec.ts and note the following:

   - The `beforeEach` method is invoked before each spec. This method configures the testing module to test the AppComponent component.

   - There are three specs (tests). Each one is invoked asynchronously using the `async` method in the testing module.

   - The first spec creates a fixture and then gets the component instance from the `debug` element. It checks that the component is *truthy* (that is, has an assigned value).

   - The second spec creates a fixture and then gets the component instance from the `debug` element. It checks that the component's `title` instance variable has the value 'app'.

   - The third spec (test) creates a fixture then gets the component's element from the debug element. It checks that this element has an 'h1' element that contains the value "welcome to app!"

4. *Run tests*: Use the following command:

   ```
   ng test
   ```

Now let's create a simple component (Figure 22-3) that allows you to increment a counter. Then we'll write a unit test for it.

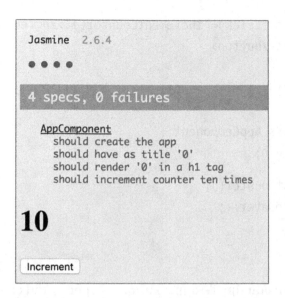

Figure 22-3. *Incrementing a counter*

This will be example testing-ex200:

1. *Build the app using the CLI*: Use the following command:

   ng new testing-ex200 --inline-template --inline-style

2. *Start* ng serve: Use the following code:

   cd testing-ex200
   ng serve

3. *Open app*: Open a web browser and navigate to localhost:4200.
   You should see "welcome to app!"

4. *Edit class*: Edit the file app.component.ts and change it to the
   following:

```
import { Component } from '@angular/core';

@Component({
  selector: 'app-root',
  template: `
    <h1>
      {{counter}}
    </h1>
```

```
    <button (click)="incrementCounter()">Increment
    Counter</button>
    `,
    styles: []
})
export class AppComponent {
  counter = 0;

  incrementCounter(){
    this.counter++;
  }
}
```

5. *Edit unit test*: Edit the file app.component.spec.ts and change it to
   the following:

```
import { TestBed, async } from '@angular/core/testing';
import { AppComponent } from './app.component';

describe('AppComponent', () => {
  beforeEach(async(() => {
    TestBed.configureTestingModule({
      declarations: [
        AppComponent
      ],
    }).compileComponents();
  }));

  it('should create the app', async(() => {
    const fixture = TestBed.createComponent(AppComponent);
    const app = fixture.debugElement.componentInstance;
    expect(app).toBeTruthy();
  }));

  it(`should have as title '0'`, async(() => {
    const fixture = TestBed.createComponent(AppComponent);
    const app = fixture.debugElement.componentInstance;
    expect(app.counter).toEqual(0);
  }));
```

```
  it(`should render '0' in a h1 tag`, async(() => {
    const fixture = TestBed.createComponent(AppComponent);
    fixture.detectChanges();
    const compiled = fixture.debugElement.nativeElement;
    expect(compiled.querySelector('h1').textContent).toContain('0');
  }));

  it('should increment counter ten times', async(() => {
    const fixture = TestBed.createComponent(AppComponent);
    fixture.detectChanges();
    const compiled = fixture.debugElement.nativeElement;
    for (let i=0;i<10;i++){
      compiled.querySelector('button').click();
      fixture.detectChanges();
      const nbrStr = (i + 1) + '';
      expect(compiled.querySelector('h1').textContent).toContain(nbrStr);
    }
  }));

});
```

6. *Run tests*: Use the following command:

```
ng test
```

Note that there was an additional test added at the end that clicks the Increment button ten times. Note also that the additional test doesn't work until the `fixture.detectChanges` method is called to perform change detection once the button is clicked.

Testing with Fake Http Responses
Introduction

In the real world, our Angular apps have to talk all the time to servers using HTTP. When we write unit tests, we cannot assume that there is an API endpoint available for us to test against. All the servers may be down. There may be no spare servers. What we need to do is to go without real servers and mock (fake) the HTTP communication between the our Angular app and the server. In this manner we can write tests to see how our App deals with a variety of responses from the HTTP server.

Luckily for us, the Google engineers behind Angular have made our life much easier, especially now we have Angular 5 and the HttpClient module, which resides in the @ angular/common/http namespace. This new HttpClient module has its own new testing module called HttpClientTestingModule, which resides in the @angular/common/http/ testing namespace and can be used to create fake http responses for your unit tests.

How to Use HttpClientTestingModule to Create Fake Http Responses

1.   Import HttpClientTestingModule into your unit test.

2.   Inject HttpClient and HttpClientTestingModule into your tests.

3.   Setup a test request object by calling one of the methods below to tell HttpClientTestingModule how many http requests it should expect to receive in the test (see below). The HttpClientTestingModule will assert that the number of requests it receives matches what it expects.

# of Requests	HttpClientTestingModule method
Unsure	match
0	expectNone
1	expectOne

4.   You call the 'flush' method on the test request object to send back the mock result.

Testing Service that Uses HttpClient: Example

For the third example, we'll create a simple component that uses a service to enable you to search for trails using an http service (Figure 22-4). Then we'll write a unit test for the service and test how it processes server responses.

1. A unit test for the component using the service and test how it processes server responses also.

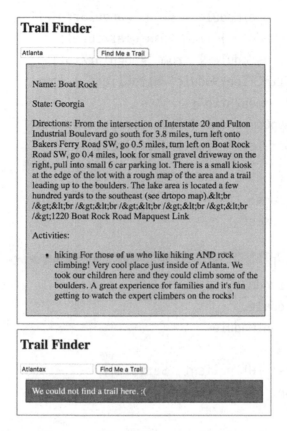

Figure 22-4. *Component to search for trails*

This will be example testing-ex300:

1. *Build the app using the CLI*: Use the following code:

   ```
   ng new testing-ex300 --inline-template --inline-style
   ```

2. *Start* ng serve: Use the following code:

   ```
   cd testing-ex300
   ng serve
   ```

3. *Open app*: Open a web browser and navigate to localhost:4200. You should see "welcome to app!"

4. *Edit module:* Edit the file app.module.ts and change it to the following:

```
import { BrowserModule } from '@angular/platform-browser';
import { NgModule } from '@angular/core';
import { FormsModule } from '@angular/forms';
import { HttpClientModule, HttpClient } from
'@angular/common/http';
import { AppComponent } from './app.component';
import { Service } from './service';

@NgModule({
  declarations: [
    AppComponent
  ],
  imports: [
    BrowserModule,
    FormsModule,
    HttpClientModule
  ],
  providers: [HttpClient, Service],
  bootstrap: [AppComponent]
})
export class AppModule { }
```

5. *Edit class*: Edit the file app.component.ts and change it to the following:

```
import { Component } from '@angular/core';
import { Service } from './service';
import { FormsModule } from '@angular/forms';

@Component({
  selector: 'app-root',
  template: `
    <h2>Trail Finder</h2>
    <input [(ngModel)]="_search" placeholder="city">
    <button (click)="doSearch()">Find Me a Trail</button>
```

```
    <div id="notFound" class="notFound" *ngIf="_searched &&
    !_result">
      We could not find a trail here. :(
    </div>
    <div class="found" *ngIf="_searched && _result">
    <p id="name">Name: {{_result?.name}}</p>
    <p id="state">State: {{_result?.state}}</p>
    <p id="directions">Directions: {{_result?.directions}}</p>
    <p>Activities:</p>
    <ul id="activities" *ngIf="_result?.activities">
      <li *ngFor="let activity of _result.activities">
        {{activity.activity_type_name}} {{activity.description}}
      </li>
    </ul>
  `,
  styles: [`.found {
    border: 1px solid black;
    background-color: #8be591;
    color: black;
    margin: 10px;
    padding: 10px;
  }`,
  `.notFound {
    border: 1px solid black;
    background-color: #d13449;
    color: white;
    margin: 10px;
    padding: 10px;
  }`]
})
export class AppComponent {
  _search = 'Atlanta';
  _searched = false;
  _result = '';

  constructor(private _service: Service) {
  }
```

```
      doSearch() {
        this._service.search(this._search).subscribe(
          res => {
            this._result = res;
          },
          err => {
            console.log(err);
          },
          () => {
            this._searched = true;
          }
        );
      }
    }
```

6. *Add service class*: Create the file service.ts and change it to the
   following:

```
import { Injectable } from '@angular/core';
import { HttpClient, HttpHeaders } from '@angular/common/http';
import 'rxjs/Rx';

@Injectable()
export class Service {
constructor(private _http: HttpClient){}
search(search) {
  const concatenatedUrl: string =
    "https://trailapi-trailapi.p.mashape.com?q[city_cont]=" +
    encodeURIComponent(search);
  const mashapeKey = 'OxWYjpdztcmsheZU9AWLNQcE9g9wp1qd
  RkFjsneaEp2Yf68nYH';
  const httpHeaders: HttpHeaders = new HttpHeaders(
    {'Content-Type': 'application/json',
     'X-Mashape-Key': mashapeKey});
  return this._http
    .get<any>(concatenatedUrl, { headers: httpHeaders })
    .map(res => {
```

```
      // return the first place.
      if ((res) && (res['places']) && (res['places'].length) &&
      (res['places'].length > 0)){
        return res['places'][0];
      }else{
        // otherwise return nothing
        return undefined;
      }
    })
    .catch(err => {
      console.log('error',err)
      return undefined;
    });
  }
}
```

7. *The app should now function*: Go back to your web browser and navigate to localhost:4200. You should be able to search for trails.

8. *Add service unit test*: Create the file service.spec.ts and change it to the following:

```
import { TestBed, getTestBed, async } from '@angular/core/
testing';
import { HttpClientTestingModule, HttpTestingController } from
'@angular/common/http/testing';
import { FormsModule } from '@angular/forms';
import { AppComponent } from './app.component';
import { Service } from './service';
import { HttpClientModule } from '@angular/common/http/src/
module';
import 'rxjs/Rx';

describe('AppComponent (data found)', () => {
  let service: Service;
  let httpMock: HttpTestingController;

  beforeEach(() => {
```

```
    TestBed.configureTestingModule({
      imports: [HttpClientTestingModule],
      providers: [Service]
    });

    service = TestBed.get(Service);
    httpMock = TestBed.get(HttpTestingController);

  });

  it('should return the first place if there is one', async() => {
    service.search("Atlanta").subscribe((res: any) => {
      expect(res.name).toContain('Boat Rock');
      expect(res.city).toBe('Atlanta');
      expect(res.state).toBe('Georgia');
      expect(res.country).toBe('United States');
      expect(res.directions).toContain('Interstate 20 and Fulton
      Industrial');
      expect(res.activities.length).toBe(1);
      });
    const req = httpMock.expectOne('https://trailapi-trailapi.p.
    mashape.com?q[city_cont]=Atlanta');
    const mockData =
    {
      "places":[
          {
            "city":"Atlanta",
            "state":"Georgia",
            "country":"United States",
            "name":"Boat Rock",
            "parent_id":null,
            "unique_id":5370,
            "directions":"From the intersection of Interstate
            20 and Fulton Industrial Boulevard go south for 3.8
            miles, turn left onto Bakers Ferry Road SW, go 0.5
            miles, turn left on Boat Rock Road SW, go 0.4 miles,
            look for small gravel driveway on the right, pull
```

into small 6 car parking lot. There is a small kiosk
at the edge of the lot with a rough map of the area
and a trail leading up to the boulders. The lake area
is located a few hundred yards to the southeast (see
drtopo map).

1220
Boat Rock Road Mapquest Link ",
"lat":0.0,
"lon":0.0,
"description":null,
"date_created":null,
"children":[
],
"activities":[
    {
      "name":"Boat Rock",
      "unique_id":"2-1012",
      "place_id":5370,
      "activity_type_id":2,
      "activity_type_name":"hiking",
      "url":"http://www.tripleblaze.com/trail.
       php?c=3&i=1012",
      "attribs":{
          "\"length\"":"\"1\""
      },
      "description":"For those of us who like hiking
      AND rock climbing! Very cool place just inside
      of Atlanta. We took our children here and they
      could climb some of the boulders. A great
      experience for families and it's fun getting to
      watch the expert climbers on the rocks!",
      "length":1.0,
      "activity_type":{
          "created_at":"2012-08-15T16:12:21Z",
          "id":2,
          "name":"hiking",

```
                        "updated_at":"2012-08-15T16:12:21Z"
                },
                "thumbnail":"http://images.tripleblaze.
                com/2009/07/Myspace-Pictures-130-0.jpg",
                "rank":null,
                "rating":0.0
            }
        ]
      }
    ]
  }
  req.flush(mockData); // valid response from server
  httpMock.verify();
});

it('should return undefined if there is empty response from the
server', async() => {
  service.search("Atlanta").subscribe((res: any) => {
      expect(res).toBe(undefined);
      });
  const req = httpMock.expectOne('https://trailapi-
  trailapi.p.mashape.com?q[city_cont]=Atlanta');
  req.flush(''); // empty response from server
  httpMock.verify();
});

it('should return undefined if there is empty response object
from the server', async() => {
  service.search("Atlanta").subscribe((res: any) => {
      expect(res).toBe(undefined);
      });
  const req = httpMock.expectOne('https://trailapi-
  trailapi.p.mashape.com?q[city_cont]=Atlanta');
  req.flush('{}'); // empty response object from server
  httpMock.verify();
});
});
```

9. *Run tests*: Use the following command:

```
ng test
```

Note the following:

- In the 'beforeEach' (fired before each 'it' test) we:

  - Configure our test bed to import HttpClientTestingModule, rather than HttpClient. This will enable us to mock Http responses.

  - We get a reference to the service.

  - We get a reference to the http testing controller.

- In each test, we set expectations on the subscription to the observable response from the service so that it can test the data coming back:

```
service.search("Atlanta").subscribe((res: any) => {
  expect(res).toBe(undefined);
});
```

- In each test, we call the method 'expectOne' in the http testing controller to tell it to expect one http request and what its URI should be:

```
const req = httpMock.expectOne('https://trailapi-
trailapi.p.mashape.com?q[city_cont]=Atlanta');
```

- The 'expectOne' method returns a TestRequest object back. On the next line, we tell the TestRequest to 'flush' back a response (in this case an empty one):

```
req.flush('');
```

- After using the 'flush' method to send back a mock response, we call the 'verify' method to ensure no Http requests are outstanding:

```
httpMock.verify();
```

Testing Component that Uses Service: Example

For the fourth example, we'll build upon the previous example. We will add the unit test for the component that uses the service to enable you to search for trails (Figure 22-4).

1. *Add component test class*: Create the file app.component.spec.ts and change it to the following:

```
import { TestBed, getTestBed, async } from '@angular/core/testing';
import { HttpClientTestingModule, HttpTestingController } from
'@angular/common/http/testing';
import { FormsModule } from '@angular/forms';
import { AppComponent } from './app.component';
import { Service } from './service';
import { HttpClient, HttpClientModule } from '@angular/common/http';
import 'rxjs/Rx';

describe('AppComponent (data found)', () => {
  let service: Service;
  let httpMock: HttpTestingController;
  let fixture, app, compiled;

  beforeEach(() => {

    TestBed.configureTestingModule({
      declarations: [AppComponent],
      imports: [FormsModule, HttpClientTestingModule],
      providers: [HttpClient, Service]
    }).compileComponents();

    service = TestBed.get(Service);
    httpMock = TestBed.get(HttpTestingController);

    fixture = TestBed.createComponent(AppComponent);
    app = fixture.debugElement.componentInstance;
    expect(app).toBeTruthy();
    fixture.detectChanges();
```

```
    compiled = fixture.debugElement.nativeElement;
    compiled.querySelector('button').click();

});

it('should display the first place if there is one', async() => {

    const req = httpMock.expectOne('https://trailapi-trailapi.
    p.mashape.com?q[city_cont]=Atlanta');
    const mockData =
    {
      "places":[
          {
            "city":"Atlanta",
            "state":"Georgia",
            "country":"United States",
            "name":"Boat Rock",
            "parent_id":null,
            "unique_id":5370,
            "directions":"From the intersection of Interstate 20 and
            Fulton Industrial Boulevard go south for 3.8 miles, turn
            left onto Bakers Ferry Road SW, go 0.5 miles, turn left
            on Boat Rock Road SW, go 0.4 miles, look for small gravel
            driveway on the right, pull into small 6 car parking
            lot. There is a small kiosk at the edge of the lot with
            a rough map of the area and a trail leading up to the
            boulders. The lake area is located a few hundred yards
            to the southeast (see drtopo map).<br /><br /><br /><br
            /><br /><br />1220 Boat Rock Road Mapquest Link ",
            "lat":0.0,
            "lon":0.0,
            "description":null,
            "date_created":null,
            "children":[
            ],
            "activities":[
                {
```

```
                        "name":"Boat Rock",
                        "unique_id":"2-1012",
                        "place_id":5370,
                        "activity_type_id":2,
                        "activity_type_name":"hiking",
                        "url":"http://www.tripleblaze.com/trail.
                        php?c=3&i=1012",
                        "attribs":{
                            "\"length\"":"\"1\""
                        },
                        "description":"For those of us who like hiking
                        AND rock climbing! Very cool place just inside of
                        Atlanta. We took our children here and they could
                        climb some of the boulders. A great experience for
                        families and it's fun getting to watch the expert
                        climbers on the rocks!",
                    "length":1.0,
                        "activity_type":{
                            "created_at":"2012-08-15T16:12:21Z",
                            "id":2,
                            "name":"hiking",
                            "updated_at":"2012-08-15T16:12:21Z"
                        },
                        "thumbnail":"http://images.tripleblaze.
                        com/2009/07/Myspace-Pictures-130-0.jpg",
                        "rank":null,
                        "rating":0.0
                    }
                ]
            }
        ]
    }
    req.flush(mockData);
    httpMock.verify();

    fixture.detectChanges();
```

```
    expect(compiled.querySelector('#notFound')).toBeNull();
    expect(compiled.querySelector('#name').textContent).
        toContain('Boat Rock');
    expect(compiled.querySelector('#state').textContent).
        toContain('Georgia');
});

it('should display a not found message if there is empty
response from the server', async() => {
    const req = httpMock.expectOne('https://trailapi-
    trailapi.p.mashape.com?q
    [city_cont]=Atlanta');
    req.flush('');
    httpMock.verify();

    fixture.detectChanges();

    expect(compiled.querySelector('#notFound').textContent).
        toContain('We could not find a trail here. :(');
    expect(compiled.querySelector('#name')).toBeNull();
    expect(compiled.querySelector('#state')).toBeNull();
});

it('should display a not found message undefined if there is
empty response object from the server', async() => {
    const req = httpMock.expectOne('https://trailapi-
    trailapi.p.mashape.com?q[city_cont]=Atlanta');
    req.flush('{}');
    httpMock.verify();

    fixture.detectChanges();

    expect(compiled.querySelector('#notFound').textContent).
        toContain('We could not find a trail here. :(');
    expect(compiled.querySelector('#name')).toBeNull();
    expect(compiled.querySelector('#state')).toBeNull();
    });
});
```

2. *Run tests*: Use the following command:

```
ng test
```

Note the following:

- In the 'beforeEach' (fired before each 'it' test) we:

  - Configure our test bed to import the FormsModule (needed by the Component to handle input) and HttpClientTestingModule. The HttpClientTestingModule will enable us to mock Http responses. We also setup the HttpClient and Service as providers. Note that we call 'compileComponents' to ensure that any components are compiled and readied.

  - We get a reference to the service.

  - We get a reference to the http testing controller.

  - We create an instance of the AppComponent in the test bed.

  - We detect changes to allow Angular to perform any change detection it requires at this point.

  - We get a reference to the DOM element for the component.

  - We get a reference to the button inside the DOM element and we click it. This simulates the user clicking the 'search' button.

- In each test we:

  - Setup different responses to the same search in a similar manner to the previous example.

  - We detect changes to allow Angular to perform any change detection it requires at this point. Angular needs to redraw the ui to reflect any changes in the model due to the response. Do not leave this line out!

  - We check that the DOM elements correspond to the expected result.

Summary

You could write whole books about testing software—in fact, nany people have. It's a complicated subject.

Obviously it's better to write more tests, and testing is a good thing. For example, unit tests are great if you have to refactor (or design) your code. If the code you refactor is well covered with unit tests and you change your code and it still passes the tests, this gives you more confidence in the correctness of your refactoring.

Writing testing code can be difficult and complicated and can take a great deal of time, so I suggest you think about focusing your testing on the most important parts of your code: where your code performs calculations, where it applies the business rules, and so on. You need to write the essential tests that focus on the most important parts of your code. After that, you can prioritize the testing of the rest of the application and adjust the amount of time spent writing tests according to the amount of time available.

The next chapter covers view encapsulation and other advanced topics.

CHAPTER 23

More Advanced Topics

This chapter throws together introductions to several more advanced Angular topics.

View Encapsulation

Remember how you can apply styles to a component using the `styles` or `styleUrls` properties of the `@Component` annotation? The meaning of the word *encapsulation* is "the action of enclosing something in or as if in a capsule."

Angular view encapsulation has to do with which method Angular uses to enclose these styles (the ones you applied the `styles` or `styleUrls` properties to) with the component.

Why is view encapsulation required? When you use the `styles` or `styleUrls` properties to style a component, Angular adds styling code into a `style` tag in the head part of the HTML document. That's fine, but you need to watch out for a few things. What happens if you have conflicting CSS style rules in different components? What if (for example) you have `.h2 {color:red}` in one component and `.h2 {color:green}` in another component?

If your components are using a Shadow DOM (or Emulated Shadow DOM) you don't need to worry about these conflicting styles. You're probably using a Shadow DOM (or at least an Emulated Shadow DOM) because that's what Angular 4 gives you by default.

However, you need to know about Shadow DOMs because if your components aren't using a Shadow DOM (or Emulated Shadow DOM), then these conflicting styles could cause you headaches.

Shadow DOMs

Scope has been a problem for some time on the browser. Developers have been able to make sweeping global changes to HTML documents easily, with little work. They can add a few lines of CSS and impact many DOM elements immediately. That's powerful but can leave your component's style easy to override or break accidentally.

© Mark Clow 2018
M. Clow, *Angular 5 Projects*, https://doi.org/10.1007/978-1-4842-3279-8_23

Shadow DOM is a new emerging standard on the web. Shadow DOMs work on most browsers (except for Internet Explorer). The idea behind Shadow DOM is to give developers the option of creating components with their own separate DOM trees, encapsulated away from the other components, contained within host elements. This lets developers have styles "scoped" to just that single component that can't affect the rest of the document.

When you write a component, you don't have to use a Shadow DOM, but it's an option that gives you control using the `encapsulation` option of the `@Component` annotation.

Component Encapsulation

The `encapsulation` option of the `@Component` annotation gives the developer control over the level of view encapsulation—in other words, to implement a Shadow DOM or not. Table 23-1 shows three variations of the option.

Table 23-1. *Encapsulation Option*

Option	Description
`ViewEncapsulation.Emulated`	Emulated Shadow DOM, the default mode for Angular
`ViewEncapsulation.Native`	Native Shadow DOM
`ViewEncapsulation.None`	No Shadow DOM at all

ViewEncapsulation.Emulated: Example

Let's create an example component with a style and specify the `ViewEncapsulation` as `Emulated`. This is the default mode for Angular. This will be example advanced-ex100:

1. *Build the app using the CLI*: Use the following command:

    ```
    ng new advanced-ex100 --inline-template --inline-style
    ```

2. *Start* ng serve: Use the following code:

```
cd advanced-ex100
ng serve
```

3. *Open app*: Open a web browser and navigate to localhost:4200. You should see "app works!"

4. *Edit component*: Edit the file app.component.ts and change it to the following:

```
import { Component, ViewEncapsulation } from '@angular/core';
@Component({
  selector: 'app-root',
  template: `
    <h1>
      {{title}}
    </h1>
  `,
  styles: ['h1 { color: red }'],
  encapsulation: ViewEncapsulation.Emulated
})
export class AppComponent {
  title = 'app';
}
```

The app should be working and displaying the word *app* in red. Figure 23-1 shows the document.

```
<html lang="en">
▼ <head>
    <meta charset="utf-8">
    <title>Ch25Ex100</title>
    <base href="/">
    <meta name="viewport" content="width=device-width, initial-scale=1">
    <link rel="icon" type="image/x-icon" href="favicon.ico">
  ▼ <style type="text/css">
      /* You can add global styles to this file, and also import other style files */
    </style>
    <style>h1[_ngcontent-c0] { color: red }</style>
  </head>
▼ <body>
  ▼ <app-root _nghost-c0 ng-version="4.3.1">
      <h1 _ngcontent-c0>
            app
        </h1>
    </app-root>
    <script type="text/javascript" src="inline.bundle.js"></script>
    <script type="text/javascript" src="polyfills.bundle.js"></script>
    <script type="text/javascript" src="styles.bundle.js"></script>
    <script type="text/javascript" src="vendor.bundle.js"></script>
    <script type="text/javascript" src="main.bundle.js"></script>
  </body>
</html>
```

Figure 23-1. *ViewEncapsulation.Emulated*

As you can see, the style is written to the head of the document. Also Angular rewrote our style for the component, adding an identifier to both the style and the component to link just the two together and avoid conflicts with other components with other identifiers. In this case, the identifier is _ngcontent-c0.

ViewEncapsulation.Native: Example

Let's create an example component with a style and specify the ViewEncapsulation as Native. This will be example advanced-ex200:

1. *Build the app using the CLI*: Use the following command:

   ```
   ng new advanced-ex200 --inline-template --inline-style
   ```

2. *Start* ng serve: Use the following code:

```
cd advanced-ex200
ng serve
```

3. *Open app*: Open a web browser and navigate to localhost:4200.
   You should see "app works!"

4. *Edit component*: Edit the file app.component.ts and change it to
   the following:

```
import { Component, ViewEncapsulation } from '@angular/core';

@Component({
  selector: 'app-root',
  template: `
    <h1>
      {{title}}
    </h1>
  `,
  styles: ['h1 { color: red }'],
  encapsulation: ViewEncapsulation.Native
})
export class AppComponent {
  title = 'app';
}
```

The app should be working and displaying the word *app* in red. Figure 23-2 shows
the document.

```
<html lang="en">
▼ <head>
    <meta charset="utf-8">
    <title>Ch25Ex200</title>
    <base href="/">
    <meta name="viewport" content="width=device-width, initial-scale=1">
    <link rel="icon" type="image/x-icon" href="favicon.ico">
  ▼ <style type="text/css">
      /* You can add global styles to this file, and also import other style files */
    </style>
  </head>
▼ <body>
  ▼ <app-root ng-version="4.3.1">
    ▼ #shadow-root (open)
        <style>h1 { color: red }</style>
        <h1>
              app
            </h1>
    </app-root>
    <script type="text/javascript" src="inline.bundle.js"></script>
    <script type="text/javascript" src="polyfills.bundle.js"></script>
    <script type="text/javascript" src="styles.bundle.js"></script>
    <script type="text/javascript" src="vendor.bundle.js"></script>
    <script type="text/javascript" src="main.bundle.js"></script>
  </body>
</html>
```

Figure 23-2. *ViewEncapsulation.Native*

The style is no longer written to the head of the document—instead it's written inside the component's Shadow DOM. To see this output, you must turn on Display Shadow DOM in your browser. Now it's easy to see how your styles are only applied to the component, which resides in the host element app-root.

ViewEncapsulation.None: Example

Let's now create an example component with a style and specify the ViewEncapsulation as None. This will be example advanced-ex300:

1. *Build the app using the CLI*: Use the following command:

```
ng new advanced-ex300 --inline-template --inline-style
```

2. *Start* ng serve: Use the following code:

```
cd advanced-ex300
ng serve
```

3. *Open app*: Open a web browser and navigate to localhost:4200.
   You should see "app works!"

4. *Edit component*: Edit the file app.component.ts and change it to
   the following:

```
import { Component, ViewEncapsulation } from '@angular/core';

@Component({
  selector: 'app-root',
  template: `
    <h1>
      {{title}}
    </h1>
    `,
  styles: ['h1 { color: red }'],
  encapsulation: ViewEncapsulation.None
})
export class AppComponent {
  title = 'app';
}
```

The app should be working and displaying the word *app* in red. Figure 23-3 shows
the document.

```
<html lang="en">
▼ <head>
    <meta charset="utf-8">
    <title>Ch25Ex300</title>
    <base href="/">
    <meta name="viewport" content="width=device-width, initial-scale=1">
    <link rel="icon" type="image/x-icon" href="favicon.ico">
  ▼ <style type="text/css">
      /* You can add global styles to this file, and also import other style files */
    </style>
    <style>h1 { color: red }</style>
  </head>
▼ <body>
  ▼ <app-root ng-version="4.3.1">
      <h1>
            app
        </h1>
    </app-root>
    <script type="text/javascript" src="inline.bundle.js"></script>
    <script type="text/javascript" src="polyfills.bundle.js"></script>
    <script type="text/javascript" src="styles.bundle.js"></script>
    <script type="text/javascript" src="vendor.bundle.js"></script>
    <script type="text/javascript" src="main.bundle.js"></script>
  </body>
</html>
```

Figure 23-3. *ViewEncapsulation.None*

The style is written to the Head of the document and this style applies to entire document, possibly conflicting with other styles from other components. Be careful with this mode.

Angular offers you the best of both worlds: view encapsulation as default plus the ability to share styles. Your component-specific styles are protected for you even if you don't add the encapsulation specification to the @Component annotation.

If you need to share styles in your components, you can use the styleUrls specification in your @Component annotation to specify shared common style files.

Styling Content Children

Remember how you can apply styles to a component using the styles or styleUrls properties of the @Component annotation? These styles only apply to the HTML in the component's own template. What happens if you go get HTML content from the server and you inject this content into your component dynamically? How do you style that?

The answer is that you use special style tags to apply styles to your component and its sub-elements (like the HTML content from the server, for example). For example, the following style rule styles all the h3 elements in your component and its sub-elements:

```
:host /deep/ h3 { font-style: italic; }
```

Summary

This chapter introduced the concept of view encapsulation and discussed how it's implemented in Angular. It may not sound very important, but you should know about it because it can affect how you write your CSS styling.

We're getting near the end. The final chapter is about different Angular resources that are available to further sharpen your Angular skills in the future.

CHAPTER 24

Resources

I hope this book has turned out to be useful to you. I didn't write it in a vacuum—I relied on many sources of information. I'd like to share a few resources that can help you in your Angular development.

Angular Official Website

The official Angular website is at `https://angular.io`, the home page of which is shown in Figure 24-1. It has a ton of great information and is well laid out. This should be your starting point for any Angular research.

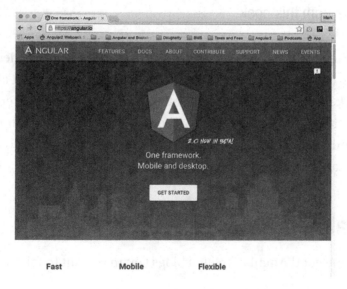

Figure 24-1. *Angular website*

M. Clow, *Angular 5 Projects*, https://doi.org/10.1007/978-1-4842-3279-8_24

I've found the API Preview page at `https://angular.io/docs/ts/latest/api/` to be especially useful. Type in what you're looking for, and it displays the search results. These search results include the objects that match the search, grouped by their packages. This package information is useful for writing the `imports` at the top of the classes. When you click an object in the search results, it shows you detailed information about its API.

GitHub

GitHub, located at `https://github.com`, is a popular web-based Git repository hosting service. Developers use it to publish their code and manage it. GitHub offers paid and free accounts. The paid accounts enjoy the advantage of private repositories. But the free accounts are popular and are frequently used when people are writing open source software projects. GitHub reports more than 12 million users and more than 31 million repositories, making it the largest host of source code in the world.

Note   Check out `https://github.com/markclow` for code samples and the example projects from this book.

Git is a widely used source code-management system for software development. Unlike older, more conventional source code management systems, Git allows developers to work in a distributed manner, managing their own local repositories on their computers, with or without a network. There's no "central" repository—there are only "peer" distributed repositories. Once a developer has completed code changes, they can merge their changes into shared repositories.

Angular-Related Blogs

Table 24-1 lists some good Angular–related blogs you may want to follow.

Table 24-1. *Angular-related Blogs*

Blog Address	Description
`http://blog.thoughtram.io`	Advanced Angular articles
`https://toddmotto.com`	Advanced Angular articles
`http://victorsavkin.com`	Angular articles
`http://blog.jhades.org`	Lots of JavaScript and Angular articles
`http://johnpapa.net`	Lots of articles, including those for Angular

Angular Air

Angular Air is a superb video podcast about Angular: check it out at `www.youtube.com/channel/UCdCOpvRk1lsBk26ePGDPLpQ`.

Summary

I hope you enjoyed the book. If you find any code that doesn't work, send me an email at markclow@hotmail.com and I will fix it. And if you feel I've left something valuable out of this book, please feel free to email me about that.

That's all, folks! I hope this book has been useful and that you download and use the code examples from GitHub (see earlier in this chapter). I certainly that site a lot when I'm working.

I'm very fortunate to enjoy doing what I'm doing. I hope you feel the same about your work and that the love of your profession keeps you motivated to keep studying.

I wish you the best in your endeavors. Never get discouraged: doing great things is difficult!

Index

A

Angular
    CLI, 77, 412
    component, 89
    detection, 398–399
    Http client, 320–321
    module system, 119
        deployment, 130
        ex100, 123–126, 128–129
        feature module, 122–123
        Node commands, 131
        root module, 121
        routing module, 122
        shared module, 123
        Start project, 120–121
    pipes
        combining date formats, 388
        currency, 386
        date, 386
        json, 388
        lowercase, 385
        percentage, 386
        predefined date formats, 387
        shortdate, 386
        UK pound currency, 386
        uppercase, 385
        variety of, 388, 390
    uses observables, 310

AngularJS
    vs. Angular
        JavaScript using JavaScript
            engines, 18
        platform, 17
        semantic versioning, 16–17
        shims and polyfills, 18
    controllers and components, 22
    dependency and constructor
        injection, 22–23
    forms, 24
    modules, 21
    module system, 116
    scope, controllers, and components, 24
    templates, 25
Annotations, 91
app.component.spec.ts, 412
Application component, 89
Asynchronous data streams
    event-based reactive programs, 291
    observable sequences, 292
    observers, 292–294
    operators
        buffer, 300
        debounce, 302–303
        distinct, 304
        filter, 304
        from, 298
        interval, 298

© Mark Clow 2018
M. Clow, *Angular 5 Projects*, https://doi.org/10.1007/978-1-4842-3279-8

K, L

M

N

Get the eBook for only $5!

Why limit yourself?

With most of our titles available in both PDF and ePUB format, you can access your content wherever and however you wish—on your PC, phone, tablet, or reader.

Since you've purchased this print book, we are happy to offer you the eBook for just $5.

To learn more, go to http://www.apress.com/companion or contact support@apress.com.

Apress®

Printed in the United States
By Bookmasters